Sandra Clayton

DOLPHINS under my bed

ADLARD COLES NAUTICAL
LONDON

Published by Adlard Coles Nautical
an imprint of A & C Black Publishers Ltd
36 Soho Square, London W1D 3QY
www.adlardcoles.com

First published by Adlard Coles Nautical in 2011

ISBN 978-1-4081-3288-3

A CIP catalogue record for this book is available from the British Library.

Typeset in 10.5 pt Baskerville by Saxon Graphics Ltd, Derby

Printed and bound in India by Replika Press Pvt Ltd

Note: while all reasonable care has been taken in the publication of this book,
the publisher takes no responsibility for the use of the methods or products
described in the book

Contents

NORTH-WEST SPAIN

THE RÍAS OF NORTH-WEST SPAIN

PORTUGAL

SOUTH-WEST SPAIN

GIBRALTAR

MEDITERRANEAN SPAIN

THE BALEARIC ISLANDS

Mallorca

Menorca

The Journey

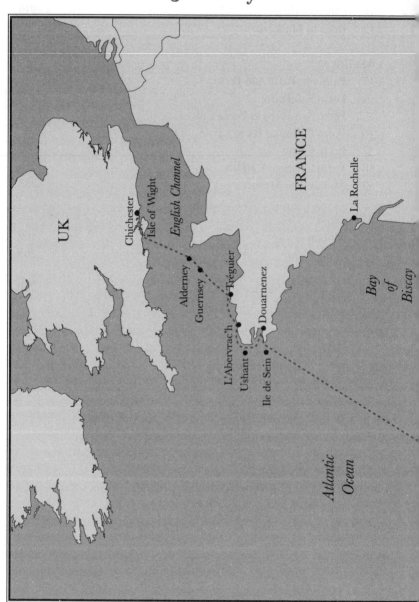

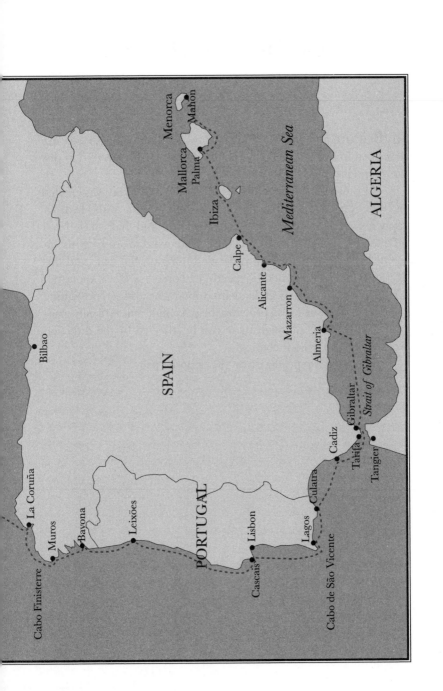

The Beaufort Wind Force Scale

In Britain and much of Europe, wind and vessel speeds are described in knots. One knot equals a nautical mile covered in one hour, and is roughly equivalent to 1.15mph.

Also used is the Beaufort Wind Force Scale. This was created in 1805 by Sir Francis Beaufort, a British naval officer and hydrographer, before instruments were available and has since been adapted for non-naval use. When accurate wind measuring instruments became available it was decided to retain the scale and this accounts for the idiosyncratic speeds, eg Force 5 is 17–21 knots, not 15–20 as one might expect. Under numbered headings representing wind force, this scale also provides the sea conditions typically associated with them, although these can be affected by the direction from which the wind is coming.

The scale is reproduced on the opposite page.

Force	Knots	mph	Sea Condition
1 Light Airs	1–3	1–3	Ripples.
2 Light Breeze	4–6	4–7	Small wavelets.
3 Gentle Breeze	7–10	8–12	Large wavelets with scattered white caps (also known as white horses).
4 Moderate Breeze	11–16	13–18	Small waves with frequent white caps.
5 Fresh Breeze	17–21	19–24	Moderate waves with many white caps.
6 Strong Breeze	22–27	25–31	Large waves with foam crests and some spray.
7 Near Gale	28–33	32–38	Sea heaps up and foam begins to streak.
8 Gale	34–40	39–46	Moderately high waves with breaking crests forming spindrift (spray blown along the sea's surface).
9 Strong Gale	41–47	47–54	High waves with dense foam. Waves start to roll over. Considerable spray.
10 Storm	48–55	55–63	Very high waves with long overhanging crests. The sea surface white with considerable tumbling. Visibility reduced.
11 Violent Storm	56–63	64–72	Exceptionally high waves.
12 Hurricane	64+	73+	Huge waves. Air filled with foam and spray.

Acknowledgements

All travellers, but especially sailors, owe a huge debt to those who have gone before and have subsequently published accurate charts and guides, as well as organisations which provide continuing support. Among the sources that *Voyager's* crew would like to express gratitude for are:

Admiralty Charts
BBC Shipping Forecast
Cruising Association
Imray Cruising Guides and Charts
Meteorological Office
Reed's Nautical Almanac
Sail & Power Nautical Almanac
Royal National Lifeboat Institution
Royal Yachting Association
UK Coastguard

The author also thanks the following for permission to reproduce copyright material:

British Broadcasting Corporation, Radio 4, London
Richard Evelyn Byrd, *Alone: The Classic Polar Adventure*
(Island Press, Washington, DC)
Jimmy Cornell, *World Cruising Routes* (Adlard Coles Nautical, UK; McGraw Hill/International Marine, US)
Cruising Association Handbook

Prelude

I came late to sailing. Actually, I didn't consciously come to it at all. It crept up on me. David and I had a brief fling with a sailing dinghy in the second year of our marriage – a disaster over which it is best to draw a veil. There were some enjoyable boating holidays on British rivers and canals. And then, for our Silver Wedding Anniversary, David asked me if I would like to celebrate with a sailing holiday in the Adriatic. To charter a yacht he needed a Day Skipper certificate. I joined him on the second of his two one-week courses and qualified as Competent Crew. The holiday in the Adriatic was wonderful. Endless sunshine, light winds and no tides to worry about.

After that, my only connection with sailing for several years was David reading yachting magazines. Then, at the age of forty-eight, I found myself joint owner of a 26ft Bermuda-rigged sloop. We kept her at Holyhead in North Wales. Between full-time employment, elderly parents a 90-mile drive away, and one of the worst summers in living memory we got to sail her only very occasionally. It was not remotely like sailing in the Adriatic. North Wales is noted for cold, wet weather and a current so strong that your destination depends on which way the tide happens to be going at the time.

Unfortunately, the deterioration in sailing conditions was matched by a similar falling off in my own performance. Even into our second season I seemed incapable of anticipating what needed to be done. I couldn't judge distances and, short of a gale, never knew where the wind was coming from. I hated heeling and a night on board turned my latent claustrophobia into full, horrific flower. The claustrophobic's ultimate nightmare is being buried alive, and the cabin of a small boat is horribly like a coffin.

I also hated putting up and taking down sails on a small rolling deck, and I didn't get on with a tiller. I always pushed when I should have pulled, so I was terrified of gybing accidentally and hurling David overboard, brained by a flying boom. Even if I managed to find him again, would my puny strength be sufficient to lift the dead weight of an unconscious man out of the water? In short, from the moment I stepped aboard our boat I was miserable. David loved her.

After my parents died we began going to the boat every weekend. I would listen to Friday evening's shipping forecast hoping for unfavourable conditions so that we wouldn't go next day. French aristocrats during The Terror probably mounted a tumbrel with only slightly less enthusiasm than I climbed into our car on a Saturday morning. I prayed the sailing phase would pass. At least it didn't cast a pall over my entire year; the British weather put an end to the season by early autumn until late the following spring.

Then, one cold, damp, winter evening as we sat before the fire – David wheezing and me aching – my worst nightmare happened. He said, 'Why don't we get a bigger boat, retire early and sail away to a warm climate? It would mean a reduced pension. But living on a boat is cheaper than a house and the benefit to our health would be enormous.' As he talked about it he changed before my eyes. The years seemed to fall away.

At 3 o'clock next morning I woke to the sound of screaming. It was me, of course. David was very understanding. Our boat went up for sale but there were no plans to buy a larger one. David went into a slow decline and I sank into self-induced guilt.

It was sad. There was so much that I liked about the idea of life afloat: the simplicity; living in the open air; travelling from place to place by water instead of congested roads; anchoring in beautiful, deserted coves; and I longed for a warmer, drier climate. In fact, I didn't mind anything about boats per se, not even the winter maintenance and antifouling. It was just the actual sailing I couldn't stand.

We kept our sloop on a mooring buoy at Holyhead. It was in the days before local entreaties prevailed, and the Irish ferries – especially the high-speed Sea Cat – roared in and out like the Starship Enterprise. An incoming ferry would send a veritable tidal wave down through the moorings. After it hit the harbour wall at the bottom it would hurtle back up through the moorings again. Then the water still travelling down would meet the water travelling back up and everything crashed about for quite some time.

The effect on a small, light boat such as ours was to send it thrashing from side to side, leaving you with no option but to drop everything and hold on to one of the boat's fixtures. If you were below, you hung onto the companionway handrails until the worst subsided. If you were in the cockpit, you crouched down low and clung to a winch.

On a rare weekend visit to our boat, to check that it was still all right, the Sea Cat roared in and the tidal wave hit. Dropping a half-prepared lunch into the sink I lunged for the handrails, followed by the breadboard and various bits of flying cutlery. With nothing else to do for the next few minutes I stared moodily out through the companionway, past David hunched over a winch, at all the other boats thrashing from side to side like ours. All except one. At the end of the moorings a catamaran rode the swell *like a plank*. In a swaying aluminium forest, its mast alone serenely rose and fell above the heaving water.

Eventually the wash subsided enough for David to let go of the winch and turn in the direction of my quivering finger. 'I'll do it,' I said, 'if we can have one of those.'

ENGLAND

▶▶▶

I

Emsworth

Major voyages are supposed to begin with a dramatic send-off. Ours doesn't. There has not even been enough water for our catamaran, *Voyager*, to leave the pontoon for a week, and she only needs a metre of water to get her afloat. Emsworth, in the upper reaches of Chichester Harbour on the south coast of England, has arranged to have a period of very low tides from July 31, which is also the day which Fate has decreed that David and I can finally set off. As a result, *Voyager's* two hulls are sunk deep in mud.

Our port hull is giving us concern. We have converted its forward cabin into a storage and workshop area, with the emphasis on storage. It has absorbed a massive amount but the weight is horrendous. We wonder if the boat will list to one side when we do finally get afloat again.

On August 9, with a sufficiently high tide imminent, we anxiously watch our port bow as the water begins to trickle across the mud flats towards our pontoon. It is above our waterline before the starboard hull drags itself free and rises from the mud with a *thhhhlock*. We sit, chin on hand, wondering if the port hull will follow. Time passes.

Getting Started

We had known before we left home that Chichester was due to have unusually low tides just now but had decided that a week on board would give us time to get shipshape and then have a rest before setting off. The first day of August was also our 34th wedding anniversary. We were unwaged now and would not be eating out as we had done when we were both in full-time employment. We therefore decided to start as we meant to go on, but still celebrated in three-course style thanks to a Chichester supermarket's gourmet counter. Dinner began with shellfish followed by stuffed bream and oriental sauce and finished off with apple and cinnamon in filo pastry with goat's cream. With a jug of carnations on the chart table and a decent bottle of wine we hadn't felt at all deprived.

The truth was that we weren't sure we should really be setting off yet. Ideally we should have waited until we were closer to our pensions. But reviewing the decline in our health over the past three years we had begun to question in what condition we should both be, in another five or six; and whether we should wake up one morning and find that we had left it too late.

In particular, David's respiratory problems were getting worse every year. He was allergic to almost everything now and despite specialists and prescribed medication he sneezed all the time, summer and winter. He would return home from work each evening congested and wheezing, from dust, pollen, perfume and traffic fumes. Latterly even newsprint could set him off, while a Sunday colour supplement would produce paroxysms of sneezing.

The previous winter he'd had fluid on his left lung. I'd wondered if this year it would be pneumonia. Worst of all, he had developed sleep apnoea. He would go to bed so congested that soon after falling asleep he would stop breathing. Just as I'd be about to shake him awake shouting, *'Breathe!'* his own diaphragm would give an almighty kick, he'd wake with a start and begin breathing again. This would go on all night.

It is odd, though, once you know what you want to do but are still reluctant to do it, how people unwittingly collude with you and all sorts of peripheral support begins to materialise. A colleague with no knowledge of our long-term plans gave me a card on my birthday that year bearing a quotation from the American explorer Richard Evelyn Byrd. It said: *Half the confusion in the world comes from not knowing how little we need. I live more simply now and am happier.*

Then one Sunday morning, washing our cars along with the neighbours in our small cul-de-sac, the subject of early retirement came up in conversation. One neighbour said it would be quite impossible for him because he would need to invest – and he mentioned a vast sum – simply to maintain his present living standards let alone improve them. But we didn't want to maintain our present living standards of a house, two cars to reach two jobs, overwork, a poor climate and declining health.

My major concern, however, was that we didn't condemn ourselves to an impoverished old age. I did not want to end up a bag lady. Nor did I want us to spend our final years in separate National Health Service nursing homes, should they even still exist by the time we needed them. On the other hand, a relaxed, physically-active lifestyle in a warm dry climate would considerably delay the need for any sort of nursing home for quite some time.

A simple question posed by an unexpected source finally transformed our dilemma into a decision. I was getting breakfast, with BBC Radio 4 playing as usual, when the seamless gloom and cynicism of national and international affairs was interrupted briefly by *Thought for the Day*.

The speaker that morning was an Anglican bishop and he began by saying, in the formal tones of the pulpit, 'Today, I want to preach to you about the Philosophy of Enough.' Then, over the next few minutes, he breezily invited his listeners to reflect on how they lived, what was really important, and how much they really needed materially to be happy.

When he had finished, I went to find David. It had been a particularly long winter. His face looked rather grey and he was wheezing from the damp air in the shower. 'How much is enough?' I said. When we both got back home that evening we sat down together and worked out the minimum we needed. The result was that we would go sooner rather than later.

It had been an unusually cold, wet spring that year. In fact, the only really good week for anti-fouling *Voyager* had been in February. Like a lot of other people, however, we had decided to ignore those few bright, dry but bitterly cold days and wait until it got a bit warmer. Like a lot of other people we also discovered too late that those few dry, bright days were all there were going to be for quite a while. March and April had brought almost constant rain.

Things weren't helped by the fact that our jobs and our home were in the north of England, while our boat was now on the South coast. Putting in an hour or two after work is not an option when it takes half a day to get to the boatyard. So it wasn't until May that we were antifouling *Voyager* on the hard.

Our transistor was tuned as usual to BBC Radio 4. The programme was Woman's Hour but, because the speaker was Mrs Bobby Moore, David had begun listening too. Bobby Moore, national hero and captain of the England football team that won the World Cup in 1966, had died of colon cancer.

His widow was spearheading a campaign to raise awareness of its symptoms and the need to take responsibility for getting treatment. Because, she explained, if his concerns had been heeded when he first began expressing them, Bobby might not have died when he did. And if someone as famous as Bobby Moore is ignored, how much harder is it for the rest of us to be heard? Caught early, she said, colon cancer can be successfully treated, but Bobby kept being told that his symptoms were normal and nothing to worry about until it was too late.

I had stopped slapping on antifouling paint and begun staring at David as she began listing nine classic symptoms of colon cancer. 'Got that one,' said David. 'And that. And that.' By the end of the list he had counted off seven of them on his fingers.

Some of them, like blood loss, he had had for a long time. Others, like fatigue and minor weight loss were more recent. Listed all together like this they sounded like a death sentence. He had visited our local medical practice only recently for the results of a cholesterol test and had promised to mention his latest symptoms at the same time.

'David!' I howled. 'You were supposed to tell the doctor!'

'I did,' he said in his characteristically quiet way. 'He said it was normal. Nothing to worry about.'

In subsequent weeks there were tests, surgery, and then more tests which confirmed that David did not have, nor had he ever had, cancer of the colon. There had been some internal damage, however, which it was hoped the surgery would correct and in fact it had. He might continue to lose blood but happily, after a few weeks, he no longer did. The other symptoms either lessened or disappeared and his general health improved. But by the time the final test results were available it was late July and the European sailing season was already half over.

There are two ways to sail a yacht from England to the Mediterranean. One is to lower your mast and motor through the French canals; the other is to sail down the Atlantic coasts of France, Spain and Portugal and enter through the Strait of Gibraltar. We preferred the latter, but knowing that this coastline is notorious for autumn and winter gales we wanted to have *Voyager* in the Mediterranean by the end of September.

We could, of course, have reached the Med in only a couple of weeks with constant sailing, but having anticipated the voyage for over five years we felt we should like to see a few places along the way. If we wanted to do that, we had to go immediately. The alternative was to spend another winter in England and leave the following spring. Since our need for a warmer, drier climate had been the major factor in our decision to go blue water cruising in the first place, we loaded the car with things crucial, things useful, and lots of things I should only have had to throw away otherwise. They had filled the boot, the back seat to the ceiling, the roof rack, my lap and all around my feet. Many hours later we had staggered down the boatyard's long pontoon with our first armfuls.

Emsworth is one of those wistful places of shallow water, salt marsh, curlews and large egrets. Unfortunately a great flock of starlings had also moved in to gorge on local crops of soft fruit and berries from the hedgerows. As a result, our boat's white polished surfaces had become purple and sticky as the starlings had excreted the seeds and a large residue of undigested fruit and juice over every inch of it. Before we could begin to put our goods on board we had to attach our hose to a tap and scrub off all the sticky purple goo that the birds were even yet depositing from their perches up in our rigging.

Getting that first load on board had been the start of more trouble. When *Voyager* had settled into the mud she had done so further away from the pontoon than was comfortable for us to climb on and off her, especially carrying heavy loads. As the tide was just then rising to its full if inadequate height, David had tried to drag her closer, and felt something go in his lower back.

Over the next few days he had taken on an increasingly disturbing shape. As he had done several times in the past, he had pulled a major muscle which had then gone into spasm and begun tilting his pelvis. The first time he had done this had been some years earlier, clearing a five-bar gate on his own when the horse that should have accompanied him decided against it at the last minute. Once weakened, the pelvis would twist if subjected to unreasonable stress. Bending double at the hips and dragging towards you eleven tons of boat with both keels firmly embedded in thick mud is about as unreasonable as it gets.

The solution had always been deep tissue massage, rest and definitely no twisting or lifting. This, however, had conflicted with

David's determination to prepare our boat for the longest voyage we had ever undertaken alone. And unfortunately there had been an awful lot to stow aboard. Like many before us, far from getting away from it all, we seemed to be taking most of it with us. Some of it, such as the new life raft, large tool boxes and spare parts were essential. Some of it wasn't. We seemed to have brought an awful lot of books and videos and … things.

'I can't believe you've brought so many clothes,' said David.

'I'd only have to throw them away,' I'd responded lamely. 'And anyway, they're cotton and you can never have too much good quality polishing cloth.'

David's back had got progressively worse until he was bent in the middle, twisted to the left and crabbed sideways when he walked. He was also in a lot of pain. Nevertheless, he carried on for several days, stowing the unstowable into small inaccessible spaces and installing new equipment. It was the life raft that finally did for him and forced him briefly to take to his bed.

In the days following, fellow boat owners stopped by to ask how he was, contemplate the encircling mud and ask tentatively when we were thinking of going. If they were dubious, no less were we. For both of us there was an unreality about all this. We had never even sailed across the English Channel alone before, never mind as far as the Mediterranean. Something had always cropped up to prevent us.

3
Emsworth to the Isle of Wight

And now we sit, head on hand, watching the water rise and anxiously eyeing the port hull. About ten minutes after the starboard side has risen, the port hull finally struggles upward with a similar glutinous sucking sound. We are afloat.

At a little after 1pm we start the engines and edge our way out through very shallow water into the channel that will take us through Chichester's large, busy harbour and out to sea. It is the usual Sunday afternoon pandemonium in Chichester Harbour. Power may give way to sail but sometimes, with a wide boat in a narrow channel, it is not always that simple. Dinghy racers, intent on holding their course to achieve the greatest possible advantage over their rivals, criss-cross the channel. We cannot risk straying onto Stocker Sands to miss them, so we slow to allow one of the little boats to pass under our bows, and then accelerate to avoid the one aimed at our beam. Meanwhile, a yacht in full sail comes hurtling towards us on our side of the channel, while behind us a fast little speedboat jockeys to get past. A subsequent survey found that Chichester Harbour is home to 11,547 boats. On this summer Sunday afternoon at the end of Cowes Week, Europe's most famous regatta, most of them seem to be out on the water.

It is the first time *Voyager* has moved in a year, and we have been unable to try anything out; not least the new mainsail we bought during the winter. Our immediate concern, however, is the electronic equipment. There are so many things on a boat to go wrong, especially one that has lain unused for twelve months.

At least the instruments all seem to be working; even the log, which usually seizes up when the boat hasn't moved for a week let alone a year. So once out to sea we decide to try out our new mainsail. One of our boat's features that we particularly prize is a self-furling main which allows us to pull this sail in and out easily by hand without need of a winch and without leaving the cockpit. This is a particular advantage for people in their mid-50s planning to sail long distances two-handed, especially when one of them is an unfit woman with weak hands and a dodgy back.

David pulls on the outhaul and three quarters of the new sail emerge from the housing on the mast. The last quarter remains stuck inside. He heaves, strains, sweats and swears. At the point where his face changes from scarlet to purple he decides to use one of the winches to pull the last section out. As is its wont at difficult moments, the wind rises suddenly and dramatically. It sends the sail flying and the outhaul thrashing. The latter twists itself round the winch in a jumble and locks solid.

For a time it looks as if we will have to cut the outhaul free. However, with the aid of a jemmy, and a large screwdriver hammered in between the rope coils, we finally manage to ease the tension enough to free it. In the meantime a supercilious couple, standing on a passing yacht with their hands in their pockets, observes us apparently knocking seven bells out of our winch with a hammer, raise an eyebrow at one another and pointedly turn their backs on us. It is not an auspicious start.

We have no sooner freed the outhaul and got the sail fully out than the wind dies away completely, so we put the sail away again and motor on towards the Isle of Wight.

As David admitted, although not until very much later, once he had put the mainsail away he had completed all the displacement activity that was keeping him from thinking about what he had committed us to: selling up, cutting ties, and not only leaving England but probably the last paid employment we would ever have. It was not even the sort of thing people like us did. We had no sailing background. No-one we had ever known until recently had ever sailed.

I kept remembering newspaper articles about people embarking on similar ventures after years of boat-building and planning, only to sink just outside the harbour mouth. We were asking for trouble; you could see that in the eyes of almost everybody we knew. At an age when our contemporaries were planning retirement bungalows, we had committed ourselves and our resources to a life afloat. And although I had every confidence in David, I knew that I was a lousy sailor. Only a very close relative, or the truly desperate, would have taken me on as crew.

Our intention now is to anchor in the Solent for the night to the east of Cowes on the Isle of Wight, near one of Queen Victoria's favourite residences, Osborne House. For in the same way that we shall not be eating in restaurants any more, we also plan to avoid the expense of marinas by anchoring wherever possible. We had anchored in Osborne Bay last summer but, unlike last year, when we approach it there are no other boats in sight. This adds to the unease that David has been feeling since leaving Chichester Harbour.

It is a year since our last sail and yachtsmen always feel a little tentative about how the boat is after a long lay-up. So he decides to head for the security of the mooring buoys outside Yarmouth Harbour. We had tied up to a buoy there the previous summer also, and though unspoken, the fact that a mooring buoy is more securely fixed to the seabed than an anchor can ever be is more than a little reason for choosing one now.

While uneasy at casting ourselves adrift, however, neither of us considers the possibility of turning back. Neither of us, we subsequently discover, had thought for a moment that since we still had a furnished house, we could always give up and go back to it. We just wanted someone to buy it, so that it would no longer be a large drain on our resources.

Our plan is to spend a year in the Mediterranean, and then cross the Atlantic to the Caribbean – if we feel like it. The problem with telling people you are going cruising is that everybody says, 'Are you going to sail round the world?' We are as well-prepared as we can be, but we lack experience and are determined not to put pressure on ourselves to do anything that we feel we are not ready for. So whenever anybody asks the question, we always give the same answer, 'No, we're just going to head for the Mediterranean and then see how we feel.'

By 5.30 that evening we are tied to a buoy just outside Yarmouth Harbour on a stretch of water called Yarmouth Road. There is a Ferris wheel behind the breakwater, but no sound at all beyond the odd seagull. A uniformed man in a small boat chugs out to collect £10 from us for a night's use of the mooring buoy, and we settle down to chicken tikka masala and gooseberry fool, courtesy of a last-minute shop-up in Chichester.

There is a glorious fluorescent pink sunset, and as darkness falls a huge russet moon rises behind the ferry terminal. The wind is from the north-east and slight, but the sea is so choppy that we are both up on deck at 1am to reassure ourselves that we are still safely tied to the mooring buoy. It is so bumpy, in fact, that I had shot awake convinced that we were about to be dashed onto The Needles, that notorious group of rocks nearby.

Actually, had we *been* adrift, we should have hit a lot of other things before The Needles, but in the dark irrational reaches of the night, a famous local landmark becomes a natural bogeyman. The truth is: it would not have surprised us at all if something had happened to end our voyage right there, twenty miles from where we had set out. But none of these things were spoken of at the time.

4
Finding a boat

When I had suggested, five years earlier, that a catamaran might be a way of overcoming my resistance to sailing, David had immediately booked a weekend trial on one, complete with a professional skipper, to see how we got on with it. I felt quite relaxed doing 10 knots in blustery conditions with all the sails up and no heeling. I observed carefully the monohulls we overtook. They were heavily reefed and heeling mightily, their crews hunched into their cockpits at an angle of 45 degrees. I was standing upright and there was no impediment to my walking upright anywhere on the boat that I wanted to go. I could live with something like this, I decided. More to the point, I could live *on* something like this.

The plan then was to find a catamaran that really suited us, and learn to handle it in all sorts of conditions. We quickly decided on a 40-foot Solaris Sunstream. Built for offshore cruising, it had full headroom for David, two roomy double cabins each with two windows and an overhead hatch for my claustrophobia, plus a generous galley for domestic harmony. Unusually for a yacht, it also had a bath. The only problem was that there were very few for sale, only thirteen of them having ever been built.

We found *Voyager* in southern Spain and spent two weeks sailing her back to the UK with the help of Ian, the skipper from our weekend trial. He was also an experienced delivery skipper and a Royal Yachting Association instructor. Having a professional skipper on board was essential for us, as we were too inexperienced to have attempted such a trip alone.

It was a fair distance to cover in the only couple of weeks the three of us had free at the same time, and most of it was spent at sea. The only time we stopped was for fuel and water or to sit out a gale. It was a tremendous experience to be under sail with a professional in our own boat in all types of conditions, especially the gales. As weekend sailors we had never been far from shelter. On a long sea passage you may not have that option.

Bringing *Voyager* home to England was memorable in many ways. It was early March and my first experience of rough weather, but she took Gale Force 8 and 20-foot waves in the Bay of Biscay ... *like a plank*. I had never seen stars in the night sky that brilliant before, nor hobnobbed with dolphins on virtually a nose-to-nose basis. I also overcame my greatest dread when I stood my first watch alone at night under full sail and coped perfectly well. Perhaps the most extraordinary event, though, occurred towards the end of the trip, as we entered the western approaches to the English Channel on our way towards Falmouth.

It was near the end of my watch when I noticed small waves breaking the water's surface irregularly beside the boat. There is a rhythm and a pattern to water as a moving boat displaces it. It rises as a bow wave and runs down the sides of the hull and these fast, erratic little flurries didn't fit. They were also a couple of feet too far away for them to be made by us.

I thought they might be caused by dolphins, and I waited for them to break the surface like they usually do once they've had a good look at you from below. But tonight they didn't. I felt disappointed, but I also felt very tired. My three hours were up and I went below and woke David to take over the watch.

'I think there may be dolphins about,' I said, as he climbed into his wet weather gear in the saloon. 'But I can't see them.'

He showed little interest. I'd woken him from a deep sleep and beyond putting the correct arm into the appropriate sleeve his main concern was forcing his eyes to stay open.

It was a raw March that year and naturally the further north we'd got the colder it had become. As we headed for the English coast I was wearing three layers of clothing underneath my wet weather gear but still felt chilled to the bone in an open cockpit in the early hours of the morning. So I was very grateful to climb into the warm bed that David had just vacated in the port cabin. He would stand watch for the next three hours and then Ian, currently asleep in the starboard cabin, would take over for the three hours after that. I was looking forward to six hours of uninterrupted rest, apart from David's chilled body returning in three hours' time.

The cold, plus the extra physical effort needed to do anything under all that clothing and wet weather gear, had made me more tired than usual. Once in bed I had curled into a tight ball to warm my knees and feet and was just drifting towards sleep when David spoke my name. I started, fearing an emergency, something round a propeller again, but he put his hand on my shoulder.

'It's alright,' he said. 'I just thought you'd want to know about the dolphins. There are dozens of them underneath the boat and …'

'I know!' I cut him short irritably, asking why he'd woken me to tell me about dolphins you couldn't see that I'd already told him about before I'd gone to bed.

'Just *listen*!' he said.

The sky through the hatch above our bunk was luminous with stars and I could see his face quite clearly. He was smiling a strange, dreamy sort of smile. So I stopped grumbling and listened. There was music coming up through the hull.

'You can't hear it up on deck,' he said. 'I only heard it when I came down to the chart table to do the log. I didn't think you'd want to miss it.' Then he went back up on watch.

I uncoiled and rolled onto my back. I was warm now and I stretched my spine and legs to their full length under the bedclothes. I gazed up through the hatch overhead and reflected on this extraordinary world of which I was going to be a part. There were stars above my head and dolphins under the bed. And somewhere in the depths of the sea something was singing. Whatever it was, it wasn't dolphins. They communicate by clicks and whistles at high speed. These were musical notes and the pace was leisurely, almost languid.

'Whales,' said Ian when the three of us discussed it in the cockpit next morning. Apparently it's not unusual to find dolphins and whales together, especially when they're feeding; although he said he'd never heard that particular sound before.

I had. More than forty years ago. And lying there in the warm darkness my memory had drifted back to my first year at secondary school and its Scots music teacher. Using tonic sol-fa, with a zeal worthy of Miss Jean Brodie in her prime, Miss Bonnell ('that's Bow-*nell*') had lashed us up the major scale: *doh, ray, me, fah, so, lah, te, doh* – and once at the top harried us back down again: *doh, te, lah, so, fah, me, ray, doh* – as if despite our industrial environment a career as opera divas awaited us all. Up and down the scale we went, lesson after lesson.

When she tired of this, she would slap her cane randomly at the notes written on the board beside her while we sang them, *ad nauseum*, at their proper pitch. And this was what I was hearing now; sections of the major scale.

It was as if each creature in the dark depths of the sea had a call sign consisting of one, two or three notes so that for example one of them would use *tee-lah-so*, another *ray-far*, and another simply *doh*. And gradually, lying there listening in the dark, these one-, two- or three-note calls became an individual, a *voice*.

What was surprising was that none of these voices ever overlapped one another. Each one, pure and unhurried, completed its snatch of song before the next began. And once you stopped concentrating on the individual notes it became music. A song from the sea. A lullaby. I listened for a long time, until warmth and tiredness became irresistible and the lullaby from the deep lulled me into one of the sweetest sleeps I can ever remember.

It stopped sometime during Ian's watch, although the dolphins remained until several hours after sunrise. They were still there when I got up, swimming on the surface now, hundreds of them. Ian said he'd never known dolphins stay with a boat all night like that. I have asked other yachtsmen since about the sound but they have all shaken their heads and looked at me suspiciously. But three of us heard it.

This trip gave us much more confidence in handling *Voyager* by ourselves, once David and I got her home, than if we had simply had her delivered to us. And the boat herself gave *me* confidence. Her self-furling main, genoa and staysail meant you didn't have to leave the cockpit to handle the sails. The cockpit itself was deep and in the centre of the boat, so you felt secure even in big seas, and she had a wheel not a tiller. Most of all, she was built for cruising so was not only stable but comfortable.

In the next three seasons, sailing two-handed at weekends and annual holidays, we explored Ireland from Carlingford Loch to Bantry Bay, and the English and Welsh coasts from the Isle of Man to West Sussex. And that was how *Voyager* came to be at Emsworth in Chichester Harbour. She was only meant to be there for a couple of weeks, and then we would collect her and take her home; but work commitments and unsuitable weather had meant that we had had to leave her there for the winter.

As things turned out, she was to remain there for most of the following summer as well. Now, however, we are finally free to enjoy what is left of it, not unmindful that David has been lucky and that we might so easily have not been making this journey at all.

Actually it's strange, looking back, to realise how very nearly our voyage didn't happen, for all sorts of reasons. Normally our boat spent her winters up on a sheltered northern river bank miles from the sea but only an hour's drive from our home. There we could antifoul, polish and spring clean her at weekends without undue travelling.

During that final winter, however, which *Voyager* spent up on the hard at Emsworth, a cyclone – not unknown off England's south coast but usually blowing harmlessly out at sea – carved its way in a south-westerly direction past Selsey Bill and then swerved inland, destroying property although happily no life.

We had felt particularly helpless that night, sitting in front of the television news watching an arrow on a map follow the cyclone's path straight towards *Voyager*. Fortunately the cyclone veered off back out to sea before it reached the boatyard. Had it travelled a bit further overland our dreams of a warm Mediterranean winter would have been buried in angst and insurance claims.

THE CHANNEL ISLANDS
⋯
5
Isle of Wight to Alderney

As we cast off from our mooring buoy at 6 o'clock next morning a ketch glides confidently out of Yarmouth Harbour, its sails silhouetted against an enormous orange sun. We put out our own sails, including the new mainsail, but the light wind soon becomes variable, and then negligible, so we take them all in again and motor.

We leave the Solent via the North Channel. It takes us past Hurst Castle, a brooding, melancholy pile built by Henry VIII to guard against the French. It was still being added to by the Victorians for the same reason. It was also here that King Charles I was held for 19 days in the December of 1648. His small cell was so gloomy, said a visitor, that it needed candles even in the middle of the day. Five weeks later he was taken to be executed in London.

Despite being garrisoned during the 17th and 18th centuries, Hurst Castle was involved in the smuggling trade, the smugglers having done a deal with the castle's officers. The contraband came from France, and often via the Channel Islands, that small group of islands in the English Channel which although close to the French coast have been British territory for centuries. Our destination is Braye Bay, on the north-west coast of Alderney, one of the Channel Islands. We are following the smugglers' route in reverse.

It is a beautiful sunny morning, with just a little haze and wispy cloud. David, however, is becoming increasingly concerned. We have never been to the Channel Islands before, and his problem is that to follow the course to Braye Bay which the GPS provides, he has to steer at an angle 35 degrees from where his calculations indicate. He repeatedly goes below to consult the chart and tide table, but can find no explanation for what is happening. In the end he decides to rely on the GPS and puzzles over whether we could be experiencing a freak tide because it is quite apparent that it is flowing in the opposite direction to what the printed tide table says. To add to his unease, visibility begins to deteriorate.

Late afternoon we see our first gannets of the year. They are cruising in ones and twos, the tip of one elegant wing not quite touching the water. The gannet is large and sleek and very white with black wing tips, a distinctive yellow head, and a droop-snoot reminiscent of Concorde. When they dive for fish they soar vertically, plummet dramatically and, after a surprising length of time underwater, rise majestically to the surface with their catch. A much-maligned bird – its very name a synonym for gluttony – the gannet's eating habits seem no different from any other bird's, while in flight it is a joy.

Gannets are usually in a flock, their flight synchronized, almost languid, although when required they can reach 60mph. Mostly, however, their rhythm is unhurried and they will pass across your stern in a leisurely glide to take a look at you, eye to eye.

Most captivating of all is when they fly in formation, for there stirs in the memory an image from all the old black-and-white movies about fighter pilots you ever saw, and a voice intoning nasally through a leather headset: 'Red Leader One, this is Red Leader One: get in line at the back there,' and the slacker at the back pulls himself together and they all flap and glide, flap and glide with every graceful wing beat co-ordinated. It is easy to become very partial to gannets.

We see only two yachts and four tankers all day. This adds to our sense of unreality because the English Channel is one of the busiest shipping lanes in the world with some 600 cargo ships and 200 ferries either crossing or passing through it daily. And we cannot see Alderney at all until we are two miles off, because visibility has become so poor. Nevertheless we arrive spot-on for Braye Bay and I tell David I think he's done a sterling job to do that, considering a freak tide and everything. That's when he confesses that he'd been working from the wrong tide chart. For the first time, *Sail & Power Nautical Almanac* has produced a two-year version and he had inadvertently put a bookmark against today's date for next year.

6
Alderney

We head for the anchorage off the town beach, between the town wall and some moored rafts, but slowly since the Channel Islands are notorious for rocks. There is a grinding sound beneath us and David throws *Voyager* into reverse.

We tear up the bilge covers to see if water is coming in, but none is. And although we see other boats taking what appears to be the same course for hours afterwards, none of them judders to a halt and shoots into reverse like we did.

The anchor bites at the second attempt, putting us a *tiny* bit closer to a small English monohull called *Antares* than we would have chosen for absolute courtesy, but the anchor holds fast and so we leave it where it is.

The art of anchoring is not simply to get your anchor firmly dug into the seabed, but also to ensure that you don't swing into other anchored boats when the tide or the wind changes direction. Nor should you drop your own anchor in such a way that it will pull up someone else's.

Most of the boats at anchor are French apart from *Antares*. Then another red ensign hoves into view and an Englishman in psychedelic shorts on a boat called *Outrageous* drops his anchor over the top of ours and spends the rest of the evening talking on his mobile phone. We dine on our favourite brand of sausages, probably our last for a long time, and are in bed by 10pm.

At 1am we are standing on our foredeck watching *Outrageous*'s stern swinging inches from our bows. David lets out more chain to avoid a collision but it is after two o'clock before we feel confident enough about *Outrageous* not pulling up our anchor to go back to bed. David is up again for the 5.35am shipping forecast, and again for the 7am tide change to ensure that the extra chain he let out to keep *Outrageous* off our bows does not put us at risk of hitting *Antares*. We sit on deck with chocolate biscuits, and coffee in the last clean cups on board because we didn't wash up last night. When he is satisfied with our position, David goes back to bed. He looks tired. I stay on deck.

It has not been a restful night, but it is a glorious sunrise; misty, with a silver-yellow sun climbing up behind the fortress on the hill above us. In the vague, shifting light it is impossible to tell where the fort ends and the headland begins. Both are draped in shades of grey-brown with vaporous mist swirling about them. What later turns out to be a concrete outcrop of the fortifications, at this moment looks for all the world like the diaphanous sail of a ghostly ship until I realise that the mast would have to be around 200 feet high. Among my numerous failings as a seaman is an inability to judge size at a distance, or to accurately gauge spatial relationships. On the other hand, they do occasionally provide some stunningly beautiful images.

Most of the French boats leave now, along with *Outrageous*. Shortly afterwards fog sets in with a vengeance, bringing cries no doubt of '*Zut Alors!*' from those who have rushed out. By 8am nothing is visible beyond the few boats still anchored around us. The life-boat's engine roars into action but it does not appear to go anywhere. Once its engine is turned off there is just the sound of water lapping around our stern, the tide sucking on the beach, a distant fog horn and faint, frenetic sounds coming from a French radio station, drifting in wisps like mist, there one minute and gone the next.

At 8.15 the beach and mooring buoys become suddenly visible again as the sun manages to pierce the fog. The young, black-bearded man on *Antares*, in his red and black check shirt and black trousers, lights a cigarette, hauls water up in a black rubber bucket and scrubs his decks with a stiff broom.

The fog closes in again and then lifts once more.

Antares' man leisurely puts out fenders along his starboard side, ties on mooring lines fore and aft and tightens his sheets, all with light, unhurried movements. He hauls up half a ton of chain, starts his engine, lights another cigarette, raises another half ton of chain plus the anchor, gazes around him to ascertain that the coast is clear, returns to his cockpit and motors slowly off towards the fuel dock. I want to do it like that; always mentally ahead of what's needed instead of perpetually scrambling up from behind. I think I must be a great strain on David's nerves.

I begin work on yesterday's washing up. I miss the dishwasher already. The fog continues to come and go. Through the galley window I look out on a sandy beach and the Sea View Hotel. *Voyager* lies between two enormous fortifications: Fort Albert, the arsenal on Roselle Point; and Fort Grosnez behind the breakwater. Military defences, from the Iron Age to the present day, exist all over the world as a testament to man's capacity for grabbing somebody else's piece of turf. Looking out on them, I am struck by the irony that these two forts, along with four others on Alderney, were all being built in the mid-19th century as a defence against the French, despite the fact that France at that time was Britain's ally in the Crimean War.

As you sail through the coastal towns of Europe, of course, the reverse appertains, and the invaders' names become English. In particular, the Elizabethan naval commander and privateer, Sir Francis Drake (c1541–1596), holds a special place in many a tourist brochure, his name preceded by the words 'burnt down by' and followed by a date. 'Don't mention the war,' is to become a refrain of our visits ashore.

We had intended leaving Alderney for Guernsey at 2.30 this afternoon, this being the time recommended in the cruising guide at which to navigate the formidable Swinge. But the Harbour Master, while delivering a Customs form for us to complete and relieving us of £2 for our night's anchorage, says the fog is due to return shortly. As we have no desire to *Zut Alors* among the rocks in fog, and are both short on sleep, we decide to remain another night.

There are rules for the sea-going; not only things like collision avoidance regulations which are designed to prevent you putting yourself and others at risk, but also measures to protect the sea itself. This includes never throwing garbage overboard. You put it in a bag, tie it up, and take it ashore for appropriate disposal. For whatever arcane reason, this is called a gash bag.

We put our gash bag into our new aluminium dinghy, and take her on her maiden voyage into Braye Harbour. We have had small rubber dinghies before but, since you travel sitting on the sides of them, in anything but dead calm water your bottom gets wet. We not only wanted one that we could sit inside, but also something we could sail, row, paddle or use with an outboard engine. We bought exactly what we wanted at not inconsiderable expense from the most offensive salesman I have ever encountered. I was for head-butting him and leaving the showroom, but David is more tolerant than me and nobody else made a dinghy like it. We only ever see one other, in Braye Harbour today, so maybe I wasn't the only one allergic to the salesman.

Sometimes, in a certain place at a particular time, for no reason you can ever determine, the atmosphere and everyone around you is utterly relaxed and happy. Alderney is such a place this summer afternoon. An island measuring only three miles by two and inhabited by less than two and a half thousand souls, it reminds us happily of childhood seaside holidays on the mainland in the 1950s.

As we land at the dinghy dock, a couple stop to tie us up and put out their hands to help us ashore. I am so startled at such unexpected courtesy I walk backwards thanking them and hit another woman on the bottom with our gash bag. I apologize profusely. David tells her I am prone to starting fights, and laughing she says it is understandable as I am obviously being kept from the pub. Sunshine, small courtesies and laughter predispose you to pleasure. It is perhaps why revisiting a place that you once enjoyed is so often a disappointment because while the physical landscape may have remained the same, the human dimension is different.

We wander the seafront and the harbour and then adjourn to The Sea View Hotel. It is light and airy with high ceilings and large windows looking across the harbour and out to sea. We lunch in the bar, in a leisurely fashion, on cod mornay and draft cider.

By the time we get back outside, it has become hot and we are drowsy. It is too much effort to climb a steep hill up to the supermarket, so we shop at a little place across the road. We buy *gache*, a local fruit loaf, and oranges and are horizontal in the cockpit under the awning by three. The forecast fog does not intrude into the harbour. There is only a little haze. If we were going to spend a contented afternoon and evening anywhere, we could not have found a more relaxed and pleasant place to be.

The following day begins overcast, but soon becomes bright and hot. We are still bothered about the weight in the bow of the port hull, so David shifts three large boxes out of it into a saloon locker on the principle that the weight will be more central. Unfortunately, almost as much weight appears to come out of the saloon locker and go into the port bow as came out of the port bow in the first place, and it gets even hotter. It is too hot to eat much, so we lunch on bananas and the *gache* loaf bought the previous day, and set off for Guernsey at half past one.

7
Alderney to Guernsey

Southbound from Alderney, the shortest route to Guernsey is through two tidal races, the Swinge and the Little Russel. The Swinge lies between Alderney and Burhou, an inhospitable island surrounded by reefs. The chart warns: *Dangerous overfalls form in the main Swinge channel. Their position varies with the tidal stream.* We are familiar with overfalls – rough water caused by two currents in conflict – from our days in Holyhead. We had found those uncomfortable enough, and they weren't even marked on the chart as dangerous. You also need to get well clear of Alderney, as the area of coast facing the Swinge has great clusters of rocks stretching a long way out from it. The tidal stream can also reach 7–8 knots at its height, so it is safest to take it at slack water.

After clearing the Swinge you then have a few miles of open sea before arriving at Little Russel, which when you look at it on the chart can be quite daunting. This channel has Guernsey to the west and the islands of Herm and Jethou to the east. Reefs and rocks stretch out well to the north of Herm as well as half way out towards Guernsey, while throughout the channel itself there is an assortment of rocks and shallow areas.

Strangely, although a narrower channel than the Swinge, the strongest currents here reach only 5 knots. We head for a waypoint to the east of Platte Fougére lighthouse and then have a series of waypoints in our GPS to help us just in case. However, it is a bright sunny day, we can spot the markers and buoys easily, and it is an uneventful passage.

From the bit of open sea between these two races the French coast is visible. It is our first glimpse of mainland Europe. So far so good. We are on our way.

8
St Peter Port

Twenty-one miles on from Alderney we approach the marina at St Peter Port, Guernsey's major town. It is packed. A harassed but polite marina manager in a dinghy shuffles us into the only space available, third in a raft-up on one of the visitors' pontoons outside the marina. Our arrival effectively cuts off the exit in front of us, as we fill the space between the two English boats on the left hand pontoon to which we are to tie ourselves, and three French boats swinging about in a louche sort of way and which are rafted up to a pontoon over on the right.

We have spent very little time in marinas and the few we have stayed in have been obscure and very quiet. I therefore feel something of a debutante in this very busy and rather fashionable one. Any chance of maintaining a low profile, however, is quickly lost as we encounter for the first time a yachting phenomenon. They tend to be short of stature, elderly, affluent, and behave as if they are personally responsible for the *great* in Great Britain. They wear navy blue blazers and caps with braid on them. They are members of yacht clubs whose names contain the word *Royal*. And to convince themselves that they exist above the common herd they name their boats with French nouns denoting superiority: *Elite* (dictionary definition 'the most powerful, rich, or gifted members of a group or community'); *Élan* ('a combination of style and vigour'); or *Éclat* ('brilliant or conspicuous success, social distinction, acclaim'). In reality they are arrogant, class-obsessed, selfish and *unbelievably* ill-mannered.

Before we can get our first rope tied, one such in full uniform bawls at us from his foredeck three boats back on the opposite pontoon that he intends to leave at 8.30 next morning and we shall be in his way. The couple on the Westerly beside us, and to which we are trying to tie up, say that they want to be off at 5am anyway so there won't be a problem. I pass this information on to the incandescent little man in the blazer behind us.

'Can't hear you!' he bawls.'

'Not a problem,' I call back. 'You'll be able to leave.'

He continues to bawl that he wants to leave at 8.30am.

I keep saying there will be room from 5am.

He begins shouting that he has a right to exit.

I say go and talk to the marina manager since he put us here.

He says he can't hear me.

'Give up,' says David.

By now, people's heads are popping up through hatches all over the marina, like gophers.

'I have a right to exit!' he roars, as if his civil liberties are being violated, and as if there isn't another exit behind him that he could use anyway.

I signal five with an open hand. 'We'll be gone by five,' I shout at the top of my voice.

'Can't hear you over your engines,' he bellows.

I climb over the other two boats to the pontoon to put on shore lines and wonder how people like him survive into old age. I can only assume it is a tribute to the tolerance and humanity of the rest of us. Deprived of one focus for his petulance, he immediately finds another and begins barking orders at the docile young woman washing his boat.

Once tied up, our location provides an ideal opportunity to observe cultural differences, given that we have French yachts to starboard and English to port.

The first noticeable difference is that each of the two outer boats in the English raft (us and the boat next door) is not only tied up to its neighbour but has ropes attached to the pontoon as well. These shore lines prevent the combined weight of the three boats from being borne by the inner boat's mooring lines. They also mean that the raft is stable and maintains a constant distance from the pontoon.

The French have not put out shorelines to their pontoon and all three boats undulate back and forth on the current like the middle bit of an accordion, sometimes almost touching us, sometimes a boat's width away. Had they used shorelines, there would have been ample space for yachts to pass between us, including that of the man in the cap and blazer three boats behind. As it is, only the operator of the little water taxi is able to do so, and only then by leaning over the side of his boat and heaving the three French yachts back towards their pontoon.

The second major difference is that while the occupants of the two English boats are closeted below, the French sit around cockpit tables, talking and eating into the late afternoon. These tables sport a remarkable array of condiments, and new dishes emerge from their galleys at regular intervals.

The town quay is only yards away from our pontoon. However, because these visitors' pontoons are attached to the seabed, and not the shore, you need a boat to reach the town. We can either crank our dinghy down off its davits or, for £1 each way, we can take the water taxi. I summon the taxi on the VHF, and once aboard David and I push the French boats aside to give the taxi driver a break. Above us their crews chew on.

St Peter Port is a real pleasure. The waterfront is a delight with its tall narrow buildings and the prominent belfry of St James. The town rises steeply with a wondrous mix of granite mansions, colonial stucco and white-washed Mediterranean-style villas. We conclude our tour at an 11th century church at the top and make the journey back down past precipitous guesthouses via steep flights of steps and narrow alleyways, and imagine staggering all the way up there with two weeks' holiday luggage.

Near the bottom we slide our noses round the door of the Royal Channel Islands Yacht Club, as recommended in the information sheet given to us with the Customs form. It is clearly not a good time, and the two women wiping tables in the deserted bar glare at us. We back out again and descend a few more stone steps to the Ship and

Crown with its ancient timbers, framed photographs of old ships and nicotine-stained ceiling. It is throbbing with life and good humour.

Channel Islanders are very polite. You collide with them, and *they* apologise. The two women from Hamburg with whom we share a table agree. They have been in the islands two weeks and are sorry they have to leave.

As we return to *Voyager* in the water taxi I discover that I have committed a cardinal sin. I forgot to turn off our VHF after calling up the taxi channel. Its cockpit repeater is currently squawking pleas for transport across the entire marina. I curse my amateurishness as we push back the French boats to get the water taxi through. Above us, dessert is now in progress.

It has been all-change in our absence among the boats behind us, according to the couple next door, who tell us they assisted, thereby protecting our boat from damage. We thank them very much, but I don't admit that I can't see any difference and that to me the boats behind us look pretty much the same as the ones that were there before we went ashore. They seem such old hands, this couple, as they talk. When we tell them our next destination is Tréguier, on the north Brittany coast, they correct our pronunciation and say we'll love it. They talk of many lovely-sounding places. They seem to have been everywhere. Before we go to bed I get David to explain what we have to do next morning to get them away at 5am in a seemly manner. I don't want to look like the amateur I feel.

Our alarm clock goes off at 4.30 next morning and we get up immediately. With my aversion for ropes, it gives me time to run through again what I have to do with the wretched things. I also don't want to be late and keep our neighbours waiting.

They do not appear on deck until 4.50am. We ask if they are ready for us to begin untying. 'Five minutes,' they say. They seem very tense.

David hovers on deck, keen to carry out a manoeuvre we have never done before: letting an inner boat out without losing contact with the pontoon ourselves – or in this case, with another boat tied up to the pontoon. It is not difficult, needing only a little preparation and a degree of co-operation. It does not require the use of an engine by the boat that is going to remain, merely judicious handling of the mooring lines. It is a standard technique and David knows it from his textbooks, although the previous day the man on the Westerley had instructed him how to do it anyway.

Now, however, despite having started their engine, instead of preparing to leave our neighbours stand about looking fraught. Taking pity on them I go below and hoik David in after me. 'I think they may be having a marital moment or something,' I whisper. 'Give them a bit of privacy to sort themselves out.'

The five requested minutes pass, and then another five. When we finally squint discreetly through the curtains what we see sends us leaping on deck. They have untied themselves from the inside boat and show every sign of leaving, despite the fact that they are still tied to us and we still have two shorelines attached to the pontoon, one of them across their bows. Our careful plan collapses in ruins.

In retrospect I could have untied our bow shore line on board, although this would undoubtedly have wrapped itself around their propeller as they left. Instead, without even thinking, I sprint over their deck, across the deck of the boat inside them, and onto the pontoon to untie it there. As David hauls it in, however, the Westerley's owners begin to pull out, leaving me on the pontoon and with our boat still tied to theirs. I just manage to scramble back onto the Westerly before the distance becomes too great and vault the guard-rails onto *Voyager* as David unties the last of the lines holding our boat to theirs.

The couple on the Westerly neither look at us nor speak, but simply motor away staring ahead, faces grim, jaws clenched. We are left to blast our engines into life and shuffle *Voyager* backwards alongside the inner boat without fouling a propeller on the stern shore line I had not had time to untie.

At 7am, the three cheerful people on the inside boat discuss their departure with us, and we are finally able to put the textbook manoeuvre into practice. It goes off without a hitch.

The man in the blazer and the peaked cap, meanwhile, has been patrolling his pontoon since shortly after sunrise and shouting orders at the young woman getting his boat ready. Having woken all his neighbours with his noise, and then instructing them on how much room he needs to exit, patrolling is all he does until 8.30 when he takes the helm of his 30-foot sloop.

As he motors past, with the docile young woman now tidying away his ropes and fenders, he eyes me triumphantly and with a toss of his head cries, 'At last!' as if he has just relieved Mafeking single-handed. As his stern passes I read the lettering on it. It says, *Éclat* and *Royal ****** Yacht Club*.

At 10am we paddle the dinghy ashore and spend the fare saved on the water taxi in the café of Castle Cornet instead. You make your choice at a counter with domestic artefacts from the museum on the wall behind it – pewter and pottery and a wooden trencher dated circa 1510 with an indentation at one corner for precious salt. We carry our coffee and banana cake outside to a small table on the ramparts, where cannon once stood, and gaze out at the sea.

The castle, begun in 1204, contains some super museums but it is the people we find most extraordinary. They are so spontaneously helpful. We are looking at the Civil War display at around 11.50am when one of the attendants climbs the stairs to tell us that the cannon will be fired on the battlements at noon if we would care to watch. At the same time she makes a special point of warning us that the explosion is LOUD.

When we reach the site there are warning notices all round the battlements to the same effect. We wait behind a rope barrier with lots of other people. First comes the sound of bagpipes through a loudspeaker, then a very thin Redcoat and a rather portly Redcoat march to the cannon. The portly one rams the explosive down the barrel while the thin one puts a brass telescope to one eye and stares at the church clock down in the town, waiting for noon.

I look around the castle walls and observe the warning signs. I had misread them yesterday. Because of my own inexperience I had accepted the couple on the Westerley at face value. Yet no-one with any skills, not to mention a basic concern for somebody else's boat and personal safety, would have cast off in such an irresponsible way. They were as phony as the absurd little man in the blazer, and a day trip from England's south coast to Guernsey is probably as far as they ever venture. And when we do reach Tréguier, even their pronunciation of its name turns out to have been wrong.

In any other circumstance but sailing I should have recognized their self-aggrandizement for what it was, but our sailing has nearly all been done in the Irish Sea. And while its conditions may be challenging, it is sparsely populated and largely marina-free. I need to be more alert to human hazards. In future I shall take better notice of the signs.

An elderly woman beside me aims her camera at Castle Cornet's cannon. I've already taken my picture so as to leave my fingers free for my ears. 'It's very loud,' I say to her. She presses her lips together and smiles in that grim sort of way you do to people stating the obvious. At noon precisely, the plump redcoat lights the fuse and, fingers in ears, David and I are ready for the bang. It *is* LOUD.

The elderly woman at my elbow is so shocked she never does take a picture. Her camera falls to the length of its strap around her neck and she just stands there with her eyes glazed and her hands still raised at the level they had been when they held her camera. Almost everybody seems to have ignored the warning notices, so the soldiers march away to stunned silence instead of applause, as people stand around blinking and waiting for their ears to stop ringing.

After Castle Cornet we go off to stock up the food cupboard, to a pharmacy for recommended anti-mosquito remedies I had failed to get at home, and for another half a pint in the Ship and Crown. Back on board I change into a swimsuit and begin to get lunch.

'David stares at me. 'How did you get all those bruises?'

They are worst on my upper arms and thighs. Several of them are whoppers in various shades of purple.

'Walked into a door,' I say. 'Isn't that what I'm supposed to tell people?'

Actually, it is not far from the truth. Three of them relate to various door handles, one to the temperature adjustment knob on the refrigerator, and the *piéce de résistance* – a real corker on my upper thigh – to the corner of the saloon table.

When you first go on board your boat after a long period you are out of the habit of both its movement and confinement. The result is bruises. The strange thing is, you are not aware of acquiring most of them; you just get up next morning and there's another bit of you turning purple. After a while, you simply get accustomed to not making expansive gestures in a confined space, and automatically adjust your balance in advance of any approaching wash. I had started every sailing season with bruises, but had rarely been on board this long before to gather so many; or found it warm enough in the Irish Sea to wear a swimsuit and flaunt them.

9
St Peter Port to Mouillier Bay

Our next port-of-call is Tréguier on France's Brittany coast and, as with any place you've not sailed before, a vital source of information is yachting magazines. A first-person account can be invaluable for discovering the hidden pleasures of a place whilst avoiding its pitfalls. A recently-published article had stressed the need to enter Tréguier's marina on slack tide because a 5-knot current rushes through on the ebb and the flood, which makes tying up very difficult.

To be sure of arriving at the marina at slack water we need to leave Guernsey marina around midnight. More boats will probably be arriving soon to replace our two neighbours from this morning. Faced with the problems of getting off the pontoon in the dark, from the inside of a three-boat raft-up, David suggests we go somewhere and anchor until after midnight, and set off for Tréguier from there.

We leave the pontoon at 2pm for Mouillier Bay. The chart warns of a large rock in the centre of it, while its shore is strewn with them. There are also a lot of fishing buoys bobbing on its surface. A cruiser's natural enemies are fishermen.

Although *Voyager* has no leaks David has apparently been mulling over possible damage ever since our encounter with rocks in Braye Harbour, so once we are anchored he goes over the side with a snorkel and mask. He surfaces to say that there is only a long thin gouge along the port keel boot. Keel boots are there to protect the bottom of the keel, and it can easily be repaired when *Voyager* is next out of the water. It is the very least we could have hoped for, and he feels much happier. It is a bumpy anchorage, though being a catamaran we don't roll too badly. The mast of a nearby monohull, however, thrashes like a sapling in a storm. We tidy the boat, have dinner and get out the hurricane lamp.

An anchored boat is required to show a light after dark to warn others of its presence, but many cruisers choose to save vital battery power by using a paraffin lamp. We fill ours, light it and hang it up on the foredeck. We go to bed at 8.30pm totally exhausted, but sleep little given the turbulence. The skipper of the monohull abandons the anchorage during the night.

We rise for the shipping forecast at forty-eight minutes past midnight and set off shortly afterwards. The forecast is for a moderate breeze from the southwest, possibly strengthening to Force 5. If it occurs, it will give us a sail. For the moment there is only the lightest of breezes and the sea is still very bumpy. The previous afternoon David had taken a compass bearing by which to leave the anchorage safely if the night was overcast. Apart from missing the rock in the middle, and the fishing buoys just waiting to wrap their ropes around our propellers, it would also make sure we kept away from the bay's rocky edges, since it is easy to stray when you pull up an anchor in the dark.

As it turns out, a clear sky allows a bright half-moon to shed its silver light around us. Unfortunately, half way through raising the anchor the chain jams in the windlass and David has to haul up the rest of it by hand. While I steer out of the bay, David takes a spanner to the windlass. Thus we set off tentatively for France. I look for signs of rain. In the past it always rained whenever we went to France.

FRANCE

▸▸▸

IO
Guernsey to Tréguier

The voyage to Tréguier is only the second night passage we have ever done alone. The first had been several years ago and forced on us when a gale kept us overlong on the Irish coast and we had to sail through the night to get back in time for work on Monday morning. Our only other experience of night passages was bringing *Voyager* back to England with Ian. He favoured three-hour watches and we plan to do the same.

We also use a tip he gave us and set a kitchen timer to ring at ten minute intervals because it is very easy at night to become drowsy or unobservant, especially into the third hour of your watch. We make it a rule that we do a complete 360° scan of the horizon every ten minutes. Having timed a commercial ship from a dot on the horizon to arriving level with us, we feel that leaving it any longer than ten minutes would be foolhardy.

Between Guernsey and Tréguier our only navigational concerns are two reefs, or *plateau* as the French call them, the Plateau des Roches Douvres and the Plateau de Barnouic. They are both marked by navigational lights at night and David has plotted a course well clear of them. He takes the first watch and I go below, but the sea is too turbulent for sleep. When I get up to take over the watch, it is cold. So I put on my oilies for warmth and rediscover, for the first time in a year, the sheer user-unfriendliness of wet weather gear.

I have a difficult relationship with my wet weather gear, or *oilies* as the two garments are still called from the days before man-made fibres when fabric had to be oiled to make it waterproof. It is also called foul weather gear as it protects the wearer from rain, cold, hail, sleet and breaking waves. *Foul* is the word that I feel describes it best, except when there's driving rain and freezing cold and then I stand around murmuring how wonderful it is.

The standard suit comes in two parts: high-waisted trousers with shoulder straps and a jacket. I find both monumentally uncomfortable. The fabric is stiff, slippery and it rasps and crackles as you move about. At the ankles, the trousers have an extra lining edged with strong elastic to deter water from going up your legs. Combined with the stiffness of the fabric itself, and the reinforcement at the knees, the whole leg is kept taut, and after an hour my kneecaps begin to ache. The trousers are good around the torso, though; coming up under the arms and keeping all your vital organs warm. It can be a little hard on the more tender parts of the female anatomy, however, thanks to its stiffening, heavy duty zip and Velcro. Like an Elizabethan stomacher, it is flat and unyielding. That's the thing with unisex, of course, it is designed for men.

The jacket has two endearing features: a high collar which stands up around the ears, and a really generous hood. The hood holds the collar up around the sides of your face and keeps out the wind, while its stiffened peak keeps as much rain off your face and spectacles as you could hope for short of an umbrella.

The rest of it drives me demented. For a start, the man-sized sleeves are too long, but the cuff has a tight inner sleeve to stop the rain from running up your arm which ensures that you can't pull the sleeves up a bit, not even enough to fill in the log or light the gas under the kettle. So I clear the chart table of instruments simply reaching for a pencil, and am an accident waiting to happen in the galley.

And then, of course, there is my special *bête noire*. Velcro. It is everywhere: at wrists and ankles so you can make them tighter and even more uncongenial than they already are; down the front openings over the zippers to make them more wind and waterproof; and as fastenings for the pockets, collar and hood. But this is no ordinary Velcro. This is commercial strength. If I ever topple overboard it will probably be because all the Velcro on my wet weather gear snaps shut like a Venus flytrap and I am rendered helpless.

Velcro is at its worst when you are roused from a deep sleep in a deliciously warm bunk to take up your second three-hour night watch in a cold, wet cockpit. Pick up the slippery trousers and they lock together at the ankles. Separate the legs and struggle in, and before you can pull up the zip you have to detach one of the jacket sleeves, the cuff of which has mysteriously leapt upwards and adhered itself to the front opening of the trousers.

Pick up the heavy, slithery jacket and its right sleeve darts around the back and attaches itself like a limpet to its own front opening, so you're effectively left wrestling a cold, damp, heavy, implacable tube. A broken nail and a strained thumb joint later and you've prized the right sleeve off the front opening, only to find it has been replaced by the left sleeve and the whole unseemly, oath-laden performance begins all over again.

The jacket is also very long. The purpose, undoubtedly, is to protect the male backside from the elements. But it means my arms aren't long enough to reach the bottom of the zipper, so I bend forward. All this achieves is that the bottom of the zipper gets closer to my knees. Soon I'm bent double and the stiff, Velcroed edges of that lovely high collar are now under my jaw bones and forcing my head back. No longer able to see the two ends of the zipper directly, I try to peer over my chin. This makes my eyes hurt so I try twisting sideways and get a stabbing pain in my neck.

To make matters worse there are actually *two* zippers, parallel to each other; the inner one to enable a buoyancy aid to be zipped into the jacket if required. The trouble is that in poor light, half asleep and giving a passable impersonation of Quasimodo, one large navy-blue plastic zipper gets confused with another. I never seem to get the two ends of the same zipper together first go and waste valuable minutes trying to force the tag of one into the clip of the other. Then that lovely generous hood falls over my eyes and I can't even see the two navy blue zippers, let alone fit the correct halves together. So I have to let both ends go while I push the hood back behind the collar.

Just when I think that either my neck will break or my eyes pop out of their sockets the proper tag finds the correct clip. In sheer relief I forget to go cautiously, wrench up the zipper and suffer excruciating pain as the large, chromium-plated steel clips of the integral safety harness crush those tender female parts. However, I cannot immediately release the zipper to relieve this pressure because the Velcro on the jacket's cuffs has adhered to the Velcro on the front fastening and with eyes watering and both hands incapacitated a voice from the helm calls, 'Aren't you ready yet?' And that's when I remember that I should have put my deck shoes on before the jacket because in my corset of stiff plastic, chromium clips, implacable Velcro, heavy duty zippers and reinforced kneecaps there's no way I can reach my feet with the jacket *on*.

When I do, finally, present myself on deck for duty there is the usual, added irritation. As well as restricting your movements, wet weather gear affects your hearing. What with that high collar, the hood, and all the attendant rustle and crackle whenever you move you keep saying 'Sorry?' or talking at cross purposes. A large French Navy boat appears behind us and I say, 'Those fire exocets don't they?'

'No,' says David, also partially deafened by his own crackling oilies, 'it's too big for a frigate.'

'I said *exocets*, not *frigate*!'

'What?' he says.

I groan and he goes below, returning with a French courtesy flag. As he raises it by a halyard on the starboard side deck I pom-pom the Marseillaise and he says, 'Shut up, they'll hear you.' And I snap, 'Not if they're wearing their bloody wet weather gear they won't.'

David goes to bed after the 05.35 shipping forecast and I take over the watch. Two gannets and a seagull come to inspect us and just after six o'clock the sun rises. It is a fiery orange-red and molten, as if it is melting and dripping into the sea. As it ascends it solidifies into a hard silver disc that is too bright to look at any more.

I feel surprisingly fresh considering that I have been without proper sleep for twenty-four hours, and settle into the helmsman's chair with a French dictionary.

It is probably fair to say that, in the main, the English and the French do not get on. Although physical encounters ceased long ago, the

Cultural Wars continue. They are forever telling us – via our own radio, books and newspapers – that our women are gauche, our clothes appalling and our food inedible. For our part, we deplore their plumbing and the way they pretend they don't understand us when we make a real effort to try to speak French to them. And then, of course, there is the Common Agricultural Policy.

Despite our best efforts, our trips to northern France during the 1970s had not turned out well and the weather was always terrible. However, we had made one last, determined effort in the early 80s to discover once and for all the magic of France that we were always hearing about but which had so far eluded us.

Our car was burgled in a car park, and subsequently wrecked on a mountain road by a French driver. The French police seemed to make a special effort to be superhumanly offensive, and we were monumentally ripped off by the garage which ultimately got around to repairing our car while allowing it to be pillaged of those possessions we had been unable to carry home with us.

The final insult had come during the stressful, luggage-laden and expensive journey back to England by public transport when an old woman on the Paris train, overhearing our English voices, began haranguing us with insults to the vast amusement of the other French passengers. And throughout this French summer idyll, for which we had sacrificed our precious two weeks' annual holiday, it had rained virtually every day.

After finally regaining our car we had turned our backs on France, and the French, for ever and discovered the magic of Italy annually instead. Accordingly, I am glad that we shall merely be passing quickly through the country. Nevertheless, I fully intend to put up a spirited English defence against Gallic hostility, and to that end sail down the Brittany coast with a French vocabulary propped above the wheel rehearsing numbers, common questions and a grammatically perfect way to ask for a marina berth for one night, please.

When David takes over the watch from me I begin work on a sinkfull of washing up. As well as the dishwasher I also miss the washing machine. The laundry bag is bulging already. Some considerable time later, my hands full of clean crockery, I turn from the sink and pitch forward. The laces of my deck shoes have come undone again.

As well as a fraught relationship with wet weather gear, I also harbour a simmering hatred for deck shoes. I find them monstrously uncomfortable especially where, despite socks, they have rubbed calluses on various bits of my feet. And they have ridiculous leather laces which you can't replace with sensible fibre ones because they go all the way round the back before they reach the eyeholes and are an integral part of the shoe.

Leather laces may be traditional, and to some eyes even attractive, *but they don't stay tied* which I would have thought was the *raison d'etre* of laces, especially on a heaving deck. So you have to tie a really tight double bow, which not only presses uncomfortably into the foot, but all this fiddling is something you really don't need, especially in the dark and/or in an emergency.

Even in double bows, however, these arcane laces still won't stay tied indefinitely, although their untying is not random. Definitely not. They untie themselves in very specific circumstances, like this one, when you're carrying the boat's entire stock of crockery. Or when you're trying to reef the genoa in bad weather and the outhaul gets stuck and you have to go to the bow to free the furling gear. As you struggle forward, with the deck heaving and waves washing over the foredeck – THEN – *that's* when they undo. The descending foot clamps down on the incontinent lace, the ascending foot rises and *Bingo!* Both feet snap together.

Then, wrenching your wrist clutching at a handrail, as the only alternative to pitching onto your face, you mutter things like, 'God bless these charming little touches of a bygone age which have survived into present times while serving no apparent practical purpose whatsoever.'

And you have to set about retying the blasted things before you can even *begin* to address the problem with the furling gear for fear of treading on them again and pitching overboard. And in your fury you tie them too tight and your insteps have little purple ridges on them for days afterwards. Unfortunately, there is simply nothing else in the world like a deck shoe sole for gripping a slippery deck.

II

Tréguier

David has chosen Tréguier as our first French stop-over en route to the Bay of Biscay because as well as convenient it is also said to be beautiful. The town, and its marina, are approximately five miles up a river called Le Jaudy. On the chart the entry into this river looks fairly straightforward if you follow the entry route known as the Grande Passe. Had we known what it would look like in the flesh – or the rock, to be more precise – I doubt we should have gone there. From the sea it looks nightmarish.

Like the rest of the Brittany coast, the mouth of Le Jaudy is littered with rocks. There are several channels through them and, like the others, the Grande Passe requires you to find an entry buoy. This buoy leads you into a safe channel running parallel with the coast for some distance – between small islands, jagged rocks and shoals – before you turn right into the actual river.

It is around 10am as we approach, but even in clear daylight it is difficult to spot the entry buoy. Ahead of us we can see a boat on the other side of the rocks heading towards the mouth of the river, and obviously in the channel. This reassures us that this vital marker buoy is where we thought it should be and we continue on our course. We have just spotted the buoy and breathed a sigh of relief when the boat ahead of us turns round and starts coming back, which puzzles us greatly.

However, everything we have read insists that entry into the marina on slack water is essential, so we press on. We reach the marker buoy and enter the channel. The other boat passes us, turns, and starts to follow us. Suddenly we realise that its skipper is using us to show him the way.

This is rash of him since not only is this our first time here, but a catamaran has a much shallower draught than a monohull unless it has a lifting keel. I should like to be able to say that this cured me forever from suggesting to David, when temporarily confused, that he should follow another boat instead of sticking to his original course; but I live in hope. Like me with the couple on the Westerley, the skipper of this yacht has been tempted to assume that everybody else knows better than he does.

Although its mouth is wide, the river itself soon narrows considerably. Its navigable channel, between submerged rocks, is narrower still and the place is littered with fishing buoys. Several times we have difficulty spotting the correct navigation buoy, and we are very cautious because apart from the Republic of Ireland this is our first real foreign port of entry. And it is *France*. After my experience with the gendarmerie and our car, there is no way I am going to tell the French coastguard that we have hit a rock and are sinking.

It takes just over an hour to reach the marina. The sun is shining and the river is glorious. Woodland tumbles down to the water's edge, with an occasional stone house among the trees. Elsewhere, fields rise steeply up from the river. In one of these fields wheat is being harvested, the sunlight turning it marigold-yellow like something out of a van Gogh painting.

David has us hovering off the marina at slack water. We know from the cruising guide that they are going to be finger pontoons. These mini-pontoons extend at right angles from a main pontoon and, unless your boat is very small, reach only part of the way down your hull. So, unless you're quick, the current drags you sideways and they grind their vicious little corners into the gelcoat near your stern. To prevent this, the helmsman needs to hold his vessel off on three sides until the crew ties ropes onto four cleats to do the job for him. If the crew gets it really wrong, the bows get mangled against the main pontoon as well. On the other hand, trying to cover four cleats at once is quite a lot for a solitary crewmember.

I have everything ready: fenders hanging over both sides and a rope on all four corners. I also have a plan in mind of the order in which I am going to tie on these four ropes for maximum protection of the boat's hulls. I am so determined to get it right in this heartland of Anglophobia that when the moment comes I throw myself over the side without taking a rope with me at all, and have to make an unseemly scramble back on board to get one.

A marina attendant appears and helps me tie up. Breathless, I open my mouth to utter a word-perfect request in French for a berth. 'One night?' he says in English, before I can make a sound. I nod. After he's gone, and as the magazine article had recommended, we put on double springs to withstand the strong current which will travel up and down the river during the three changes of tide that will take place during our stay.

My next priority is a shower. French plumbing has always been notorious among British travellers. Naturally, we do not approve of open-air public toilets in town centres, nor mixed-sex ones even when they have a roof and doors, but most appalling of all to us are the 'squatties', the hole in the floor with grooves for the feet.

Surprisingly the marina's shower block has real pedestal lavatories, but smaller and lower than anything seen since infant school. The floor is also under water. The reason soon becomes clear. The moment the flush button is touched, water blasts across the seat, your shoes and the floor where it adds to the slick that met you at the door.

The showers respond to 9 francs, which release a cistern of water above your head that you operate by a chain with a handle on it, like a 1950s outside privy. After seeing what the lavatories can do, I decide to bathe on *Voyager*.

We open a bottle of wine. So far so good, we say. So far so good. We have corned beef sandwiches for lunch and the last of Alderney's gache bread with blackcurrant jam on it. Tired from a night's sailing but happy, I nap for an hour and wake feeling relaxed and smug to have arrived safe and sound with more personal dignity than expected.

David, meanwhile, has been looking at the charts for the next stage of our journey and we have a leisurely discussion about crossing the Bay of Biscay, which will be our next big challenge. A weather window has appeared in the shipping forecasts. There is currently an area of high pressure stationary over Biscay which promises a period of settled weather. We want at all cost to make our way across this notorious bay during these few days of calm.

We plan to leave tomorrow around noon on a falling tide, after first getting diesel from the fuel dock a short distance from our finger pontoon. Nothing is left to chance. We even go and have a look at the fuel dock. It is very narrow for a catamaran, but we pace it out to ensure we can get *Voyager* in. The approach to it is also rather awkward, with a semi-submerged ramp and a wooden stake warning of shallows, but they will not be a problem at slack tide.

One of our two bottles of propane gas, which we use for cooking, refrigeration and hot water, runs out so we decide to amble over to the service station across the road to see if we can get it refilled. There is not only a fast current on Tréguier's river, but also an 8.5-metre drop in the water level at low tide. Already the ramp leading from our pontoon up onto the quay is getting quite steep.

The service station does not fill gas bottles on the premises. It sends them away to a refilling facility which takes a day or two, so we wander back to the marina and fall into conversation with the English-speaking marina attendant.

Intuition is a strange thing. For a long time I tried to suppress mine, but finally succumbed to it, even if it does sometimes mean appearing a little odd. As we part and go our separate ways, and almost in spite of myself, I stop and call after the attendant, 'We're going to buy fuel tomorrow.'

David looks at me sideways with the sort of expression which says, 'Why did you do that?' But the attendant doesn't think me odd at all. Walking back to us he purses his lips and shakes his head. The fuel dock, he says, is not run by the marina, but by the service station across the road. When you want fuel, you have to go there and ask for someone to come here and serve you. No-one will be working at the service station tomorrow because it is a public holiday, and the following day is Sunday, so it won't open again until Monday. He looks at his watch. They will be closing soon.

We are mortified. If we have to waste two days of this precious weather window waiting for fuel we could end up in the middle of Biscay when the weather breaks. Although we had survived gale-force winds and 20-foot waves there once before, bringing *Voyager* home to the UK, it had been with an experienced sailor. We would prefer not to do it again now if we can avoid it.

We run back up an even steeper ramp, and back across the road to the garage. Since it is late Friday afternoon, as well as the eve of a public holiday, there are a lot of cars on the forecourt. They will have to serve these first, they say, and then they will come. We rush back to the boat. After all that careful planning and self-congratulation we are going to be shunting out of our finger pontoon, into and out of a narrow fuel dock, and back into our vicious little finger pontoon again in a 4-knot tide. I want to weep, but there isn't time.

We manage it, despite *Voyager*'s notoriously slow-filling fuel tank. I muck up the ropes again, but a Frenchman who has tied up next door in the meantime joins me and we get *Voyager* in before the infamous current reaches its full force. The man is dark-haired and plump with a kind, sad face. His wife, who stays aboard their boat, is unsmiling, detached, elsewhere. They have a little dog with them, a concoction of English breeds in surprising combinations but the overall result is a cheerful curly brownness.

We put on double springs again and indeed use virtually every rope we possess, on the better-safe-than-sorry principle; the way you get when you are rushed and stressed and all rationality has gone. When we have finished, our boat resembles one of those book illustrations of Gulliver after the Lilliputians have captured him and tied him down.

Our berth has cost £21 for the night and the fuel £54, which hasn't left much of our £100-worth of francs, so we set off to have a look round the town and replenish our funds at the same time. It is a pretty town centre up a steep hill with a lot of traffic and pavements only one person wide.

Unfortunately all the cash points refuse to provide any money. We cannot find out why, because all of them have instructions in French only. However, we discover the town's launderette, the restaurant where we will have dinner, and the medieval cathedral of St Tugdual with its spire of delicate stone tracery that lets the sky shine through.

'Five minutes,' says the woman in the cathedral doorway apologetically. A service has just finished and the clergy can be glimpsed disrobing in the panelled vestry. 'We close in five minutes. So sorry.'

We use the five minutes to take in the beautiful interior, a heart-rending Christ on a crucifix, and two wonderful carved wooden figures: St Peter with the keys of the kingdom and St Paul with his epistles.

Tréguier lies in an area called Trégor, one of the four ancient regions of Basse-Bretagne where Breton is still spoken and traditions and local costumes are preserved. The town itself was founded in the 6th century by St Tugdual and was once a place of learning and a centre for the arts. The cathedral's doors open onto a square. Around it are medieval shops and houses. They are mostly of stone with steep slate roofs. Some have towers, and a few have a black-and-white lath-and-plaster upper storey overhanging the street. An annual event here is a May procession called the Pardon of St Yves, the patron saint of lawyers. I never knew they had one.

We've been back on board *Voyager* only minutes when a large motor yacht collides with the pontoon on our starboard side. The force of the tide is turning the vessel sideways. We go to assist, and fend off while its French skipper hops off and ties up with four short lines little thicker than parcel string, and no springs.

We feel we have to warn him of the dangers of the tide here and tentatively explain the problem to him in a combination of halting French and mime. He thanks us most politely in impeccable English but says he thinks he'll be OK as he's kept his boat there for the past seven years. David and I sidle away from him, arranging ourselves so as to obscure his view of the cat's cradle pinning Gulliver to the cleats behind us.

'Shall I take some of them off?' I whisper, as the man sprints up to his sun terrace for cocktails with his elegantly-dressed wife.

'Nah,' says David, beginning to droop with tiredness. 'Leave 'em.'

Word obviously gets round, though, because during the course of the late afternoon people going ashore from other pontoons make a detour via ours to look at our mooring ropes. And a very old couple – she in traditional black with a headscarf, he leaning heavily on a stick – come from the town and spend quite some time contemplating them, as if they are a harbinger of approaching catastrophe, like a strange light in the sky or the village well overflowing.

We dine this evening at a whitewashed, green-framed, lace-curtained little place near the quay. We eat seafood off wooden trenchers not unlike those behind the counter of the teashop in Castle Cornet circa 1510. The bill comes in a little square straw basket with a lid on. We have eaten royally and relaxed, thanks to a litre of smooth red wine, for £8.50 a head in the restaurant's former cellar, now the Smoking Salon.

When you have been stressed, and then you become relaxed with food and wine, there is a tendency to gaze around you as if you are in a gallery looking at paintings: still life, portraits, scenes of everyday life. Everything becomes vibrant, there is no self-consciousness. You don't so much observe as absorb, and you are not so much a spectator as a medium for recording these things. And you capture on the canvas of your mind this restaurant and these people, for no other reason than that they, and you, are there, and they last for as long as memory lasts.

In the far corner a small man wearing a skullcap, bookish, with a young woman of an age to be his daughter. To the left of our table, a swarthy man with a woman; both thin, cynical, sardonic. In front, a family: he round, in a spotless, high-necked, buttoned white top, the baker in medieval portraits; two women with him, one with the serene smile of a madonna and a small male child. Behind, two couples and a sun-bleached youth. The blonde woman wears shorts, her right leg jerking up and down as she relentlessly strokes her thigh with chewed fingernails. The man beside her (not her partner) talks endlessly, his dark-haired wife nodding approval. The youth, like a beached windsurfer, wants to be anywhere but here with them. Oddly, no likeness of the blonde's partner is captured, only her restless attention to the other man.

Contrary to belief, part of the pleasure of foreign travel is *not* being able to speak the language: of being excluded from the rush and stress, the petty snobberies of class and the country's economic, political and cultural dilemmas; while at the same time getting a break from your own. People, we will also discover, are particularly kind to those without their language, as long as their assistance is asked for with care.

Back on board, I sit in the dark cockpit, in my favourite spot beside the companionway doors, with my back against the saloon bulkhead and my knees up under my chin. On the boat to my right, the man with the dour wife and the cheerful little brown dog smokes a last cigarette and sings very softly to himself in the darkness before going to bed.

To my left, the shapes of the medieval town are outlined by street lamps. The cathedral spire with the delicate stone tracery lets the lamp light shine through and seems to tilt a little to one side. A house near the quay is squat and square. It has a round tower on its corner with one of those typically French conical roofs whose curve defies the very nature of flat, brittle slate.

The lamps along the quay are yellow; up on the hill a church is lit from below with white spotlights. Between them they send slender shafts of gold and silver shimmering across the surface of the dark water towards our boat.

On the bank an unseen woman recites a poem in a high, clear voice. The words are lost to me, but their rhythm turns them into music, rising and falling like notes from a flute. And then there is silence. The river is still. It has been a good day.

12
Tréguier to L'Abervrac'h

Next morning we wash *Voyager* down, fill our water tanks and go into town. It is our first experience of a French launderette, or indeed of any launderette since the early days of our marriage. There is no indication as to what value coins should be used in the washers or driers. There is, however, a French woman, folding linen on a large table, helped by a small girl.

'*Pardonnez moi, Madame.*' I have my French currency spread on my palm as I approach. I don't want her to think I'm asking her for money, or for change.

'*Ah!*' She smiles and pounces on a coin. *This one:* she holds it aloft and points to the washer. *These two:* the drier. *And this:* she points to a little machine on the wall in the corner I hadn't noticed which dispenses soap powder, something I'd forgotten to bring. Not satisfied that she has done enough for me, she begins to explain in French how to use the machines.

I put coins into the wall machine for 4 francs-worth of little individual packets of surprisingly pungent soap powder. For weeks afterwards its distinctive smell will waft out of any locker where anything that has been washed in it is stored.

While I get the washers going, David sets off on another attempt to get some French currency. He returns triumphant brandishing cash. He has finally worked out that unlike English ATMs at the time, but typical of every European one we would subsequently encounter, after you put in your pin number you have to press the button *confirmer* – confirm.

It has become hot and airless in the launderette so David takes a chair onto the pavement outside where it is pleasantly cool. He settles himself there with a magazine, ready to load the driers at the appropriate time. Clutching French currency I set off up the steep hill to the shops. I buy bread and some gorgeous caramel custard pastries, big juicy pears, brie, tomatoes and ten views of medieval Tréguier to post home. In between times I can't help noticing a decidedly stop/start quality to the town's traffic. For no apparent reason, at one moment it is clogging up the streets and the next it evaporates.

As I walk back down the hill I see a car stop outside the launderette and its driver accost David. Other cars pull up behind it. David lifts his shoulders, raises his palms and shakes his head. The traffic then moves on. Moments later another car stops, other cars pull up behind it, David gives the same shrug and the cars move on. It happens several times more before I reach him.

'What are you doing?' I ask.

Tourists, he says, seeing him in his chair on the pavement, take him for a local and keep stopping to ask directions. None of them speaks English and his first few attempts to explain that this was his first visit here only resulted in grid-locking half the town. So he has resorted to a Gallic shrug and Tréguier's traffic keeps flowing.

We leave the marina at noon, just as the tide begins to ebb. We intend to travel through the night, arriving at L'Abervrac'h around dawn the following morning. The estuary of the River L'Abervrac'h is a good place to rest and wait for the right tidal conditions for the passage through the Chenal du Four. We have a mountain of rope to remove. When we have done so, the Frenchmen from the boats either side of us materialize to fend us off the pontoons if necessary and wish us *bon voyage*.

The falling tide carries us down the river and back out to sea. Once clear of the rocky entrance we let out the sails but, because the wind is very light and almost on the nose, we motor-sail. We make good speed throughout the afternoon, around 7 knots with the current behind us, but keeping well out to sea to avoid outlying rocks. It is a very pleasant sail in bright sunshine.

Early evening, after passing the group of islands and reefs called Les Triagoz, we alter course which brings the light wind into a more favourable position. To maintain our present speed, however, will get us to L'Abervrac'h, and another rock-strewn river entrance, while it is still dark. So we cut the engine and purely sail for the first time this year, ghosting through the night in a gentle breeze with the shadowy mainland in the distance.

So light is the wind, and with the tide slowly turning against us, that progress drops at times to barely a knot. But sitting in the cockpit there is no urgency. The sky is clear, with a bright quarter moon and Venus beside it, like the star and crescent. The night is calm and cool. The only movement apart from us is from two shooting stars and the lights of a few distant boats.

Five miles off L'Abervrac'h the wind becomes too light and variable for the sails so we take them in and turn on the engine. As we near the rocky reef at the entrance to the river, the GPS screen displays the message *No Position Found*. It is hard to describe the effect of arriving at a difficult river entrance in the dark without an accurate course to follow. *Panic* is the word which springs most immediately to mind.

When this initial moment has passed, David remembers that months earlier he had bought a hand-held GPS as part of his planning for emergency situations and equipment failure. He fetches it, gets it out of its box, turns it on, and while it searches for satellite signals to lock onto and find our present position, he feeds in the co-ordinates for the waypoint to which we are heading. Just as the hand-held GPS begins showing a course, the other one comes back on again. It is to become a regular feature of our main GPS that when approaching a dangerous entrance to a harbour it will stop functioning and display the message *No Position Found*.

We arrive at L'Abervrac'h at 7.15. It is a cold, damp morning. We tie up to a buoy and are in bed within half an hour. The alarm clock is set for a little before noon. We are both tired after a night passage, but fail to sleep nevertheless and are pottering around by eleven. We break our fast with tea, French bread and blackcurrant jam and listen to the 12.02 shipping forecast – Variable mainly NW backing SW with gentle-to-moderate winds. As we slip our mooring and head for the Chenal du Four it is almost calm.

13

The Chenal du Four to Douarnenez

The Chenal du Four is a stretch of water between the French mainland and a group of islands, the largest of which is Ushant. There is a romance attached to some place names, and an evocative one for British sailors is Ushant. In the days of clipper ships, and limited navigational aids, ships' captains used it as a waypoint. When they saw it they knew exactly where they were, and could then set a course for the southern English ports of Plymouth, Southampton or Portsmouth.

The Cruising Association Handbook, 8th edition, warns: *It is important to note that with strong winds against tide, severe steep seas build up in the Chenal du Four which may be beyond the capabilities of the average small yacht.* It has a wicked current and is littered with shoals, rocks and marker buoys and care is needed to take it at the right state of the tide; hence our short stop at L'Abervrac'h. Take it against the tide and you make very slow progress. Take it on the flood and there's a chance you will not have enough control to avoid its rocks and shoals.

There is a famous lighthouse here. Anyone who has browsed in a poster shop will probably have seen an arresting picture of gigantic waves crashing against a lighthouse with such force that they reach its light. That is the Chenal du Four lighthouse, with the channel's violence at its height. Today, despite the forecast, there is so little wind we have to motor all the way. And it gets so hot that I have to go below for a shirt to keep off the sun. It is redolent with the smell of French washing powder.

By the time we've got through the Chenal du Four, the tide is about to run against us and our timing will be wrong for going through the Raz de Sein. David consults the cruising guide and, seeing no suitable anchorages, decides to head for a marina at a place called Morgat.

Mid-afternoon we pass the entrance to the Rade de Brest, an enormous bay containing the city of Brest and France's premier naval base. Two French Navy boats, leaving a massive wake, roar into the bay, scattering two old wooden-masted, gaff-rigged boats as they go. One has buff-coloured sails and a buff hull. Against a dark cliff-face it looks two-dimensional, like a picture in a children's book. The other, with traditional red-brown sails, has an extraordinary prow. When they have finished bouncing in the Navy's wash they continue on their stately way into the Bay of Brest.

By 8pm we have entered the huge Bay of Douarnenez but have still not reached Morgat, and seeing three boats anchored in a small cove decide to join them for the night. The anchor slips off weed the first time and we move to another spot to try again, bringing us closer to the three other boats. David drops the anchor again, but before we can be sure it has bitten *Voyager* begins circling wildly.

The most successful method of anchoring that we have found is for me to take the controls while David goes up front to the anchor. Steering into the wind, I bring the boat to a stop at the chosen place, David drops the anchor and lets out chain with the boat in reverse (either from the wind or by my putting both engines into reverse). We then test the anchor several times by motoring towards it and then putting both engines gently into reverse until the anchor pulls us up sharp as it digs firmly in.

When David is satisfied, he puts on a snubbing line to take the strain off the windlass and then we take transits. Taking a transit involves standing on your boat and stretching your arms out wide so that your finger-ends point at a fixed object, or transit point, on either side of the boat. If, when you adopt the same position later, your hands no longer point at the same two objects you know the boat has moved. It is a very effective method but we rarely see anybody else do it.

Tonight, however, when I try to motor forward to test the anchor the starboard engine sticks in reverse. With the port engine going forward, and the starboard engine in reverse, the result is to drive *Voyager* in circles around her anchor.

The people on the other boats come up onto their decks to watch. We turn the starboard engine off and anchor with just the port, which is less satisfactory than using both engines. While David goes below to find the cause of the problem, I take transits and keep going back on deck to check that they remain constant. The bay's shoreline is rocky and I am worried about drifting onto it if the anchor doesn't hold on the weedy bottom.

David traces our mechanical problem to the Morse controls but is unable to solve it. I become convinced we're dragging our anchor and am determined to be sure before it gets too dark to see. It may have unnerved our French neighbours – first, an English catamaran spinning like a whirling dervish and then this anxious-looking woman constantly materializing on deck and impersonating a tree – but for whatever reason, all three boats up-anchor and leave. Fortunately for us it turns out to be a quiet night.

While David looks through the cruising guide for a Yanmar engine dealer, I get dinner: tomatoes in olive oil, basil and black pepper, green salad, French bread, brie omelette with *herbes de Provence* topped with parmesan cheese; caramel egg custards, coffee and Belgian chocolates. Not bad, really. Considering.

According to the guide there is a Yanmar engine dealer across the bay at Douarnenez, a large commercial port. We shall go there in the morning. We put up the paraffin lamp on the foredeck, light the wick and go to bed. David looks very tired. I expect I do too. It is always the way with a sudden disappointment. We have only just been thinking how well we are doing, and that we shall be in good time to tackle the Bay of Biscay in a day or so. Now we have dark thoughts about how long the weather window for Biscay will last, how long it will take to get the Morse controls repaired, and how much it is going to cost given our last experience of French mechanics. Our rest would have been even further disturbed had we known that tomorrow is a public holiday.

We leave our solitary anchorage at nine the next morning for the two-hour journey to Douarnenez. It is France's fifth busiest fishing port and fishermen have used it since Roman times. Nowadays, it is mostly seasonal fishing for sardines and tuna. In the main, trawlers head south for the Bay of Biscay, although some fish off the coast of Africa.

During the journey I get out our French vocabulary to prepare for a French mechanic. I memorize the salient words but just in case he can't, or won't, understand my efforts to speak his language I also write a note in French. It is succinct: *Excuse me. English. Don't speak French. Starboard engine reverse, oui; forward, non. Problem – the Morse control gearbox. Can you repair, please?*

14

Douarnenez and through the Raz de Sein

At Douarnenez we aim for a small cove called the Rade de Guet. Given our limited manoeuvrability with only one engine we anchor well away from half a dozen local boats on buoys so as to avoid embarrassing situations we can't steer out of. Despite giving the boats on the mooring buoys a wide berth we still think we have parked relatively tidily until we look back from the dinghy on our way to the marina and see that *Voyager* is slap in the middle of the route in and out of the bay.

When you leave the Rade de Guet for the town by dinghy you cross a stone causeway called the Passe du Guet that is impassable at low tide, and which connects a small wooded island called Ile Tristan to the mainland. This little isle has several lovely, crumbling old houses on it. Once over this causeway you are in the river. Dog-leg across the river between the sandbanks and you enter a little marina in the village of Tréboul. We arrive there at 12.30.

Now, some behaviour patterns are inherited through the genes, and some are learned. Whatever the cause, one of David's is to arrive everywhere at lunchtime. If we're talking behaviour patterns, heaven knows I'm in no position to criticize, although that never stops me unfortunately.

'It's lunchtime,' I grumble as we cross the submerged causeway.

'So?' says David.

'So this is France,' I snap. 'The whole country closes for lunch between noon and five. It is also approaching the hottest part of the day.'

David, however, is the supreme optimist. His response is always the same: 'Oh, somebody will be open/We can have a look around the town/I'll buy you lunch/It's not *that* hot.'

Everywhere, including the Yanmar engine dealer, is closed – not just for lunch but for the holiday – except the patisserie and a clothes shop. Food and fashion. I find that very French. We buy a baguette and an amazing baked plum custard from the patisserie, and then take a detour to the office of the Capitaine du Port to explain our being in the middle of his patch rather than have him arrive angry on our doorstep. But the harbour master's office is shut as well.

On our way back to the dinghy we press our noses against the Yanmar mechanic's window in the vain hope of detecting signs of life within. There are none, but someone passing by, who speaks a little English, says very helpfully that the mechanic will be there at two o'clock.

The bad news is that the town is hosting some sort of regatta, so the chance of getting a mechanic quickly seems rather remote. Looking down into the packed little marina it is obvious that there isn't a berth available for *Voyager* while he works on her either. The weather window for Biscay seems to be slipping out of our reach.

We return to *Voyager*, finish Tréguier's brie with some of Tréboul's freshly-baked baguette, and devour the baked plum custard. This type of pastry must surely have been what was in the mind of the person who coined the word *ambrosia*. We set off again at 2 o'clock and are just within reach of the marina's outermost pontoon when the outboard runs out of fuel.

It is probable that the mechanic, a rather shy young man, has gone into work on a public holiday so that he can get some work done in peace. However, once we spot him through the window of his locked shop we eyeball him until he feels obliged to come out to us. I try my French on him. He blinks at me sympathetically, but is at a genuine loss to understand. So I rummage in my trouser pockets. He backs away. I pull out my crumpled note and offer it to him. He takes it gingerly, reads it and relaxes into a stream of rapid French. In among the torrent of words I recognize only four: *demain, du matin* and *neuf*. I translate for David. 'Tomorrow morning at nine.'

David's face brightens in anticipation of getting the job done so soon; then he looks down apprehensively into the crowded little marina. With two engines, *Voyager* will turn in her own length;

with one, it can be ignominious. 'Where does he want us?' he asks resignedly.

The mechanic begins speaking again.

'What's he saying?' asks David.

I don't know. I can't find a single familiar word to grab hold of, but with his right hand he seems to be clutching an imaginary tiller and with the left pointing at David. Then he grins at me, taps his chest, points to the dock beneath his feet, and with his palms pressed together against his chest makes a coy little diving motion towards the water below us. Light dawns and I translate. 'He says will you collect him from here in our dinghy tomorrow morning at nine? Otherwise he will have to swim to us.'

'Delighted to!' says David pumping the mechanic's hand.

We begin paddling back to *Voyager*. There is a strong current in the river combined with a strong head wind. And as well as avoiding sandbanks we are soon dodging aged wooden boats motoring up and down the narrow river. They have their sails furled and look rather grim.

'What are they doing?' I ask, paddling furiously from under a wicked-looking bowsprit.

David has a standard answer for my how, what, where and why questions, which tend to occur over-frequently and especially under trying circumstances. '*I* don't know, Sandra,' he says. 'How the hell would *I* know?' This is a variation of, '*I* don't know, Sandra, go and ask your father,' which I encountered quite a lot as a child.

As far as I can work out, between my increasingly ineffective paddle strokes, one old boat motors down the river while another disappears back up it. It seems an odd sort of carry on to me.

The wind gets even stronger as we leave the river and cross the causeway into our cove. I am quite weary by the time an inflatable dinghy approaches from behind making a huge wash. It slows as it gets level with us, to avoid overturning us, and the man in it stares first at our paddles and then at the outboard engine on our stern. I smile and point to the outboard. 'Kaput,' I lie then continue paddling bravely. Well, I'm not going to admit we've run out of fuel. And I don't know the French for it anyway. But I *am* getting very tired. The man throws us a rope and gives us a tow back to *Voyager*. I am very grateful.

Back on board David refuels the outboard engine and then goes below to work out a course for the Raz de Sein, ready for when we can set off again. The Capitaine du Port's boat comes whizzing towards us and I begin marshalling my French excuses for our being plonk in the middle of his busy cove, but he passes without glancing our way.

Had we *been* tidily anchored, of course, we should not have seen them. We should have been tucked into the corner, near the moored boats behind the Ile Tristan, with our view obscured by its trees and crumbling old houses. Instead, we have an uninterrupted view from our little cove into the enormous Rade de Douarnenez. And drifting across it that afternoon are the tan sails of what we later identify as an Essex fishing smack and a replica 18th century two-masted warship rippling with white canvas and complete with gun ports.

'Good grief!' I say, darting below for the camera. 'Come and look.'

By the time I get back on deck there are several more. They are motoring down from the harbour further up the river, past Tréboul's little marina where we'd dodged a couple of them in our dinghy, down to the mouth of the river, raising their sails as they turn right at the Ile Tristan and emerging into the Rade de Douarnenez under full, glorious, billowing sail.

The ones we had seen off the town of Brest, being buffeted by the French Navy, must have been just two of the dozens making their way here for the regatta. There are huge sailing trawlers, tiny fishing dories, beautifully restored yachts, old workboats with barely any paint at all and enormous luggers. There are bowsprits, figureheads, wooden masts galore, tan sails and white sails, square rigs and gaff rigs and every boat has every bit of canvas it possesses aloft and silhouetted against a backdrop of gently rolling summer fields and a blue sky.

We open a bottle of Soave, put our feet up, and spend the rest of the afternoon on deck, under straw hats, just gazing at them. It is like watching a nineteenth century painting come to beautiful stately life.

At a quarter to six a church bell begins tolling. Most of the boats are gone now. David is asleep. He was up several times during the night to check our anchor, and again to get the 05.35 shipping forecast. The BBC has changed its times and the forecast is earlier than ever now. I go below to prepare an evening meal. A random twiddle of the radio dial produces a familiar signature tune: *The Archers*, an everyday story of country folk and the BBC's longest-running radio soap opera. Tony Archer is complaining about his milk quota. The last time we were in France, shortly before we abandoned the country for ever and immediately before the French driver hit us on a mountain road leaving us with a catastrophic repair bill, our car radio had been playing an episode of The Archers. I hope tomorrow isn't going to be a case of *déjà vu*.

In the absence of any shopping I raid the store cupboard for dinner: spaghetti, pepper & garlic sauce with a few anchovies, parmesan cheese and French bread. The Tréguier water in our tank also makes very good coffee.

One of the things you notice in this kind of life is the great differences in drinking water. One source will leave a brown residue on the inside of your cup while another is indistinguishable from spring water. The ultimate test is smell. If it has one, you wait until you get to another town before you fill your tank. Before you do any of that, however, you ask somebody reliable if it is actually meant for human consumption, no matter what it looks or smells like because unlike Britain, where we even flush our lavatories with drinking water, what comes out of a tap in mainland Europe may only be intended for washing your boat.

We look out on a cathedral tower, and the setting sun turns the commercial dock behind us honey-coloured. Two Frenchmen in a small day boat, faces glowing red from a day fishing hatless in the sun, grin and wave as they hurtle past our stern to their dinner. The big bay is empty now, except for one tan-sailed gaff-rigger and one white-sailed schooner having a last unimpeded sail. It has been a lovely day. Even my deck shoes are almost comfortable.

Next morning David sets off in the dinghy at 8.30. Before picking up the mechanic he also needs to call at the Bureau de Change for more French currency. He soon comes hurtling back again. It is low tide and, despite a draught of only inches, our dinghy won't go over the causeway. As he shoots past me on his way out of our small bay and into the larger one, which is quite choppy, I call out, 'What about a life jacket?' He waves and smiles, the way he does. 'Well, how about one for the mechanic, then?' I yell at his disappearing back, but he can no longer hear me. Remembering the massive charges for our car repairs in France, I can only suppose its absence will be reflected in his bill.

The mechanic, when he arrives, shows no resentment at our lack of care for his safety, nor at the wet bottom he has acquired on the journey out. Indeed, he is not only polite and cheerful, but very quick. Not only is he very quick, he is also at great pains for David to understand what has gone wrong with the gearbox control cable and how to fix it himself if it happens again. Having solved the problem on the starboard side, he then goes off to check the port gear box to ensure the same thing is not about to happen to that one, too. When we return him to his shop we find his charges very reasonable. Then we go and stock up the larder.

The supermarket is small and cramped, but the atmosphere is delightfully amiable as you dozie-doe and two-step around other customers that you suddenly encounter nose to nose around the shelving. We find everything we want except eggs, and the French word for eggs eludes me. In desperation I eyeball the owner.

'Madame,' I say, 'Si'l vous plait,' make a small ellipse in front of her eyes with my index fingers, then pump my elbows and cluck like a broody hen. She bursts out laughing, dives under the vegetable counter and emerges with a box of six.

Maybe coastal French are different from metropolitan French, or times have changed, or maybe we just smile more nowadays. For whatever reason, we have encountered nothing but civility. We also discover, despite what everybody says about the French, that they queue as well. We join a huge one outside the patisserie, single file and straight out of the doorway down the middle of the street so that the traffic coming down the hill has to struggle round it. And the lady in the Tabac not only sticks the stamps on our postcards for us but directs us, unasked, to the furtive little post box, tucked away on the edge of the quay, on the wall of the office of the Capitaine du Port.

We return to *Voyager* with two bottles of wine, peaches, greengages, tomatoes on the vine, port salut cheese, pâté and tinned sardines, six brown eggs, some more of the glorious pastries and a warm loaf with a fleur de lys pattern baked into its crust.

At 11.30 we up anchor and set sail for the Raz de Sein. This is the entrance to the Bay of Biscay. Like the Chenal du Four, catch it wrong and it is very inhospitable. It is particularly dangerous when the wind is against the tide, causing a steep breaking sea. Strong westerly winds also cause breaking seas.

On top of this, the tidal stream attains up to 7 knots during spring tides. The next spring tide is seven days away and, apart from taking advantage of the Biscay weather window, has been another reason for wanting to go now. At present, half way between spring and neap tide, the tidal stream will be a maximum of 5 knots even if we should miss slack tide.

By 12.30 the promised wind speed of up to 16 knots is a mere four. At 3pm we turn left out of the Bay of Douarnenez and into the Raz de Sein with all three sails up. We have the timing right and sail through it without being aware we are anywhere special. Twenty five minutes later we are into Biscay.

15
Crossing Biscay

The Bay of Biscay is part of sailing folklore. For Northern sailors like us, taking the Atlantic route, it is an obstacle to be overcome before achieving the sunnier climes of southern Europe. It is notorious for bad conditions and as a graveyard for ships. Even at temperate times of the year, when the sea areas adjacent to Biscay are expecting moderate winds, the shipping forecast for the Bay will often be for gales.

World Cruising Routes, a publication which informs yachtsmen planning voyages when they can hope to encounter the best conditions, explains its inherent violence as follows: *Because of the abrupt change from deep to shallow waters in the Bay of Biscay, seas can become extremely rough even in a moderate storm. The situation is sometimes exacerbated by a high swell generated by a hurricane blowing thousands of miles away. ... Towards the end of summer the frequency of gales increases and some attention should be paid to the forecasts from the middle of August to the end of September when some of the most violent storms have been recorded.* Today is August 18 and there are hurricanes on the other side of the Atlantic.

Our objective is the North West Spanish town of La Coruña and the crossing will take around 55 hours. It comes as a surprise, when making your first crossing of a large expanse of water, how little you need to do. Inevitably, the focus of the day becomes mealtimes and our evening meal at sea becomes supper rather than dinner.

Tonight we have tortellini with a tomato and basil sauce. Pasta is quick to prepare, requires a minimum of pans on a moving boat, and is hot, tasty and filling. A deep soup bowl and a spoon are also easier to handle, while perched on the helmsman's chair or the cockpit coaming, than a plate and a knife and fork.

Hot enjoyable food, eaten together, is not only companionable and comforting as night falls, but for the person taking the first watch it provides necessary warmth and energy as the temperature drops. For the off-duty crew member, with only a few hours in which to get some rest before taking over the watch, it can be sleep-inducing when combined with a warm, comfortable bunk.

As well as bodily comfort, solitary night watches require something to occupy the mind which will not distract from the act of observing. This is particularly crucial as you approach the end of your last watch of the night, when all your mind can think about is its crying need to go to sleep. In an attempt to reduce this tiredness we have decided to experiment with a four-hour watch this time as on our previous night-passage we found that three hours' sleep did not refresh us enough for the next watch. I stand the first one, from 8pm until midnight, as I prefer the natural transition from daylight to dark rather than go to bed in the light and get up into blackness. I also like to see the sun set.

We are under sail only, so it is wonderfully quiet, and for once there are no worries about collecting fishing buoys around our propellers. After all, who in their right mind would drop lobster pots all the way out here? At around 8.30 half a red-gold sun breaks through the cloud just before it sinks into the sea, leaving little white puff-clouds on a strip of pink horizon back-lit in gold.

As daylight begins to disappear I switch on our navigation lights. The night's traffic consists of two black-backed gulls, three yachts, a fishing boat and a couple of lights too far away to identify or matter. The sky clears a little later on, enough at least for stars to become visible in the west.

Some time before midnight the wind drops away and it becomes necessary to switch on some power. There is no quiet way to start an engine under a bed and it is something David has never experienced before. I have, a long time ago, but unfortunately I have forgotten what it is like to be deep in the arms of Morpheus when a 27 horse-power diesel engine clatters into life directly underneath your mattress. After the silence of sail, that initial cacophony is transformed by the sleep-befuddled brain into your worst nightmare: a collision at sea at night. David materializes on deck in seconds, his eyes wildly searching for the source of the calamity.

'Sorry,' I mumble guiltily. 'I should have come and woken you first.'

The cold air hits him and, fully conscious now, he totters back to bed.

I don't wake him at midnight to take over the watch, but leave it closer to the 00.48 shipping forecast which we will need to take together. Out here the radio is inaudible with the autopilot on, so while I listen to the forecast David steers with one hand and aims a torch at the manual compass with the other. He's spent ages trying to get the console lights to work but without success.

It is necessary to start listening to the radio a few minutes before the forecast is due. The reception is so poor that it takes a while to attune your hearing to it, even with one ear pressed against the speaker. I am also confused on this particular night by a strong Spanish accent and demands for a kidnap ransom. Unsure what station I am tuned into, I am just about to start trawling through the wavelengths when it becomes clear that it is after all the BBC, and what I am hearing is the end of an item on bandit activity in South America. It is followed by another announcing that President Clinton is taking a holiday with his family after admitting sexual relations with Ms Lewinsky and that Mrs Clinton has already forgiven him. The forecast is for a moderate breeze from the northwest, which would have been a broad reach and a super sailing wind had it materialized, but it doesn't. The wind comes from the north and is very weak.

I am in bed by 1am and on watch again at five. At six I have plump, sweet greengages for breakfast. I have to get David up around eight to help me get in the mainsail. The wind has shifted towards the northeast causing the main to shadow the genoa and leave it flapping uselessly. Since the latter is our most powerful sail, we take in the main and motor-sail with just the genoa. David returns to bed.

A short time later, glancing across our starboard quarter, I am startled to see what looks like a large cliff with a lighthouse on it doing 22 knots across the horizon and then realise that I have just seen my first super tanker. I watch a yacht beating northwards and envy its full main and genoa. A small, scruffy white aeroplane begins flying around us, very low and very close.

It is quite eerie to sit in your cockpit in a grey empty sea on a grey murky morning and look up into an aeroplane's windows, every one of which contains an impassive face staring back down at you. The minutes pass. The faces continue to circle *Voyager* and stare. It's odd, the thoughts that flit through your mind. Alien abduction. Drug smugglers. The riders in the chariot.

I can see no markings on the 'plane but finally assume they must be French customs officers. They monitor craft in French waters and if they form any suspicions about you will summon up their coastguard to search your boat. A friend had his boat searched three times on a four-day passage down the French coast. I am curious as to what it is that makes them decide in the end whether to have you intercepted or fly away and leave you alone.

Ultimately I become irritated by their staring faces. I feel like shouting up at them, 'Just give me a call on the VHF and I'll tell you anything you want to know!' But that really would get us stopped and searched so I just continue to stare back at them.

Maybe one of them checks out our yacht's registration details and finds nothing suspicious. Or maybe they decide the grumpy-looking middle-aged woman glaring up at them doesn't really fit the profile of an international drug-runner. For whatever reason, after another circuit of our boat, they fly away.

I am supposed to wake David at 9am, but he seemed very tired when he went off watch. His sleep keeps getting broken, usually by me. I decide to leave him where he is for a while and organize some Spanish ready for our next landfall.

My ancient teach-yourself-Spanish book, that I haven't looked at in decades, provides examples such as 'Milk is cheap' and 'Old Martin did not see us, because he was blind.' Guaranteed to impress even the most hardened immigration official I should think. The tense of the second sentence begins to fascinate me. *Was* blind. Shouldn't that be *is* blind? Has Old Martin *been* blind, but by some miracle can now see? I seem to be losing my way. A basic vocabulary and politeness is the best thing to aim for. I've left it a bit late for grammar.

I begin practicing numbers: *uno, dos,* er ... Three is invariably the number where I revert to the previous language. Fortunately I still have another couple of days. Looking away from the page to try and memorize the numbers my gaze becomes riveted by the instrument panel. It may simply have been a shoal of fish passing under the boat that has caused the depth gauge to show such a dramatic drop. But when you are 70 miles offshore and it suddenly registers only a metre of clear water under you, the blood runs cold.

I have a French peach for tenses; when you breakfast at six, elevenses get earlier. The peach is red on the outside and almost white inside, sweet and *very* juicy. While mopping up afterwards I spot what look like two yachts on the horizon, but after I clean my glasses they are no longer there. The sun comes out at last and I can remove some clothing.

By 11.45 we are dodging fishing buoys. Seventy miles from shore, in two and three-quarter miles of water, and somebody plants pots! Hardly worth the diesel and all that string I should have thought. At its maximum, Biscay is three and a quarter miles deep. We lunch on Breton pâté, and the last two crème caramels from Tréboul's patisserie which tremble when you lift them.

There are no birds out here.

I do the 8pm to midnight shift again, using the genoa, stay sail and port engine. It is one of those wonderful, warm, dry, starry nights when you feel it is a gift to be alive and just exactly where you are at this moment. There are only three other boats during the whole watch and I don't have to get David up once. When it is quiet like this, apart from a search of the horizon every ten minutes, the night is yours to write, read, daydream – or fiddle with things. Accordingly we now have lights for the instruments and the manual compass.

It will no longer be necessary to read them at night using a torch. When David gets up I demonstrate.

'Brilliant!' he says. 'How did you do it?'

'Easy,' I say, 'I just got a screwdriver and …' I finish the sentence with a shrug.

He looks so impressed I'm almost tempted to leave it there.

'Actually,' I say, bending double under the wheel and pointing upward, 'There's this switch...'

Today is Thursday and our third day at sea. At 05.35 I listen to the shipping forecast while David steers. I sometimes wonder why we go to so much trouble to get a forecast because it so often fails to reflect what really happens. The expected NW backing W3 or 4 increasing to 5 in the north fails to arrive and although we still have the genoa up, the breeze is so light that we turn on both engines. Then David goes to bed.

In the eastern sky the moon is a thin crescent of russet-tinted silver, although the reflection from the rising sun completes the circle by creating a wafer-thin silver rim all around it. More surprising still, the angle of the sun's rays reveal the dark three-quarters of the planet, its craters and even its roundness. I have never seen the moon as a sphere before, only as a flat disc.

The sun is hidden by cloud, but it is soon hot enough to get out the shorts. The surface of the sea becomes flat and shiny. It undulates very gently somewhere deep below the surface but there isn't a breaking wave as far as the eye can see. Finally even the light breeze falls away to nothing. This fearsome stretch of water, this bogeyman of mariners famous for its murderous rages and mountainous waves is currently undergoing a period of calm.

With the wind gone the genoa droops. By the time I've pulled it in, and remembered to re-set the alarm clock for the next shipping forecast, I discover that I have forgotten to do the 6am log.

We keep an hourly log, recording weather conditions and all our instrument readings. It has two purposes. Firstly, it makes you look at your situation on an hourly basis, because it is easy to drift off mentally on a long passage and not notice things like a sharp drop in the barometer. Its other purpose is that should you lose all or any part of your instrumentation you would at least know where you were within the last hour and be able to navigate your way by dead reckoning.

Nothing stirs for a long time. Around 8am I lean over the side to observe a piece of flotsam that we pass. Around nine, with the help of radar, I finally work out that what looks like two ships towing a road bridge directly at us is actually a tanker travelling at a slight angle down our starboard side. At eleven David withdraws his head from the locker in the port cabin where the fuel gauge resides, goes up on deck and turns off one of the engines.

We have done a stupid thing. Before leaving Douarnenez we should have topped up our fuel tank. But it was so terribly crowded with the regatta, and hot, and everybody knows that in Biscay there is more wind than you know what to do with. The last thing you expect is light airs followed by a dead calm. This is no excuse. When going offshore you fill up with everything – fuel, water and food – because you never know what will happen at sea, as has just been proved. The result is that we are now running very low on diesel.

Fortunately we are not short of food. We lunch on pâté, Port-Salut cheese and French bread, followed by almond cake and fresh peaches. We have the bread with the crusts cut off, not out of delicacy but because, like our voyage, the loaf with the fleur-de-lys motif is also in its third day and its crust resembles concrete. After all, the popular image of French people trekking through the streets several times a day clutching the staff of life has less to do with cultural traits than the minimal keeping quality of the nation's bread.

After lunch I write a letter to a friend, have a nap and when I wake David points to a patch of the horizon ahead of us that is a bit darker than the rest. The coast of Spain is visible. By 4.30 we can smell it: wild herbs, scrub, earth and tree bark, all baked by a hot sun.

By now we have the genoa and the main out again to take advantage of the little wind that has returned, but it keeps fluctuating.

Throughout the afternoon one or other of us keeps trudging down into the port cabin to stare at the fuel gauge and David picks out several places on the chart, before La Coruña, that we could go into and probably get fuel. But as the day progresses, and having calculated miles-per-gallon to a nicety, he decides to head for La Coruña after all.

At 9pm I put out the fenders as we head for La Coruña's harbour wall. A long, long line of fishing boats passes down our port side, heading out to sea. Doubtless we will become re-acquainted with them when they all hurtle back during the early hours of the morning in the race to be first onto the fish dock.

The setting sun, on our starboard side, is the most magnificent I have ever seen. Great coils of cloud blaze scarlet against a gold and azure sky. In front of it, bathed in the same scarlet light as the clouds, stands the stately Tower of Hercules, begun by the Romans and the oldest working lighthouse in the world. It looks stunning in this incredible red light but it never occurs to me to photograph it. My mind is too full – of tying on fenders and mooring lines, of running out of fuel at the last minute and there not being enough wind to get us under sail into water shallow enough for us to anchor in – to think of cameras.

It is dark by the time we enter the harbour. There is a big Ferris wheel lit up on a distant quay but the marina itself is indistinct. The approach to it appears to have some sort of barrier, or boom, across it that is not shown in the cruising guide. There are also lots of buoys and odd clutter in the water and it seems prudent to anchor in the main harbour, with several other boats, and enter the marina in daylight.

We turn off the engines at 9.20pm: 58 hours, or three days and two nights, after leaving France's Rade de Guet and having covered 370 nautical miles; the longest single passage we have ever done with just the two of us. We are very glad to be here, especially as the weather could break at any time. As if to prove how contrary this sea area is, while the latest forecast for Biscay is still gentle breezes, its surrounding areas – Sole, Plymouth and Finisterre – are expecting Gale Force 8. For us though, the worst is done now. There's just Cape Finisterre to go. But when David calls his brother, to say that we have crossed Biscay safely, he learns that their mother has died suddenly. Tomorrow we will make arrangements to fly back to England.

NORTH-WEST SPAIN

▸▸▸
16
La Coruña

Our two objectives on Friday morning are to find somewhere safe to leave the boat, and to book a flight home. We pull up our anchor and motor into the marina. A strong wind that we could have done with over the last couple of days has now got up and keeps blowing us off the reception pontoon. A silent Swede emerges from his boat and helps us tie up.

We have forgotten to put our timepieces forward an hour from French to Spanish time and have arrived at the marina at noon, instead of eleven as we thought, and the office is closed for lunch. A Belgian, cruising single-handed, comes to talk to us. Old hands tell you to beware the solitary sailor. They go for long stretches without speaking and, like the Ancient Mariner in Coleridge's poem, once they buttonhole a listener they can sometimes find it impossible to stop. We have an hour he's welcome to, before the marina re-opens.

When it does, the young woman in the office says we are too big for this marina, but we can go to their other one on the other side of the little fort that juts out into the harbour. She says a boat is just leaving round there and we can berth against the wall, which will save us the trouble of a lazy line. We have never used a lazy line and from their reputation among British yachtsmen we are in no hurry to.

Before we dare go anywhere, however, we have to refuel. After hovering for ages, waiting for another boat to come out of the tiny fuel dock, it takes all David's concentration to squeeze *Voyager* into it. As we approach, a young Spaniard on a shiny new jet ski roars up from behind and streaks in ahead of us. It is a very short dock with boats moored all around it and, given the fact that our current fuel supply may quit at any moment, once committed David has no option but to keep going. I am at the bow with a shore line, ready to tie up fast to the high stone quay and look down anxiously at the queue-jumper directly below me. His eyes widen in his upturned face as *Voyager*'s bows slowly cast their shadow over him, like Coyote in the Roadrunner cartoons just before a piece of mountain falls on him. The young man on the jet ski revs his engine and leaves.

There is a passage in the Anglican funeral service, which I have sat through more times than I care to remember, that begins: *In the midst of life we are in death.* In the midst of death we are also in life this August afternoon. It vibrates all around us. There is a wedding party on the quay above us. The bride and groom are being photographed in the bright sunshine against a backdrop of moored yachts and a bright blue sky. Below us, on a large square pontoon, children are putting away sails from their fleet of little Optimist dinghies and leaping into the water with shrieks of pleasure. Fairground music throbs across the water from the direction of the Ferris wheel; there is the whine of bagpipes from a street musician and the chanting of male voices at some distant football stadium, rising and falling like a church organ.

When we finally get to the other marina we hover for some time but nobody has left – or looks about to leave – a wall. There is no space against any wall anywhere, nor is there anyone around to ask. The only place to tie up alongside is a small pontoon and most of its length is taken up by a Guardia Civil patrol boat. Its crew will not be best pleased if they are unable to respond to a call because they are trapped in a corner by us. We troll up and down each side of the visitors' pontoon. There are very few spaces, none of which is wide enough for us to get into.

Then half a dozen cheerful young Poles appear and wave us to a space beside them. We should never have attempted it ourselves, it is too narrow for us, but they push and pull and get us in. *Voyager*'s high sides and ample girth – compared with their long, low, slender monohull – amuses them. Elderly but well-maintained, it probably began life as a racing yacht.

'You are very wide,' one of them says, 'while we are very ...' he holds his palms a few inches apart. They are indeed extremely narrow; beautifully, elegantly so, but I do wonder how all six of them manage to fit inside.

The ropes on the quay are too short to reach our bow cleats, so we tie on our own, and the Poles hold our bows off the concrete quay while we confront our first experience of a lazy line. With eight people involved, however, and *Voyager* wedged in like a tinned sardine, we do not have a problem.

We are now into the hottest part of the afternoon in Spain's high summer. After three nights of broken sleep and the last four hours in the broiling sun berthing three times and refuelling, David and I are wilting. We eye each other with the same unspoken thought: it is now so late that we could just as easily go in search of 'plane tickets first thing tomorrow morning, when it will be cooler and we are less tired.

The six young Poles are scaling the ramp and disappearing across the quay. The last one turns at the top. 'Fiesta tomorrow!' he calls, pleased to be offering us a treat. 'And the next day, *and* the next!' David and I watch him disappear after his friends in horror. A three-day Fiesta means today will be the last day anywhere will be open for business until next Tuesday and the funeral is on Thursday. We hurry from the boat without stopping to change.

La Coruña is the town's Spanish name. In the language of the Province of Galicia, in which the town lies, it is called A Coruña. The British know it as Corunna, and the relationship has sometimes been a turbulent one. It was from here that Philip II of Spain's Invincible Armada sailed for England's south coast in 1588 with 130 men-of-war, ostensibly to punish Queen Elizabeth I for the execution of Mary Queen of Scots but also to extend their empire and return the English to the Catholic Church. Sixty three Spanish ships and 15,000 men were lost.

A year later, in 1589, Sir Francis Drake, with 30 ships, led an assault on Corunna, but the town was saved by local heroine Maria Pita whose statue stands in the town's main square.

In 1809, during the Peninsula War, at the Battle of El Vina just outside the town, Marshal Soult led Napoleon's forces to victory over British troops led by General Sir John Moore. General Moore died of his wounds and is buried in the Old Town.

Today La Coruña is an industrial town of around a quarter of a million residents, which is not a size one normally associates with friendliness. A yachtsman we once met, who had used it as a bolt hole while waiting to get round Finisterre, had declared it was the pits. We expect the next couple of hours to be difficult, if not downright unpleasant. We are wrong.

17

Booking a Flight Home

To get from the marina to the town involves walking along the pontoon, up a ramp, across a car park, through a small inner harbour and across a multi-lane highway. This highway runs parallel with the waterfront, but none of the rather grand buildings lining it contains anything resembling a travel agent. They are mostly foreign banks, marble-fronted and with acres of plate glass.

In one of them I catch sight of my reflection: baggy cotton trousers, loose long-sleeved shirt and straw hat. David looks a little less eccentric, but not much. In fact, we look like the sort of foreigners that in an earlier age any self-respecting townsperson would have thrown stones at.

We can't spot a tourist office and, since it is siesta, everywhere is closed and there is barely a pedestrian to be seen. We finally manage to trap one, on a traffic island with a little circular news stand on it, although like everywhere else the news stand is closed. Only as we corner the pedestrian do we realise that in our hurry we have left our Spanish/English dictionary behind.

The man is elderly and has a kind face. 'Excuse me,' I say in Spanish. 'Do you speak English?' I have never in my life seen anyone sorrier at being unable to fulfil a stranger's request. He puts a hand to his mouth and shakes his head sorrowfully. Then he brightens and thrusts both hands forward, nodding encouragingly, in a gesture that says: *Try anyway, you never know.*

'Travel agent,' we say in the unlikely event that the two words sound similar in both languages.

He makes a painstaking, almost heroic attempt to discover what we need, but we cannot bridge the gulf. His shoulders sag, his hands drop, and his eyes fill with sadness. We are consumed with guilt and do our utmost to cheer him. We cannot abandon him in his present state. I take both his hands in mine; we thank him repeatedly for his efforts, and finally leave him smiling.

We make our way up a steep, narrow side street into the upper town, but there is nothing resembling a travel agent up there either, so we look for someone else to ask. There are only two people in sight: an unusually tall young Spaniard with an empty fish tank under his left arm, talking to a friend in an open doorway.

I offer my apology in Spanish and ask if either of them speaks English. Both shake their heads, but with no-one else in sight I feel I have to persist. The expression of the tall one with the aquarium is so amiable, and he is so obviously willing to help, that I decide to concentrate on him. I sigh. Miming *eggs* in a French grocer's was child's play, but how do you perform *travel agent?*

Half-expecting both young men to rush inside the house hooting with derision, I thrust out my arms and sway slowly forward. My impersonation of an aeroplane could just as easily be interpreted as a mad Englishwoman in baggy clothes and a straw hat who thinks she is a seagull. Indeed, the shorter of the two men does begin to edge discreetly inside his doorway.

'Aero port!' says the tall one smiling, and is about to describe how to get there. Suddenly I am into Charades mode: the left index finger raised, accompanied by a smile celebrating his identification, then a cautioning right hand. The young man's amiable face is a study in concentration. His dark eyes never leave my hands. As a much-criticized hand-waver myself, it confirms my theory that the hand ballet of southern Europeans is not the empty exhibitionism claimed by northern sceptics. Hands can be read like print.

Nevertheless, I'm not sure how to move from the simple concept of flying to the complexity of airline ticket sales. *Tickets.* I flatten my left hand, and raise it palm uppermost to chest level, supporting an imaginary book of airline tickets. Then, with my right hand, like airline check-in staff, I snap out a ticket in a crisp gesture, and hand the imaginary ticket book forward with my left.

'Ah!' he says, and begins to describe in Spanish the compli-cated route to the town's nearest travel agent. Fortunately he keeps the words to a minimum, and the accompanying hand signs make them easy to follow: *Up here, second left, 3rd right, down a steep hill, follow the road round to the right, then take the left fork …* From there it is straight on. We thank him very much.

We get as far as the fork in the road and then our memories give out – or rather David's does. My ability to follow directions extends only to a factor of three: in this case as far as 'Up here, second left, 3rd right.' Unfortunately there is no-one around to ask. We stand at the junction while David racks his brains to remember whether we are supposed to take the left fork or the right.

'I suppose logically it has to be the right …' he begins, when a sound close behind us makes us turn. An unusually tall young Spaniard with an amiable expression and a fish tank under his left arm points to the left fork with his free hand. David grasps it in both of his and shakes it warmly. I do too, though I really want to hug him for his kindness. We plunge on.

In her middle years, and of grim expression, the woman presiding over the travel agent's counter sits sideways-on to it and gives most of her attention to the computer screen in front of her. She glances at us only rarely, obliquely, over her spectacles. She also teaches us a meaning of the word No that you won't find in a Spanish dictionary.

'Do you speak English?' I ask.

Her right hand moves fast towards her left shoulder and from there it slashes across her body towards her right hip. 'No!' she snaps.

Given a choice we would undoubtedly have left at this point and gone elsewhere, but time is running out and we have to persevere. In doing so we discover that her response, whilst initially off-putting, really means: *Actually I speak quite a bit, and understand even more than I speak, but am not terribly confident about it and get lost if I'm deluged in too many words at high speed, but I'll do what I can for you.*

We British are renowned, not least among ourselves, for the way we speak to people whose language is foreign to us. We say, 'Do you speak English?' and if the person asked says, 'No,' we continue in the expectation that they will inevitably understand as long as we speak loudly and slowly enough. If, on the other hand, they say, 'Yes,' we immediately assume that they are as fluent as we are and confuse them with complicated sentence structures and a flood of unnecessary words. The woman tenses, waiting.

I point to David. 'Madre,' I say, 'morte'; then indicate both of us: 'Inglaterra, por favor.' She relaxes, and goes to work immediately on her computer. Gradually her language skills begin to emerge. There is a severe shortage of seats because of the holiday, she explains in English. However, she has found two on a scheduled flight, although not together, and they are expensive. We accept them gratefully and she telephones to reserve them.

After looking at us briefly, however, she purses her lips and turns back to her computer for some considerable time.

'What's happening?' I whisper at David.

'Dunno,' he whispers back.

After surfing endless computer pages she emerges triumphant with two return tickets on a charter flight departing earlier and at half the cost of the ones she has just reserved for us. She confirms them, writes out tickets, and cancels the reservations on the scheduled flight. Yet still she is not finished.

The airport, she explains, is a long way from the town, and gives us the name of the hotel where we can buy tickets for the airport bus at a fraction of the taxi fare. The bus will pick us up outside the hotel. She gives us a timetable, advises us to buy the tickets beforehand, and to be at the stop ten minutes in advance of the bus departure time. And all this from someone who denied speaking a word of English. She looks rather startled at having her hands squeezed affectionately by two oddly-dressed gringos with sun-burnt hands and faces. There are two days until our flight.

18

Fiesta and Leaving La Coruña

We are woken at 7.30 next morning by cries of 'Arriba, arriba, uno, dos, tres,' and the sound of rasping breath. Five Guardia Civil officers are hauling a RIB over the stern of the patrol boat that we prudently didn't block in yesterday afternoon. Massive engines throb and the RIB rumbles out. Half an hour later it rumbles back, by which time the quay has become a hive of activity. People are erecting scaffolding, and sound equipment is arriving.

We go ashore and, as instructed by the other marina, pay our fees at the Real Club Nautica of Coruña, a magnificent building, elegant with panelling, chandeliers and sparkling glass. This is a strange setup for a yachting centre so crucial to yachtsmen travelling to and from northern Europe. For non-members the shower block and other facilities are ten minutes walk away at the other marina and I have a fleeting vision of trekking through the fairground and down an elegant avenue in bathrobe and fluffy slippers with a towel round my head.

However, as berth-holders we do have access to the Club's lavatories on the first floor. They are sumptuous, with black and white diamond tiling, large white panelled doors and gleaming brass fittings, although the mirror filling one entire wall really belongs in the fairground across the way because despite being tall and thin my reflection in it is short and plump. As you walk back down the stairs you look through the Club's dining room of starched white cloths and napkins and down the long wide veranda which runs along the front of the building with its wonderful view over the harbour.

Out on the street, and determined to locate a launderette, we stumble upon the tourist office. It is a completely anonymous building from the pavement as you leave the quay. Only if you turn and look back as you cross the multi-lane highway into town do you see its sign and entrance. Someone inside tells us where to find the launderette and gives us a map. We go back to *Voyager* and load the large rucksack.

A passing Pole, seeing us disembark with it, wishes us a good trip.

'Going to the launderette,' we say.

'Happy laundry,' he says cheerfully.

It is a long walk uphill which takes us through the old quarter's back streets and narrow shady alleys, past small, peaceful squares and Romanesque churches. When we get to the launderette its steel shutters are down. A sign says it opens Monday to Friday. Today is Saturday. We have coffee under the striped awning of a pavement café and take our laundry home again. We meet the same Pole. He looks at his watch, surprised.

'Launderette closed,' we say.

He shrugs sympathetically. 'That's España.'

Although overcast, the day is very hot. When the sun breaks through, the deck beyond the awning's shade is too hot for bare feet. Yet on the boat opposite a woman in a black swimsuit lies out in it all afternoon, rising only to hose herself down periodically and then fall back onto her towel again.

Meanwhile the scaffolding opposite lives up to its threat of becoming a sound stage. First it is draped in black fabric decorated with stars, and then the sound arrives. No people; just a massive sound system pumping out noise so loud that initially it stops you in your tracks and ultimately prevents you from thinking. We put in earplugs but it makes little difference. The boat and our bodies are vibrating with it.

Around 2pm we wave off the Poles in their elegant, slender yacht. 'Good time to go,' I yell through the wall of sound coming from the empty stage. They nod with pained expressions. 'Thanks again for helping us in yesterday,' I shout, but several feet away by now they are unable to hear me.

The noise ceases suddenly at 3pm. Its absence is disorienting. We are just getting used to it when an unseen hand starts it up again. After the brief respite it sounds worse than ever. And this, of course, is only the beginning. The electronic guitars and vocalists, all megamicrophoned, are still to come. We decide to put as much distance between us and it as possible by going into town and remaining there for dinner.

A short time later, bathed and respectably dressed, we step ashore. Our first stop is the posh loos of the Real Club Nautica of Coruña. A diminutive, anxious man in a white jacket blocks the main entrance. He is obviously under orders from a management in fear of being overrun by the hoi polloi during the fiesta. He seems to be asking if our name is Judd. David's face brightens the third time he repeats the question, as understanding suddenly dawns. 'From *Voyager*,' he says, pointing down into the basin below us. We are allowed upstairs to the WCs.

The town is incredibly full of people. And lots of small children. Yet, despite being shoulder to shoulder in a few places, everyone is polite and good humoured – strolling, chatting, drinking coffee.

We accost a matron at the top of the hill and ask for Maria Pita Square, where David thought he saw restaurants while we were walking our laundry. We have climbed too high. She accompanies us back down the hill with rapid instructions, in Spanish but clearly about which roads *not* to take when she leaves us and continues her own journey. Then, realizing we are not understanding, she abandons her own destination and escorts us to ours.

The square's eateries do only snacks, but in a side street running off it we find the seafood restaurants. The waitress, unusual since Spanish restaurant staff is usually male, speaks no English but has a lively personality. Because I carry out all negotiations in foreign languages, along with the meal I also order the wine. When she brings the bottle to our table she pours it into my glass for me to taste. I am quite startled to realise that this is the first time I have ever been invited to taste the wine at a table which contained a man.

There is a radio playing in the restaurant kitchen which you only hear when the door opens briefly to let the waitress in and out. It's interesting how you can not be listening to a broadcast that is incomprehensible to you anyway, but are immediately alert to the inclusion of any words from your own language. I recognize the words 'Ralph Feinnes' and 'The New Avengers' before the door closes but even that is almost overwhelmed by the rock concert half a mile down the hill. Dessert is almond tart. When it comes it is stabbed with a fork and has Jerez sherry poured into the holes.

Back out on the streets the atmosphere everywhere is extraordinarily good-humoured. There are no gangs, no drunks, no fights, no pushing, no shouting. A small, elderly man hunches on a narrow pavement with a sign in Spanish and English saying he is an out-of-work English seaman. Two Guardia Civil officers wait patiently until a large African street vendor completes his sale of a leather belt from a well-stocked suitcase before moving him on. A couple of sly 20-somethings pose in a doorway with a neatly written sign claiming dire poverty. They are well-dressed and with such obviously feigned expressions of suffering that they fool nobody. A saxophonist plays a particularly plangent version of the Django Reinhardt classic, *Nuage*, while from a distance comes the ubiquitous sound of bagpipes.

Late evening, and back on the quay beside our boat, the rock concert's decibel level has soared above the pain threshold. Dominating the stage, a pink latex pig in a green shift sings aggressively into a microphone to the immense delight of a large number of small children. Then the heavy metal returns and children and parents melt away. Today's music is as incomprehensible to me as '60s music was to my parents. The only difference being that, courtesy of technological advances, nowadays it is much louder. It is currently bouncing off the buildings and making all the masts and rigging in the yacht basin rattle. There is no point in trying to sleep, so we continue walking.

Tied up to the quay, a 70ft schooner is putting on a pirate play. A pirate play is easy to follow in any language: lots of shouting, macho posturing, leaping through the rigging and waving swords about. After a while we join a throng of amiable strollers that takes us back onto the main road again and into the fair. Neither of us has been to a fair in decades. The years fall away. It is fragrant with candy floss and diesel fuel, bristling with shooting galleries – darts, air guns, bows and arrows, corks aimed at miniature bottles – and brimming over with food.

The exterior of the Ghost Train looks particularly ghoulish with its painted corpses rising from broken tombs. In its ticket booth a young woman, dressed as a zombie, is watching the sit-com *One Foot in the Grave* on a tiny portable TV.

As soon as the concert finishes we go to bed, although the fair is still going and the pirate play has yet to reach its climax. We assume that the loud bangs we can hear is the pirates firing the small canon on their stern, but when we stick our heads out of the hatch above our bed we see that it is their stupendous firework display, so fast and furious that it sends their remaining patrons reeling back against the sea wall. It is so good, in fact, that when it finishes a huge cheer goes up from all around the quay and the fairground.

After breakfast on Sunday morning we top up our water tanks, and then walk round to the other marina to make arrangements for the week we shall be away. We have decided to leave *Voyager* on a mooring buoy there as it will be a fraction of the cost of our present berth. There will be a buoy available late afternoon. With that settled we set off on a long, slow walk around the deserted headland to the Torre de Hercules, the world's oldest working lighthouse that we passed as we sailed into the harbour.

It is one thing to wander among Roman ruins and imagine what the buildings must have looked like. It is quite another to look up at this great stone tower, whose light has been trimmed through two millennia; to think of the generations who have laboured up its steps, and the lives its light has saved from the surrounding sea. For Galicia's northern coast has witnessed countless shipwrecks. Its storms and jagged rocks have earned it the name Costa da Morte, coast of the dead, and overlooking La Coruña is a cemetery for drowned sailors.

From the lighthouse we take a short-cut through the dunes and scrub to get back onto the road. Families are picnicking under brightly-coloured umbrellas. On the steep coast road back to the quay we stop at a small café. It has half a dozen tables single-file along the narrow pavement. None of them is occupied. We choose the one where the conjunction of umbrellas gives the most complete shade. The proprietor comes out to us.

'Do you speak English?' I ask in Spanish.

His right hand shoots up to his left shoulder and then slashes downwards past his right hip. 'No!' he says emphatically. *'Dos cerveza,'* I say, *'Por favor.'* Our drinks arrive. We say *thank you* in Spanish. The man moves a short distance away, hovers, then disappears into his café.

He emerges a few minutes later with a tiny girl in a pink embroidered dress and a tiny denim baseball cap worn back to front. Her fair hair and skin and delicate features give her the look of a porcelain doll. In hesitant, economical English he introduces us to his 16-month old daughter.

There is a noise behind the man as he is joined by a robust dark-haired boy in a pedal car. The little boy's face is a picture of pleasure as his plump brown knees pump vigorously at the pedals. The man introduces his three-year old son to us. And as we slowly drink our beer, this man with no English tells us in English the best place to watch the fiesta's main firework display tomorrow, and the route of the pageant that will carpet the street with flowers; and talks of family life and parenthood and the surprising differences between raising a boy and a girl.

The door behind our chairs, he says, is the entrance to their grandmother's house. His son loves to visit his grandmother. 'But the girl…' He throws out a despairing hand. And the words tumble out. 'Two children: good. But no more! And the difference! The boy, he sleeps all night.' His daughter? 'Arghhh! Awake at 2.30am!'

'Wait 'til she's sixteen,' we say.

'Arghhh!' he says again, looking at her with a combination of bewilderment and adoration. 'Always on the move!'

As if on cue, the tiny dynamo sets off for pastures new, trailing father and brother behind her. We finish our beers and contemplate youth and age; life and death and how quickly time passes. For in our two families, we are the older generation now.

Late afternoon we motor *Voyager* back round the little 18th century fort to the marina we started at and tie her to a plastic mooring buoy. An attendant comes out in a dinghy and insists we move her to a large metal drum instead.

A narrow strip of gold behind the Ferris wheel is all the sunset we get this evening. But by 9.30 the sea and the heavily-clouded sky become deepest pink with a strip of gold at the horizon. It is most beautiful.

Monday morning is grey, bleak, windy and overcast. Outside the Hotel Atlantico we board a neat little bus with red curtains for Santiago Airport and begin our journey home.

19

Return to La Coruña

We return to La Coruña at the beginning of September. The harbour is hectic and we want to be quiet. The weather is too rough to attempt the passage round Finisterre for the time being, so the answer is to go and anchor in one of the adjacent *rías* until it improves.

When we'd got back to *Voyager*, however, we'd found that a piece had been chipped out of her port bow by the metal mooring buoy and the refrigerator would not ignite on gas. So before we can go anywhere we need to repair the gash in the gelcoat and get the refrigerator fixed. We also need to replenish our food supplies and there is still the laundry waiting to be done.

It is a long, long walk, culminating in a steep hill, to the premises of the authorized Electrolux refrigerator repairer listed in our owner's manual. We arrive at his metal shutters promptly at 9am. A sign on them says they open at 9.30. We find a street café and order coffee. The man behind the counter has a bad case of the shakes so we wait there while the coffee reaches the cups and then carry them outside ourselves so that there will still be something left to drink.

When the repair shop's shutters finally roll up we learn from the men inside that they are no longer Electrolux agents. If we want our fridge repaired we will have to wait a few days for them to come out to look at it. Then it would take three or four days to get parts from Madrid, and then they would have to see about coming out to fix it. They don't seem keen, and we have begun to mentally add up the time this is going take, not to mention its potential cost.

We say we'll think about it and go off to check out the launderette before lugging our washing all the way up here again. Now that its steel shutters are up it is apparent that this is not a self-service launderette after all but a drycleaners and service laundry. This means it could take three or four days to get our laundry back. We set off for the supermarket.

When you travel in the way we do, you become a connoisseur of supermarkets. Each has an ambience of its own. As soon as you enter it you know whether it is run for the customers' convenience or the owner's. The floor plan dictates whether you are a contented shopper or an irritable one. Wide aisles plus a ticket dispenser at the wet fish, cheese and bread counters make all the difference between leaving cheerfully or with gritted teeth. Add friendly staff, and it goes into a sort of private pantheon of cherished supermarkets. La Coruña's is one of these.

It is on the ground floor of a large square market building, up a steep hill and a long way from the harbour. In Spain, we discover, supermarkets are invariably a long way from the quay and up a steep hill. At its self-service fruit and vegetable counter we reach for a bag and begin making our selection. We are the only people there apart from a mature lady replacing empty crates with full ones. After a minute's uncertainty she comes over to us, coughs discreetly then politely, wordlessly, indicates a small dispenser we hadn't noticed. It contains disposable plastic gloves: a simple but civilized means of ensuring that when you've selected *your* apples, subsequent customers don't go home with your finger prints all over *theirs*.

It has been a disappointment to us that only relatively large towns seem to sell fish. Whenever I grumble about it people point out that the sea is full of them and there are fishermen everywhere – which is true – but there is rarely a fisherman around with a couple of fresh trout handy when you want them, and David and I don't fish. I know this is moral hypocrisy, as we will buy them lifeless off a slab, but hauling one up by a hook in its throat and observing the fatalism in its eyes as you kill it is beyond us.

La Coruña's supermarket has a wet fish counter. I order two trout from the tall young man standing behind it. He tries to converse, sociably, but my Spanish is too limited so he concentrates on the fish. After opening the first one he inspects it with a pained expression, shakes his head, lifts it by its tail and drops it at arm's length into a waste bin. The second trout soon follows. With the sweep of an eloquent hand across a tray of local sardines, and a brush of the fingertips past his lips, he invites me to consider an alternative whose internal hygiene he can personally guarantee is beyond reproach. Then, with a plastic bag on each hand, he selects a dozen of them individually and guts every tiny one. 'With garlic,' he says, 'onion, tomato, potato.' He raises his fingers to pursed lips again in a way that says *delicious*.

They are. And as we lunch on them back at the boat we have a crew meeting. The damage to the port bow can only be reached by either drying *Voyager* out somewhere and standing on a ladder, or going into a marina and dangling off the pontoon. Our fridge is powered in three ways: by gas when we are at anchor; by 12-volt electricity when one of the boat's engines is running; or by mains electricity via a shore line. The meeting concludes with the following decisions: the hull can wait; we can still chill the fridge when we're travelling and won't store perishable goods when we're not; the larder is now full; and as for the laundry, we still have a few items we haven't used yet.

THE RÍAS OF
NORTH-WEST SPAIN

▶▶▶

20
La Coruña to Ares

We leave **La Coruña** after lunch and head for the anchorage at Fontan. One of the unexpected pleasures of this part of our journey is the undeveloped *rías*. They are long narrow inlets in the coastline, former valleys that have become submerged by the sea and peculiar to this part of Spain's north-west Atlantic coast. La Coruña is a *ría*, but it has developed into a large town and a busy commercial harbour. Most have remained relatively undeveloped.

This region is very attractive anyway, with a rugged, hilly coast and trees coming down to the water line, but there is an added pleasure when you enter one of these quiet *rías*. They are all quite different. One will have a long, deserted, sandy beach with a path leading up a hill through woodland to a hamlet. Another will have a fishing village around a small harbour. Yet another will have a small rural town at the end of it, but all of them have one thing in common: they are largely unspoilt. Nor do they have the intense summer heat that southern Spain can produce.

Intense or not, one of the essentials of a life afloat is shade from the sun. And if you don't create some shade in your cockpit one of two things will happen: either you fry out in the open, or you spend all your time cowering below in the only available shade. We knew our fair English skins wouldn't cope with too much direct sunshine and, alert to the risks of skin cancer, we'd spent quite a bit of time designing and making awnings for the boat before leaving England. The one going over the boom and providing maximum cover, headroom and airiness we had already put to good use. A smaller one, to be slung under the boom, had been designed to allow unrestricted movement of the mainsail. The journey to Fontan is the first time we have wanted to use the mainsail at the same time as needing shade, and the small awning works very well.

Unfortunately, when we arrive at Fontan the anchorage is littered with buoys. Worse still, there is a large fishing fleet. Fishermen are a cruiser's natural enemy. They plant lobster pots and discard netting where they are most likely to wrap themselves around your propellers, and the sea is their workplace so they have a tendency to resent leisure sailors. One way of demonstrating this is to roar past anchored yachts at full throttle in the chill early hours, comforted in the knowledge that their massive wake will have thrown a yachtsman or two out of his warm bunk and turned more than one galley or saloon into a disaster area. So, if you're looking for a quiet night, as we are, an extensive fishing fleet is something to avoid.

David consults the chart and cruising guide and decides to try the next *ría* along the coast, which is Ares. As we approach Ares I sit on the side deck with binoculars while David steers towards the centre of the long strip of sand described in the cruising guide. I squint hard at it and then say, 'You're heading for a breakwater.'

Like a man with his hand on the Bible affirming his faith, he says, 'There *is* no breakwater. I've got the cruising guide in front of me.'

'Well, I've got the binoculars in front of me,' I say, 'and you're heading for the centre of a sand-coloured stone wall.'

David has a touching faith in cruising guides. Me, I trust what I can see, even obscurely through salt-smeared lenses.

'Oh, yes,' he concedes with *hauteur* some minutes later. 'It must be new.'

There are no fishing boats visible, which means either there are none or, more likely, they are small ones that go out and return during daylight. The only sound coming from the village is a rather mournful church bell. The trees above the beach are tall and lush, and overlooking the bay is a mature hacienda-style house with carved stone balustrades and decorated eaves.

We have dinner on deck in a lovely quiet evening that is overcast but warm. Beyond the new breakwater, men are now fishing out of dinghies, two to a boat, in stark relief against a flat grey sea and a misty grey sky. During the evening they return to the village, their small, wooden dinghies painted inside and out in red, blue and green, some with classic high prows, some pram-shaped with flat bows. A man hauls one of the latter out of the water on a handcart, helped and hindered by children who chatter and laugh, admire his catch and get under his feet.

Some of the smallest boats have integral wheels and are pushed up the ramp like wheelbarrows. The fishing fleet proper, when it returns shortly after, turns out to be mostly small, one-man vessels, trim and freshly-painted, lobster pots stacked 2 or 3 high in tidy rows around the rails and half-way up the wheelhouse. They return at modest speed. More to the point they are back before dark. We have high hopes of a quiet night.

We don't get one. The wind gets up. It sends the sea banging under our bridge deck and sucking noisily through the drain holes under the companionway grid. And having dutifully put our black plastic ball up in the rigging to signal that we are anchored, it collides remorselessly with a steel shroud with a clang even more mournful than the village's church bell. The day, when it arrives, is grey, cloudy and damp and it rains a little. We stay in bed late, propped up with books and mugs of tea and remember when we used to get up at dawn on days like this to sit in a traffic jam.

Although the alarm clock is still set to go off before dawn, for the shipping forecast on BBC Radio 4 Long Wave, it doesn't mean much now that we are in the meteorological area of Finisterre where forecasts for this area are notoriously unreliable. Nor do they come without effort. We can only get Long Wave here by teetering on tip-toe on the edge of our sloping cabin roof, with body and arms at full stretch, while holding the portable radio's fully extended aerial as far up *Voyager*'s steel backstay as we can get it. Reception of Short Wave is more accessible, so for news and programmes we use BBC World Service.

We lunch on board and, when the weather brightens, take the dinghy ashore. While the few modern houses out on the headland are large and spacious, those in the village seem to be almost in miniature, with green shutters, tiny balconies and chaotic terracotta roofs. It is 4.30 when we arrive and everywhere is still closed except for a small café. After a stroll we have coffee there, overlooking the harbour. It is a lovely, peaceful bay. Before we return to the dinghy, we pace out the new breakwater, so that we can let the Cruising Association have the details for the next edition of its cruising guide.

At the ramp a young man, noticing us about to embark, comes across and holds the dinghy for us to get in; for which we thank him very much. As we push off I express my regret to David that, given the kind of courtesy we consistently receive here, Spain should receive so much that is less than the best of British. Last week a newspaper reported that the Vice Consul in Ibiza had resigned 'because of the depravity' that young British tourists wreak on the island, not to mention fifty drug-related deaths a year. But as David points out, before national guilt can completely overwhelm me, the holiday resorts do advertise for them. Not comforted by this thought, I accidentally turn the air release knob on the outboard engine the wrong way, it jams, and the engine won't start. David has to row us back to *Voyager* and spends the next half hour releasing and repairing the spring which operates it.

As we dine in the cockpit that evening two Optimists wobble out onto an almost windless sea.

'Look,' I say. 'Little Angelas.'

Wherever there is water there will usually be Optimists (variously and affectionately known as Oppies or Optis), the little dinghy with a single sail in which young children around the world learn to become sailors. Because of the shape of the sail, and the gentle airs they tend to go out in, at a distance they look like a flock of butterflies resting on the surface of the water with their folded wings quivering. In the shelter of harbours, Oppie sailors – a surprising number of whom are girls – practice capsize drill.

Our earliest encounter with them was during our first trip to Ireland. One chilly afternoon, a short distance from our stern, the class instructor told the group to capsize its boats. His small pupils looked down into the cold, diesel-dappled water and hesitated. The instructor, desperate to motivate his class under the very windows of the yacht club that employed him, called out, 'Come on, Angela!'

The bold eight-year-old rose to the challenge and began hauling with all her strength to pull the resisting little boat over onto its side. As it passed its point of no return and she began her slow slide into the uninviting water she cried out triumphantly, 'Wheeee! I'm going!' to the cheers of her fellows.

'Well done, Angela!' cried the instructor, watching with relief as all the other Oppie sailors threw themselves into the water after her.

David and I had adopted Angela and the Oppies into our personal folklore. If the Oppies were out it meant conditions were mild and the auguries good. Angela herself became a symbol of optimism and that liberating sense of all things being possible. Even years later, at moments of petulance when I stand stiff and resistant to the unthinkable task before me, David will call out briskly, 'Come on, Angela!'

It is so still, lying off the sleepy shore of Ares, and yet the sea roars at the beach behind us as if six-foot breakers were crashing onto it. It remains overcast, but warm.

Without television or newspapers you rediscover books, chess, backgammon, card games, conversation and, when reception is good, BBC radio. Tonight David wins a game of Scrabble. This I perceive as a betrayal. While I expect him to beat me at chess, Scrabble is *mine*.

The night is as still as the evening had been, but it also becomes rather humid. I opt to sleep in the other hull and wake around 2.30am, steaming. I also become aware of a dull, regular thud. Behind the headland I can see an intermittent flash followed by a dull bang. I wonder if it is heat lightening but the flash seems too contained. I get up for a glass of water from the galley.

In a boat, getting water from a storage tank to a tap requires a pump of some kind. Ours is electric and my glass of water seems to cause an unseemly racket in the silence. After the cold water hits my stomach I set off for the heads. The loo pump sounds horrendously loud with someone sleeping, and the washbasin tap provides a rat-tat-tatting reprise of the one at the galley sink. I think: why don't I tap-dance in wooden clogs in the cockpit over David's head and *really* wake him up.

'Heard you get up,' he says some hours later when he brings me breakfast in bed. I mention my damp problem during the night and ask if he'd experienced the same.

'Skippers don't suffer that sort of thing,' he says. 'Only other ranks.'

Voyager is brown this morning. It is a constant source of wonder to us how she gets so dirty in such out-of-the-way places.

21
Ares to Laxe

We leave Ares on a collision course with a late-rising seagull. It is too languid to fly away. It simply paddles out from under our bows and down our starboard side towards a fishing boat where it waits patiently for its breakfast.

The sea is still. There is no wind. It is overcast and humid. Beyond the beach and around the headland there is a huge quarry, so what I heard and saw in the night may have been blasting. There are also a lot of tall chimneys heaving out noxious-looking smoke. This probably explains why our boat is brown this morning.

We are visited by dolphins. At first it is just odd splashes on the starboard beam that do not quite belong to the natural wave patterns. Then the fins appear above the water. And when we are leaning over the side rail they arc up out of the water in twos and threes so fast that while you are still trying to glimpse their faces their dorsal fins are already going back down into the water.

A fellow-comedian once joked that the late Sammy Davis Jr was such a consummate performer that when he went to the kitchen for a midnight snack, and the refrigerator light hit him, he would be into the second half of his act before he remembered about the sandwich. Dolphins are like that. Provide an audience and they will go into their act. Their performance space of choice is in your bow wave, so to get the best of both worlds they have to lure you onto the foredeck. First they attract your attention by arriving beside your cockpit where you can see them. Then, when you are on your feet, they leap forward so that you have to climb out onto the side deck if you want to go on watching them. When they've finally got you hanging over the bow rail, looking down onto them between the two hulls, *then* they put on a show. There are seven of them below us this morning.

Everyone is familiar with the dolphin's extraordinary communications system, but it still takes your breath away to see them criss-cross above and below one another at high speed while at the same time maintaining only an inch or two of clear water ahead of your moving hulls. They do not so much avoid the sharp edge of a bow as compete with it, individually and en masse. They are the ultimate in synchronized swimming. Their enjoyment is tangible. When they leave, it's as if a cloud has temporarily covered the sun.

We have sail out for a while but, despite a forecast for a gentle breeze from the southeast rising to Force 6, the wind dies away completely and we haul everything in. Then it rises to 13 knots from the south-south-west so the main and genoa go out again. It falls away and the genoa comes in again; then out again, like washing on a wet Monday and then it settles at 22 knots straight on the nose and we take everything in.

It turns into a bumpy, squally passage gusting to a near gale force 32 knots. It's a bit squally on board, too. On his second sortie out to the foredeck to tighten the luff on the genoa, David finally kicks overboard a winch handle that I had twice asked him to move, and in between hauling sails in and out we reach an agreement that he will be slightly less focused on the immediate task and a bit more in tune with what is under his feet while we still have some possessions left. And while we are at it, there's his habit of standing things upright on a moving boat and expecting them not to fall over. We also agree that I will try and focus on nagging less and not saying, 'I told you so' all the time.

By 5pm we are glad to enter Laxe (pronounced *Lashay*). There are a lot of small boats on buoys, and fishing boats packed tight round a corner of the sea wall. We anchor off the beach. With 32-knot gusts on the nose driving us backwards it is difficult to hold the boat in place long enough for David to drop the anchor where he wants it.

One of our transits is an ancient stone church, just above the waterline, with a square bell tower and terracotta roof. Even at slack tide, with the water still, the force of the wind on its surface makes a rattling sound like the kind you get when people tie polythene bags to their rigging to scare birds away.

The log shows that we have covered 700 miles since leaving Emsworth a month ago. One of our water tanks is empty again. It is a cold, wet, windy evening. We dine indoors on corned beef and fresh vegetables, served hot with butter melting on them and black pepper. David concedes two games of Scrabble. We have a restful night.

By next morning, after a night of light, intermittent rain, the dirt from up in the rigging has joined the dirt down in the cockpit. Unless it is torrential, instead of removing dirt rain simply shepherds it into corners and around fittings. It forms brown stains where you are going to want to sit in light-coloured clothing when the sun comes out again, and every rope you lift reveals a coiled serpent of fine grit just waiting to grind its way into your gelcoat. The best way to get rid of it all is lots of soapy water. With seawater incompatible with soap and one tank empty we don't have fresh water to spare for washing the decks.

There is something eccentric about somebody washing things in the rain, but on a boat you learn to take whatever opportunities are offered. By mid-morning the downpour becomes moderate and constant so, while David spends some time with the chart and cruising guide, I go out in wellies and bright orange waterproofs with washing-up liquid and a large sponge. It is like being a child again, playing in the rain. And at the end of it the boat is clean. The sun comes out and dries it and we lunch in swimsuits at the cockpit table, on tuna and butter bean salad, in blazing sunshine. We had always assumed such erratic weather was quintessentially English. Yet wherever you go somebody will say of these sudden bursts of cold and rain in high summer, 'This is so typically French/Spanish/ Portuguese.' And it amazes us how often it rains on Sundays and public holidays, just like at home.

The Guardia Civil roars into the bay, hovers near the beach, ferrets about with fenders and shore lines and then shoots into the fish dock causing a mammoth wash; the only one thus far since the fishermen here are perfect gentlemen.

The forecast says possibly Gale Force 8 so we decide to leave *Voyager* where she is for another night and go ashore late afternoon, when the shops seem to open. In the meantime David catches up on our mail and I am lazy. *Ría*s are such pretty, languid places and, since there are few bolt holes along the Portuguese coast, while the weather is so unsettled there is no better place to be. Two other boats come to anchor in the bay. The Englishman settles down with a fishing rod off his stern, while a couple of Swedes in a dinghy spend some time recovering a lost anchor.

We take the dinghy into the village around 4.30. Initially we go to the ramp at the fish dock, but a small boy begins untying our dinghy before we have even turned away from it. We shoo him off and retie her, but when we look back a larger boy is jumping up and down in it. Afraid that we shall return to find our dinghy either under water or floating out to sea, we take it round to a beautiful long beach of fine sand and drag it up above the waterline. Directly in front of us, above the beach, is a building. In one of its upper windows is a small sign. It says *Spar*. This is most unusual in Spain. They tend to put supermarkets where only the locals know where to find them and visitors would never think of looking.

Before shopping, however, we wander round the town, starting with the church that forms one of our transit points. It is very old, and locked, its dirt yard sheltered from the open sea by a high wall with funerary niches in it. The winding street leading from it into the village looks as if it hasn't changed in centuries and is so narrow that the two facing rows of houses are joined by a small archway. At bedroom level, the houses on the sunny side of the street are festooned with laundry.

We have a beer at the Bar Mirador off the square. It is owned by a descendant of a family of photographers active from the 1870s whose pictorial history of the area covers its walls. Their pictures of the village, not least the road with the arch, look as if they might have been taken yesterday. Only the villagers' suits – as they haul boats up the beach or enjoy local celebrations, and the formal poses that getting the right exposure with early cameras demanded – set them in the past.

A young girl with a cough is running the Spar supermarket single-handed: weighing fruit and vegetables; cutting, weighing and wrapping at the cheese and the meat counters; receiving deliveries from impatient van drivers and manning the checkout. Everybody else in the town seems to be either standing about talking, or sitting on a wall dozing. It is still siesta, after all. We buy chicken, which is yellow, and I hope this is because it is corn-fed. It smells all right which is usually a good indicator. Back on board David cuts himself boning it and I end up dismantling a locker to find a plaster.

Before leaving England I had emptied our home medicine cabinet as well as buying from the local pharmacy all those things I had been advised were necessary to be self-sufficient in isolated places. Then I had stored them in the lowest locker in the port hull, below water level, where they would remain cool.

Accordingly I pull out an emergency kit for burns, another for injections (in case one was needed where hypodermic needles were suspect), Jungle Fever drops, aspirin, homeopathic rescue drops, eye drops, cough mixture, cold cures, antiseptic dressings, bite cream, sore throat remedies, a sling and enough rolled bandages to stock a cottage hospital. But a small plaster? I finally find a box, see to my patient and then set about putting everything except the box of plasters back in the port hull locker. Cold remedies in a Continental summer seem a bit pointless, yet everywhere we go in Spain people are sneezing, so they might be needed yet.

When we had set off for distant shores I'd wondered if buying food in foreign languages would be a problem for the linguistically-challenged like us, but in Spain food shopping is made simple by the supermarket labels. They contain a picture of the main ingredients, and a can of pâté, say, will have a leaping tuna or a sedentary duck on it. A jar of spaghetti sauce will show a tomato, a red pepper and a clove of garlic; a meat sauce will include a stylized bit of steak. They may do this at home, too, but in your own country you tend to read the words rather than look at the picture. And in ours the picture is likely to be a *serving suggestion* which in today's compensation culture is probably the manufacturer's self-protection against being sued for not including the plate shown on the label as well.

At breakfast next morning, however, I discover that a picture on a product is not infallible. The carton of red grape juice I'd picked up from among the fruit drinks at Spar the previous day, and which I now serve chilled with breakfast, turns out to be rosé wine. Sipping it with his cereals, David frowns at me over the rim of his glass. 'Starting a bit early today, aren't we?' he says.

The shipping forecast now threatens the possibility of Strong Gale 9. There is a danger with shipping forecasts which for a period are consistently wrong. For days you shelter from threatened gales that never come, sitting at anchor in sunny, windless conditions or – even worse – perfect sailing weather. This leads to frustration and, after a time, a tendency to say, 'Oh, sod it! We could sit here for weeks like this. Let's go.' This has led to many a sea-going disaster.

For short journeys, however, the other side of the forecasting equation is to look out at the conditions around you, divide this by the estimated length of the passage to be undertaken, subtract the general difficulty of entering the new anchorage in the event that the endlessly-promised blow should finally arrive, and with all things being equal to shove off.

Our objective has been to get *Voyager* safely into the Med before September is out. She spent ten days longer in La Coruña than expected and now the first week of September is almost gone. Despite the seductive charms of these lovely *ría*s, we need to push south whenever we can.

Laxe to Ría de Camariñas

Next morning, under a cloudy sky, we set off on the 19-mile passage to Ría de Camariñas. There is a 12-knot wind on the nose, so it is a lumpy passage. Camariñas is a long and very beautiful *ría*. At the bottom of it is a sheltered little bay called Ensenada de Merejo and four hours and forty minutes after leaving Laxe we negotiate its mussel beds and anchor off its long, beautiful, pale sandy beach. In the afternoon we take the dinghy to a little cove with two small wooden fishing boats pulled up the beach above the rocks, a path leading up past a solitary house, and a lane leading to a narrow road.

An elderly, dapper man in a three-piece suit and black beret desperately wants to engage David in conversation, in Spanish, about *Voyager*'s twin engines. Sadly this is not possible as we don't have the necessary Spanish words. The road into the village is heavily wooded, mainly with pine and eucalyptus. A large pine tree has recently been felled and its trunk cut and neatly stacked ready for winter fires. The smell from it is heavenly.

Although our journey to this *ría* had been overcast, windy and cold, its village is sunny, warm and windless. Everywhere is closed, except a couple of family bars. Apart from us there is no-one about. We have a beer in one of the bars. Its only occupants are the family matriarch all in black, the bar owner, his wife and one other customer besides ourselves. They are all very civil with greetings and farewells.

It is a quiet night, but towards morning it becomes windy and wet. The forecast is again for Strong Gale 9 but this time we stay put, for though the wind early this morning is relatively slight, it soon begins to rise and the incoming sea is *wild*. Enormous breakers come thundering in through the heads and crash against the eastern headland at the entrance to our bay. Gradually the surging water rushes down through the mussel beds and tumbles even our secluded little corner.

It is our first experience of lying at anchor in a gale but the anchor is well dug in and although the wind screams in the rigging and everything around us rattles and shakes we feel reasonably comfortable and secure. Not everyone is so fortunate. Late afternoon, when the worst of the wind has abated, two unhappy men from the village begin collecting fragments of one of the small wooden fishing boats. It had not been beached high enough above the rocks to escape these particularly violent, wind-driven waves. The latest shipping forecast, meanwhile, is favourable for travelling tomorrow.

When we set off next morning it is still heavily overcast but our little bay is nowhere near as turbulent as yesterday. As we approach the exit from Camariñas itself and out to sea, however, it is a different story.

There is a reef reaching out from the southern headland, and shallow water stretching some distance out from the northern headland. This affects the movement of the water passing between them and, despite only a light southerly wind, the exit is *very* rough, exacerbated by a swell created by yesterday's huge tide. We bounce and crash, and mutter through rattling teeth that if the open sea turns out to be as bad as this we will come back into this *ría* until things get calmer.

In the event, the Atlantic Ocean is much calmer than the entrance to the *ría* and it is quite a pleasant passage in bright sunshine. The forecast is WSW up to Force 7 although it never reaches more than 8 knots as we head down towards Finisterre, which is fortunate since the wind is actually from the south which means it is directly on the nose.

The heavy sea swell persists, despite the light wind, although happily the rollers are behind us and send *Voyager* surfing at speed. There is also a lot of flotsam around us: broken wooden crates washed from the decks of boats and branches from tropical trees.

This stretch of shoreline between Ría de Cameriñas and Finisterre is the most westerly point of Europe's Atlantic coast. The name *Finisterre* – from the Latin *finis terrae* meaning *end of the earth* – was just what it seemed to be to the Roman expedition brought to a halt there by what they imagined to be an endless sea.

Once we have rounded Finisterre the wind is no longer on our nose and we are able to put up the sails. It is a very pleasant sail; not at all what we had expected from Cape Finisterre. Had it not been for its notoriety we should barely have noticed it at all. In fact, it is so quiet and pleasant that there is no risk at all in taking the shorter inshore passage, between rocky shoals, to get to Muros.

The Ría de Muros is a huge bay and it is a very hazy day. Initially there is some hesitation as to where the anchorage is, as it is some distance after entering the *ría* before you can see it. However, once we round Cabo Reburdino we can see the little town of Muros and quite a few yachts already anchored there.

Muros is a super little billet. We anchor a few yards off the town quay, near a house whose garden juts out over the water, and well away from the fish dock and the fishing fleet. Variety, as they say, is the spice of life. Deserted bays are restful; town quays are fun. With the latter you can pop into town in your dinghy in the cool of early morning and then watch the passing throng from the shade of your cockpit in the heat of the day.

Once anchored, we go ashore. Muros rises in tiers from the seafront and some of Galicia's best traditional architecture is to be found in the narrow streets of its Old Town. The fact that it has all been built in stone also gives a special unity to its arches and columns, squat buildings, flights of steps, benches built into the walls of houses and water troughs for washing clothes. In a back street the market traders are putting up their stalls.

We climb a steep hill. At the top is the cemetery. It is crowded with religious images and artificial flowers and overlooks the sparkling sea.

We take the route back down via a very narrow, winding street of very small houses. A man is renovating one of them. He has the tiniest works van we have ever seen, with just enough room inside for his tools and a pane of window glass. But then, a tiny van is all anyone could possibly get up a street like this.

The kindergarten, half way down, has big flowers cut out of paper in primary colours on its windows, and at the bottom a mature woman in a floral overall decorously sweeps up leaves. As time goes by we will come to realise that mature women with house brooms are responsible for much of the cleanliness of Spanish streets. Back on the quay we sip cold beer among some of the town's ancestral arches while the cheerful bar owner gives us directions to the *supermercado*.

We select masses of fruit and vegetables (remembering the little plastic glove) but on reaching the checkout are sent back round all the boxes again to find the number identifying each item so that we can key it into the electronic scales we had failed to notice the first time around, then weigh each bag and stick on the price ticket.

We buy some steak and enjoy it hugely with onion, red pepper, garlic and mushrooms and a bottle of Faustino. Foolishly we start drinking the red wine while I am cooking, after the beer and on an empty stomach. This is a mistake. I wake next morning with my first migraine in a long time. Even David, most unusually, gets up with a hangover. We leave Muros for Bayona sometime after 10am.

24
Bayona

We have been to Bayona once before and remember it, and a particular seafood restaurant, with enormous pleasure. I make a hot drink to have after weighing anchor, but the chain sticks and by the time we get to the drink it is tepid. The nine-hour passage to Bayona exacerbates the migraine.

I haven't always had migraine. It was a side effect of prescription medication I didn't want to take in the first place for symptoms it failed to relieve anyway. Then I spent a year on other pills to get rid of the migraine. I don't take any pills at all now, but once in a while I still get a migraine, usually connected with red wine drunk under the wrong conditions. It makes me even more cross knowing that it's my own fault, than it did when it was somebody else's.

The first half of the journey is most unpleasant; rough enough for the foredeck to be awash. The sea is also full of flotsam again, this time with the wreckage of small boats and refuse blown off boatyard quays added to the stuff washed from the decks of ships and bits of trees. There is also a navigational warning on our Navtex.

The Navtex system provides vessels with navigational and meteorological warnings and other urgent safety information. It is a component of the International Maritime Organisation and all member countries transmit their information in English. We have a small receiver above the chart table and the information appears on a screen. Among today's warnings is one about six containers washed from a cargo ship and which may not be visible above the surface.

When your life is spent on land, cargo lost overboard means little beyond another increase in the cost of living through bigger insurance premiums; or, to a very tiny minority, something useful washing up on their doorstep. To seafarers, however, an encounter with one of these containers can be catastrophic. The reason so many of them end up in the world's oceans is the way in which they are transported. Since only cargo carried below deck attracts port levies and canal tolls, shipping companies stack containers on deck, as many as seven high or 60 feet.

Figures are scarce since shipping companies are reluctant to admit their losses, but in 1994 Cape Town's harbour master said that in recent years over 40,000 containers had been officially reported as lost from the decks of Atlantic container ships. In October 1998 one ship alone lost 406 in a storm in the Pacific. A single ship can carry over 5,000 at a time. Estimates of losses vary from 1,000 to 10,000 a year.

The problem for the likes of us, as today's Navtex warning has highlighted, is that containers toppling off a ship's deck do not immediately, or inevitably, sink to the sea floor. Some are so buoyant that they travel hundreds of miles with the tide before sinking. Some never sink at all and float ashore with their cargo intact, as the refurbishments in many a small coastal village will testify. Containers of frozen meat, on the other hand, float 9/10ths under water for some time, sink as air is lost, rise again as the meat putrefies and then finally sink to the bottom.

To put things in context, *Voyager* is 40 feet long, made of fibreglass, designed to cut through water and weighs 11 tons. An industrial container is 20' x 8' x 8' 6", built of steel with heavily-reinforced edges and sharp corners, designed to resist damage in collision with similar materials and weighs anything from 20 to 40 tons.

Six of them, which may or may not be visible above the surface, are not a happy prospect, especially in the present rough sea. With several feet exposed above the water they are relatively easy to see in good conditions if you are keeping a constant lookout. Viewed from the deck of a yacht, however, where your line of vision is only about eight feet above sea level, they can be invisible among even moderate waves until it is too late. In poor visibility or at night, or floating just below the surface, you have no chance at all of avoiding them.

The sea calms gradually and happily there is no sign of any floating containers. The sun comes out and it gets very warm. At 1pm we alter course sufficiently to turn off the engines and beat our way under sail. But early evening, just as we have to make our final turn between two reefs into Bayona, the GPS shows *No Position Found*. Nor can we see the buoy in the water, nor the marker on the shore, that are there to lead you into the harbour via a safe channel through the reefs. Staring across sunlit water looking for the markers causes starbursts to explode inside my throbbing head.

Despite the best efforts of both of us, the markers remain elusive. However, David calculates that when we are one and a half miles north of Cape Silleiro we can turn safely towards Bayona. We use the radar to tell us when we are the necessary one and a half miles north of the cape.

Despite our intention to anchor wherever possible, we plan to spend three days in Bayona's marina. The prime reason is so that David can repair the damage our port bow sustained in La Coruña, but we also need to get our gas tanks filled and find a launderette. We should also like to spend a little time in the town. Our previous stopover here had been very brief and it is somewhere we have always wanted to revisit.

As David makes our approach I go out on deck to tie on mooring ropes and fenders. It is hot and muggy now and the sea is very choppy. Far from relishing the prospect of getting re-acquainted with Bayona all I really want to do is lie down in a darkened room.

'Fuel?' shouts a man in blue overalls leaning against a pump when we are still some yards off the waiting pontoon, which doubles as a fuel dock. I am about to say 'No' when David says, 'Yes.' It *is* the sensible thing to do. It will save trouble later when the dock might be crowded or weather conditions bad, and with full tanks you can leave whenever you want. My head is roaring.

In addition to the turbulence of the water, there is the usual strong wind blowing that always materializes whenever you approach a pontoon. So, while David concentrates on not demolishing our starboard hull, or the dinghy somebody has abandoned just where our bows really need to be, I straddle the foredeck rail with my bow rope, waiting to jump.

This is just the moment when the man leaning against the diesel pump starts to interrogate me about whether we want a berth or not, how big we are, how long we want to stay and what sort of fuel we want. With the pontoon rising and falling quite vigorously to a different rhythm from that of our boat, I judge my moment and running to a cleat on jarred ankles tell him yes, diesel, and three nights, please.

He says two nights on a pontoon and one on a buoy; but as I rush for the stern rope before *Voyager's* back end takes off I'm of a mind to agree to almost anything. By the time we've tied on a spring and are ready to receive the fuel gun from him – he's gone.

We stand around in the heat for 10 minutes and just when we've decided to hell with it and head for Lisbon, he comes back and hands over the diesel gun. I pass it across to David. He puts the nozzle into the tank, touches the lever, and a blowback sends diesel flying all over the cockpit. I rush to the galley for a pair of rubber gloves, washing up liquid and kitchen roll to clean it up before it can get walked into the saloon carpet.

Diesel is foul stuff. Get it in fabric and you never get rid of the smell. Get it in a small break in your skin, and the resulting infection can take ages to heal. Your heart aches for marine life every time you hear of a major diesel spill at sea. Even the unregarded minor spillage at the world's refuelling docks, commercial and leisure, must maim a multitude every day.

So here I am, all diesel slime, Marigold gloves and migraine and cue the Cruiser from Hell. This lovely-looking young Irish woman with long, lustrous red hair is half of a couple, although the young man with her says nothing beyond a brief initial greeting. Their boat, it seems, has been at anchor for some days and they have come over to refill their water tanks.

It is only later, in a more charitable frame of mind, that I wonder if perhaps this is what happens when a taciturn man and a vivacious woman spend days isolated in close confinement together: she becomes effectively a solo sailor and when she corners someone she won't stop talking.

She immediately demands a blow-by-blow account of our journey. I can't understand why, because they have recently travelled the same route as us. So why does she want intricate information about every stop we've made getting here?

Where have we come from, she wants to know. *And where are we going? Which stops have we made along the way?*

I wonder briefly if she might be working undercover for Customs and Immigration.

Which rías have we stayed in? Worsened by the bending and the diesel fumes, my head is so bad now that I can't remember.

Did we stop in Viveiro or Ribadeo? I don't know; all the names have merged into one. I suggest she asks David, who is hunched over the diesel gun trying to prevent another blow-back but he keeps his head well down and she continues interrogating me. *Did we stop off at Pontevedra?* I didn't think so.

I'm getting little coloured lights zigg-zagging down my peripheral vision now. *What was the passage like between Ares and Laxe? Which other boats did we see?*

Why does she want to *know?* I keep wondering. Why does she never stop asking questions? Why doesn't she get on and fill her bloody water tank and just *leave me alone?* I listen to the knocking inside my head and wonder if I might be having a stroke.

At last David hands the fuel gun back to the attendant. All we need now is a berth to be allocated and directions how to find it and I can escape her; not rot in a Spanish jail for the inexplicable murder of a lovely Irish colleen. The attendant clunks the gun back into its holster and asks laconically if we are all right for water as he isn't sure if there's a tap where we are going.

And so it goes on. While David goes to the office to pay for the fuel, I wait for her to finish using the solitary water hose. *Had we come across a young English couple with engine trouble? Or the Swedes with the two children?* Even after she has finished filling her tank and passes me the hose she shows no desire to leave the dock. *Had it rained while we were in La Coruña?* I don't *remember*. I don't have a single memory left about anything anymore; just an all-consuming desire to garrote her with the water hose and hurl her lifeless body into the sea.

Our berth, when we finally reach it, has *two* water taps on it and I am pettishly pleased that the fuel pump attendant hadn't received a tip.

It is 9pm before we are tied up and we are too tired to get bathed and decently dressed and leg it across town to enjoy the promised meal. Instead I heat up some curry and cook the last of the brown rice. It is *definitely* the last brown rice I shall ever buy. It takes forty-five minutes of gas to cook it and despite its much-vaunted life-enhancing properties always tastes like boiled sand with grit in it.

When gas has to be lugged aboard by hand you begin to read cooking times on the back of packets before buying them. You also begin to ignore traditional cooking rules, especially those involving boiling rice or pasta in gallons of water in an open pan, and then rinsing it afterwards in gallons more. It's a waste of water as well as gas and all that steam just makes your boat damp. A minimum of water with a lid on does just as well and I doubt that any but the most discerning palette would ever tell the difference. As for rinsing boiled rice, after throwing decades of culinary wisdom out the window I read that a research team somewhere has concluded now that it simply rinses away valuable nutrients anyway.

Because of the direction of the wind, *Voyager* snatches violently at her mooring ropes all night.

The following day is grey and overcast with intermittent drizzle. The lovely Bayona of happy memory looks like your worst British Bank Holiday Monday ever. At least the migraine has gone. We go in search of propane gas and a launderette. 'Gas,' everyone tells us, 'is available in La Coruña. It's the centre for gas.' Nor does Bayona have a self-service launderette. There is a place at Vigo just down the coast which will collect your laundry and return it washed, ironed and aired four days later. And somebody on the pontoons thinks there *might* be a self-service place in the next town, a taxi-ride away, but it all seems like too much effort. When we get back to *Voyager*, David hauls out our remaining gas tank, estimates its contents by its weight, and decides it will last until Gibraltar. I decide our linen supply will too.

We fill up the water tanks and give *Voyager* a thorough wash. A French woman from a neighbouring boat spends several hours on her knees beside us washing, rinsing and wringing nappies at one of the taps. Not for the first time do I reflect that a boating holiday with very young children is not much of a break for women.

In the evening we walk into town for that shellfish we have been promising ourselves. The place hasn't changed in the intervening years. The table legs are still uneven and the chairs don't match. The seafood is even better than we remembered; a great platter piled high with scallops, king prawns, snow crabs, cockles, mussels, crab claws and barnacles all freshly-caught and cooked, and served hot with crusty bread and green wine. As you dine, the local fishermen pass along the far wall of the dining room, between the entrance and the kitchen, to hand over a bag of mussels or a lobster to the chefs. Back on board it is another choppy night of snatching ropes.

We wake next morning to a beautiful, sparkling, sun-shining blue day, the Bayona of happy memory, and set about some of the more critical areas of our laundry. Another French boat with a baby on board has arrived and both mothers put small baths under the two taps and set about their laundry.

We do ours aboard then fill up our tanks again later when they've finished. It is much easier than crouching on a pontoon anyway. I wash. David rinses and wrings. The boat rails are soon festooned with it. By the time we have cleaned up *Voyager*'s interior, and showered, the laundry is dry enough for ironing.

In the afternoon we wander around Bayona. It is a lovely old town of narrow cobbled streets and long narrow shops of the bit-of-everything variety. It also has an impressive fortress begun in the 15th century, some wonderful old churches and some strange legends.

The last two combine in the ancient Santuario da Santa Liberata. According to the breviary of Tuy, the Roman emperor Hadrian installed Lucio Catilio Severo as governor of Gallicia in 119AD. Both he and his wife were pagans. The legend, recorded on the door of Liberata's sanctuary, says that Lucio's wife gave birth to nine daughters in her only pregnancy. Believing her husband would suspect the multiple birth (I have yet to work out the logic of this reasoning) she ordered her nurse, Sila, to get rid of them.

Instead, Sila found separate homes for them all, where they were christened and raised in the Catholic faith. When Hadrian later ordered the prosecution of Christians all nine of them, along with the nurse Sila, were brought before their father, the governor, and ordered to abandon their faith on pain of death. All refused and fled in different directions but were caught and martyred.

Liberata was the last to die. She was crucified in Lusitania, a Roman province on the Iberian Peninsula during this period. She was the first Christian woman to be crucified. One of her arm bones rests on the altar of her sanctuary in Bayona and every July 20 the people of Bayona honour their patroness.

A reminder of more recent events is berthed in the harbour: an exact replica of *La Pinta*, the caravel which arrived at Bayona on the first day of March 1493 with news of the discovery of the Americas. Bayona thus became the first place in Europe to learn of the existence of the 'new' world

When you look at this replica caravel, built for the fifth centenary celebrations in 1993, it seems hardly less unbelievable than nine children from a single pregnancy. When setting out to cross the Atlantic nowadays the modern sailor has charts, weather forecasts, GPS, self-furling sails, dehydrated and frozen food, one or more diesel engines and the certainty that there is actually something out there.

None of these things was available to Columbus and the crews of the *Pinta* and her sister ships, the *Niña* and the *Santa Maria*. And looking at the Pinta it does seem so very *small* for a voyage of over

2,800 miles in uncharted waters. Where on earth did they fit the crew needed to man a sailing ship, or store all the food and water required for them all? And yet people who know about these things maintain that the ships were ideal for their purpose. And all three of them did return, after all.

In between browsing through Spain's cultural heritage we do a little shopping. There is no wet fish shop, but we are able to buy huge frozen scallops and prawns for supper at sea the following night; and being frozen they will keep well.

We also need a post office, but the building shown on our map has no sign on it to say it is a post office and it is locked anyway. As we stand hovering, a spry, elderly man comes down the road towards us. 'Do you speak English, Señor?' I ask. He inclines his head and flutters his fingers near his mouth to indicate *very little*. 'Post Office?' I say, 'por favor.' He is tiny and probably in his eighties. His very little English emerges. 'Tomorrow morning,' he says, '8.30 until 2 o'clock. It is here.' He turns and indicates the anonymous, dark, glass-fronted building behind him. 'Muchos gracias,' we say. His smile lights up the street.

Spanish post offices are something of a challenge. Like supermarkets, they often have no sign on them, as if trying to keep their existence secret. Even when a resident points one out to you, its opening hours or even which *days* it opens may not be shown on its frontage. You just keep turning up with your postcards and hope to catch it unawares.

The counter clerks are invariably thin and stressed and use rubber stamps with a degree of violence that is quite unnerving. Even apparently simple transactions, like dispatching an ordinary-looking brown envelope, requires them to consult huge directories, their supervisor, and each other, in low whispers while the queue on the other side of the counter droops in the airless heat behind a yellow line painted on the floor. The culmination of every trans-action is signalled by slamming a rubber stamp from ink pad to envelope or document half a dozen times with a force that makes the windows rattle but also brings a brief tremor of hope to the wilting queue of people behind the yellow paint.

The most memorable one was in an old worn building in a narrow street. The big, square room had a bare wooden floor, flaking walls, a large old-fashioned, slow-moving ceiling fan and looked like a scene from a 1940s movie set in war-torn Europe. We couldn't work out what was happening at the long, high wooden counter ahead of us where several elderly people stood hunched in front of the right-hand clerk. They had younger members of their family with them, apparently to take it in turns to wait because periodically a couple of them would go outside for some fresh air, leaving other members of the group to take their place at the counter; holding vital documents aloft, baton-style, like in a relay race only waiting instead of running.

Meanwhile, at the left-hand side of the counter, a middle-aged man had waited so long for his envelope to be processed that as soon as the clerk raised her rubber stamp he lurched away, blank-eyed, towards the door and had to be called back to pay. The fee had been overlooked among the whispered consultations, enormous directories and hammer blows of the rubber stamp. It was all probably futile anyway, since the contents of his lumpy manila envelope would never have survived the rubber stamp. We took his place at the left-hand end of the counter, hoping the foreign destinations of our envelopes would not consign us to a fate similar to that of the family on our right, and flinched in spite of ourselves when the rubber stamp finally fell.

With such hushed, bureaucratic complexity on one side of the counter, passive endurance on the other, and the execution-like effect of the rubber stamp, I have since wondered if Franz Kafka got the idea for his novel, *The Trial*, from a Spanish post office.

We never did work out what the family at the right-hand side of the counter were trying to achieve. Whether it was registering a birth or a death, buying a marriage license or querying their social security cheque, their documents were still unstamped when we staggered out into the sunlight with our letters pummelled and a vague feeling of relief to find ourselves still alive and at liberty.

David finally manages to get some gelcoat repair into the gash in our port bow. Unfortunately, with the water so choppy and the boat plunging up and down so much all he can really do is aim the filler at it. The result is a bit like a small carbuncle, but it will do for the time being. The marina attendants also come by and say we can stay on the pontoon tonight and not have to move to a buoy after all, and that they will only charge us half price. That really means full price if you are a monohull. Like many marinas, it has charged us double for being a catamaran, even though *Voyager* is only a couple of feet wider than some monohulls of an equivalent length.

We dine out again in the same restaurant, this time on sea bass. *Voyager* snatches at her mooring lines all night again, and before we can leave next morning we have to take a hammer to them. The bowline knots, normally so user-friendly, have been pulled so tight that loosening them with a hammer is the only way to prize them off the cleats. As we set off the wind is moderate and near the nose. We are able to beat but need an engine to help hold our course. The sky is heavily overcast.

PORTUGAL

▸▸▸
25
Bayona to Leixões

The border between Spain and Portugal is defined by the River Miñho, and as you leave Spain's Galician coast you also leave behind its rugged mountainous coastline. From here southwards, as far as São Vicente, the coast gradually flattens into sandy beaches backed by dunes.

This northernmost region of Portugal is known as the Costa Verde, the green coast, since behind its endless miles of deserted beaches it is lush and green. Contributing to this lushness are the vineyards which produce *vinho verde*, the young, dry and very inexpensive green wine that is so refreshing on hot, summer days.

Among its many pleasures, cruising is a living geography lesson. It is not like a series of airports nor an atlas showing different colours. When viewed from a boat the land – as Native Americans and Australian Aborigines have always known – transcends the ownership of man and his artificial borders. And although I get a childlike pleasure from standing on the foredeck watching Spain morph into Portugal I know that the distinction is entirely arbitrary; just as the distinction between land and sea is arbitrary. For land and sea make one living planet. The sea is not the *finis terrae* of those expeditionary Romans whose world ended where the land did. The sea is, after all, from where we all come. It produced the oxygen that led to life on land, provided food to support it, and it continues to produce the rainfall which sustains our daily existence.

It begins raining about noon and visibility is poor. Our destination is Leixões, a big commercial port and only a bus ride from Oporto. A famous advertising slogan from our childhood was 'Port comes only from Portugal' and Oporto is home to the world-famous port cellars. Yachtsmen wanting to visit them take the bus from Leixões because the River Douro, on which Oporto stands, has a ferocious current at its height and only those who know the river attempt to sail up it.

Something else we have heard about Portugal since childhood is that it is England's oldest ally, although neither of us can remember anybody ever saying why. So David looks it up. Our special relationship dates from 1385 when English archers helped free Portugal from the Castilians at the battle of Aljubarrota. It was put to the test in 1807 when Napoleon gave Portugal an ultimatum to declare war on Britain. Since Portugal was dependent on Britain for half her trade at the time, and on the Royal Navy to protect her trade routes, the Portuguese refused. The French invaded. Britain sent Sir Arthur Wellesley (later the Duke of Wellington) and he defeated the French.

Around 2pm we are approaching the entrance to the Portuguese town of Viana da Castello and, because it has been such an unpleasant, choppy journey we decide to go in there for the night. By the time we have taken down the genoa, however, the rain has stopped, visibility has improved, and we decide to carry on. We soon wish we hadn't. Within half an hour the rain and visibility are as bad as ever, and we now have the added hazard of hundreds of fishing buoys. Watching for obstacles over a long period in poor visibility is very tiring on the eyes.

We arrive at Leixões at 8pm. The large harbour there contains an anchorage, a marina and commercial docks. The anchorage is very crowded. We can take our chances rather too close to the sea wall, or drop our anchor behind all the other boats. David chooses the latter. By the time sufficient chain has been let out, however, I am unhappy with our position. I feel we are too close to the shipping channel between the commercial docks and the harbour entrance. My skipper disagrees, probably because he is too tired to try somewhere else.

'See,' he says, pointing a finger over our stern in justification. 'There's a tug boat over there. If he was bothered, he'd come and tell us to move.'

I am to become on quite intimate terms with that tug boat during what turns out to be a long night.

Sometime after midnight I am woken by *Voyager* vibrating to a loud throbbing noise and stick my head out through the hatch. A huge – and I mean HUGE – container ship is turning round only feet from our bed. I get a crick in my neck just trying to look up at its vast rear end as it circles above me, blotting out the stars. It is so close I could lean out and scratch my initials on it. Having turned it, the tug boat guides it slowly out through the harbour entrance.

'David,' I whimper, shaking him.

'Gotosleep,' he mumbles and sinks back into oblivion.

The arrival and departure of container ships continues throughout the night. It doesn't help that the outgoing tide has left *Voyager* lying even further out into the shipping channel than when we'd anchored. I have never been this close to big commercial ships before. I never want to be again.

26
Leixões to Cascais

Next morning a number of yachtsmen go ashore to get the bus for Oporto, but the forecast is good and conditions perfect for a passage down the coast. Even Navtex can only come up with one hazard – a ship anchored off Cascais, our destination, which is carrying vinyl cyanide and not to be approached under any circumstances.

It turns out to be the most brilliant sail of the trip so far; all sails up in a northerly 15 knots and a following sea which gives us 8 knots. And it is sunny into the bargain. I do the 8pm to midnight watch and it is sail-only all the way.

Sometimes, night watches can be magical, and this one down the Portuguese coast is one of them. Without an engine on there is just the occasional sound of a wave splashing against the hull. The sails sway gently in front of you and the sky is full of stars. Two hundred billion of them, I read somewhere. And on a clear moonless night at sea, miles away from land and all its electric lights, you would swear you could see them all. They sparkle like diamonds scattered on dark blue velvet and the Milky Way just blows your mind.

With binoculars you can see the red of Mars and Orion's Betelgeuse and the beautiful shimmering star cluster in the Pleiades. Even with the naked eye you rarely look up for more than a few minutes without seeing shooting stars. And I once saw a dozen glittering specks of silvery blue, but what they were is still a mystery. Another mystery was a green planet I watched with a mounting sense of awe until after a good ten minutes it revealed itself to be a distant airliner when it turned to port and its green starboard wing light changed to red.

When Venus is low in the western sky, during the last watch of the night, it is the colour of old gold and so bright that its light reflects off the sea like moonlight. Named for the Roman goddess of love, Venus is the Sun's second closest planet and comes closer to Earth than any other heavenly body except the Moon. As a consequence Venus shines very brightly and its presence as the Morning and the Evening Star has made it an object of affection among sailors from time immemorial.

As the Evening Star, the planet appears as daylight is fading and provides a cheerful light through the gathering dusk before any of the other stars become visible. As the Morning Star, it is at its brightest just before dawn when the night is at its coldest and greyest.

The fact that Venus's surface temperature is between 400° and 500°C, with an air pressure more than 90 times that on Earth, is irrelevant. Its bright golden light gives comfort to the long watches of a dark and solitary night and its morning brilliance heralds the imminent return of the sun and the start of a new day.

27

Cascais

By 3 o'clock the following afternoon we are in the large bay into which the River Tagus runs. On the north shore of this bay is Cascais (pronounced Cashkesh). A few miles up the river lies Portugal's capital, Lisbon, but Lisbon has no anchorages, only marinas. So, after giving the ship carrying vinyl cyanide a wide berth, we anchor off the rather lovely resort of Cascais. The waterfront has a wonderful mix of architecture: towers, loggias, fort, modern hotels, classical palazzo, French chateau, stucco and terracotta, stone and tile. There is also an apartment building which from a distance looks as if it is crumbling at the edges, but as you sail closer you see that each storey has a terracotta roof over the corner apartment, creating a sloping, tumbling effect. We anchor beside a 45-foot yacht flying an American ensign so faded that all its stars have disappeared. We are tired and stay aboard. The temperature at 6pm is 32°C.

We take the dinghy in late next morning, motoring between the supports of a large pier and into a small, high-sided pool with some small local boats in it and a railing around the top. While David holds the dinghy steady I get out and begin to climb up the pool's steep side. As my head rises above the quay a fisherman with a mass of black curls tinged with grey and a strong, weathered face leaves his nets and approaches. Given the cruiser's relationship with fishermen I assume he is going to express the Portuguese equivalent of 'Sling your hook!' but instead he puts out his hand to help me over the railing. It is a lovely welcome to a new country.

For a very modest amount of escudos we have lunch near the quay at an open-air restaurant. The wine arrives with crusty bread, soft white cheese and green olives, followed by fresh sardines grilled in brown sugar crystals, salad, and boiled potatoes the colour and texture of butter. Then we set off for a look around the town. It is attractive and busy, with trees everywhere and pavements treacherously shiny.

Portuguese pavements are made from tiny squares of polished stone laid as mosaic. It is delightful but your shoes can skate over it. This might explain the amount of people in the town on crutches or with their arms in slings. One man has a sling like a string shopping bag, and has tucked his newspaper and other odds and ends inside it.

Our next objective is to locate the post office for the morrow, choose some postcards and buy something for supper. We accost the first person we come across who does not look Portuguese; a tall, fair-skinned, bewhiskered man in a baseball cap carrying a copy of the New York Herald Tribune under his arm. He turns out to be Tom, our neighbour on the American boat with the faded ensign. He and his wife have been cruising for 10 years. He hails from Michigan and is as helpful as they come. Nevertheless, as he talks he seems agitated, waving his newspaper and passing it from hand to hand. What incenses him, it transpires, is Bill Clinton's definition of sexual relations. 'If she does it to him,' Tom says stabbing a finger at a photograph of his President in disbelief, 'it's not adultery!' He sets off back to his boat, with his Herald Tribune back under his arm, a troubled man.

We supper on oily yellow cheese so blissfully mature that it makes your gums throb, the most wonderful bread and a ridiculously cheap, very palatable dry white wine. Portugal's national palate seems to be less sweet than Spain's.

It is a blustery night, with the wind howling in the rigging and a rattling for which, no matter how hard you try, you can't find a cause. It is not particularly bouncy; the wind is blowing off the shore so there is no time for waves to build. But the holding here is not very good, and the likelihood is that we or some of the boats around us will drag, so we share a watch until it blows out around 3am.

We spend the following morning aboard, writing letters and postcards. It is afternoon when we reach the post office but the queue is so long that we buy our stamps from the newsagent next door. Meanwhile, my attention is caught by one of the postcards David has written. The picture is of Sintra, site of the summer palaces of the kings of Portugal and of the Moorish lords of Lisbon before them. It's a pretty picture but puzzling as we haven't been there, so I turn the card over. It is addressed to David's brother Tony and his wife and the message written on it says, 'This is Sintra. We haven't been here. Hope you're both OK. We are. Sandra & David.'

'David!' I protest. 'Is this the best you can do?'

He is unrepentant. 'Tony won't mind.'

The Jumbo supermarket has an amazing fish section, more a department than a counter. There are acres of trestle tables covered with salted fish: cod fillets three-feet long and preserved in salt, dry and stiff as cardboard. Since it takes hours of soaking in fresh water before you can even begin to think about cooking it, and the residual salt must have a devastating effect on the blood pressure, it is hard to imagine why anyone would buy it when fresh fish is so cheaply and abundantly available. But then, of course, in time you discover that it is part of the culture and a national dish, and that if you'd given it a moment's intelligent thought you would have realised that salting fish has been a timeless way of keeping perishable protein without refrigeration. At the fresh fish counter, where I join a queue of local women, they automatically scale your fish for you, trim its fins and tail with scissors, and gut it through its mouth. It takes forever, and the queue is enormous but quietly resigned.

The wind gusts all afternoon and by evening the wind speed indicator shows 34 knots or Gale Force 8. We share a watch again. Apart from concern about our own anchor holding, a Frenchman has dropped his own very close to our bow, and a small Australian sloop with a barbecue on its port side, has squeezed in between us and the American boat. When I go to bed at 2am the town is still busy with traffic, the streets having been regularly grid-locked with cars throughout the night, despite the availability of endless buses and trains.

28
Lisbon

We catch a train next day. The journey from Cascais to Lisbon takes only thirty minutes but is a scenic tour in itself. It follows the coastline as far as the estuary and then it runs beside the River Tagus. It passes through the large town of Estoril, a name made famous by the Portuguese Grand Prix; and through smaller towns and villages in a way that is sometimes surprising. It leaves you wondering if they ran the railway down an existing street or built the village round the railway, for in places the train is hard up against pavements and house fronts. In between you hurtle through open countryside of fields and small farmhouses and get a splendid view of Lisbon's famous suspension bridge.

Julius Caesar used Lisbon as his capital in 60BC when he set about integrating the Iberian Peninsula into the Roman Empire. And it was from here in 1497 that Vasco da Gama set out on his voyage to find the passage to India around the Cape of Good Hope. This discovery of the sea route to the Orient ushered in Portugal's 'golden age'.

What you see today is an 18th century city because in 1755 Lisbon was hit by an earthquake so great that its shock waves were felt as far away as Scotland and the Caribbean. It struck on a Sunday morning during Mass and the candles from all the altars added to the inferno that consumed the city. Fleeing inhabitants sought refuge at the waterfront, only to be swept away by a huge tidal wave. Around 15 per cent of the population was lost.

Portugal's king, Dom José, who preferred courtly pleasures to rebuilding the city – or even running the country – gave a free hand to the Marques de Pombal who not only took control of the rebuilding but re-organized the whole country as well. The centre of the city was rebuilt, to neo-Classical design, in less than a decade and the result is elegant and integrated. Built on a grid, it has spacious squares at either end while the names of the streets running between them reflect the crafts, such as silversmiths and shoemakers, which originally flourished there.

It is a most pleasant city to walk around because, as well as the squares, one of the long central avenues and many of the side streets are pedestrianised which means they are filled with people and street cafés instead of traffic. However, it can be a little hard on the feet, being laid in mosaic, each little square of polished stone being not quite flat and thereby making its presence felt through the sole of your shoe. Its maintenance is as original to Portugal as its universal usage. No tar trucks here, nor cement nor heavy duty rollers; just two or three workmen on their knees, hidden by the passing throng until you almost fall over them, replacing missing pieces by hand.

As if to make up for the pedestrianised areas, in the main thoroughfares motorists hurtle through at ferocious speed, or gridlock the few side streets still available to them.

Although Pombol himself appears to have been something of a control freak, his achievement is still celebrated in a quite personal and unexpected way. It is somehow touching to go into a tiny shop in a small Portuguese town hundreds of miles from Lisbon and see on the wall above the till an icon of Pombal, fashioned in blue and white tiles with a candle in front of it, in the style usually reserved for the Virgin Mary.

Lying between a triangle of hills, the city is built on two levels: the Baixa, Pombol's city-centre grid; and above it (as viewed from the river) to the left the Bairro Alto and to the right the Alfama district. Both survived the 1755 earthquake and retain the jumbled houses, narrow alleyways and winding steps of their Moorish and medieval past.

One of the ways to get up to the Bairro Alto is by Eiffel's elevator, a wonderfully eccentric structure with design echoes of Paris's Eiffel tower. Alfama, on the other side, produced not only da Gama's sailors but also the lament for lost sailors and lost love known as *fado*, a word meaning fate. Once heard only in local bars and cafés, Portuguese singers now perform it around the world.

Up a street only slightly less perpendicular than Eiffel's elevator is Lisbon's cathedral, or *Sé*. It is not somewhere for the halt or the lame to attempt on foot; they would never make it up the hill. As we climb a pavement with the type of incline that in other places you'd consider using crampons, a young boy on a bicycle sails past holding onto the rear of an ancient yellow wooden tram.

The cathedral was founded in 1150 to commemorate the city's re-conquest from the Moors. It is built like a fortress, and its organ pipes jut horizontally across the chancel like two brace of canon ready to do battle on behalf of the Church Militant. A marble knight at rest on his tomb has a smug-looking dog at his feet; while his wife opposite, prim as a nun, has a nasty-looking gargoyle under hers, chomping its way through a chicken's head.

The cloisters are being excavated but visitors are still allowed in. We navigate our way between stone sarcophagi shaped inside to give a snug fit to the head and shoulders. And teeter across planks balanced over trenches which reveal the odd human bone sticking out of the soil and medieval drains. A row of burly men sit on the steps of the private chapels, hunched over buckets of water, scrubbing small finds from the dig, with a kitchen glove on one hand and a toothbrush in the other, gossiping like fishwives. Real fishwives, stately, black and silent, also with buckets at their feet, stand outside in the square, selling the day's catch.

On the way back to the railway station we take a detour into a dark, cluttered shop that seems to sell every foodstuff and drink you can imagine. Shelves of groceries rise from floor to ceiling, counters are piled high with cheeses while cooked hams hang from hooks in the rafters. Edging sideways past trays of salted fish, we make our way to the rear of the shop and enter the grotto where the port is secreted.

It takes us a while to decide, among a wide range of prices and vintages going back to the 1920s. The owner materializes silently a couple of times behind us, two gringos with a backpack in his cellar of expensive port, but too polite to tell us to leave it outside. We keep it with us because it has our own valuables inside it, not least our ship's papers and passports, but we have no way of explaining that.

At the cramped little till he hovers at a discreet distance. While David pays, I studiously empty our camera and telephoto lens from the backpack and put the two bottles of port into its obviously empty insides. Then I put the camera and lens on top. The watchful man relaxes and wanders off. Only Christmas will tell us if this is a good buy.

It is at the railway station that we discover Portugal is one hour behind Spain. It says something about the pace of our life nowadays that it has taken us four days to notice.

We had fancied visiting the famous monastery of Jeronimos at Belam, which survived the great earthquake and is about 20 minutes away by tram. It was begun in 1502 to celebrate the return of Vasco da Gama whose body is buried just inside the doorway. But it is hot, and we are getting tired, so instead we return to *Voyager*, put up the awning, open all the windows to create a cool breeze and languish in the shade with a glass of cool white wine. The monastery will still be there another time.

It is a gentle afternoon and evening and we dine on deck on a blue sea under a blue sky. It is a quiet, restful night.

29

Cascais to Lagos

It is a long sail to Lagos (pronounced *Lagoosh*) on Portugal's southern coast. This is the area known as The Algarve, after al-Gharb, a Moorish kingdom. We can't hope to reach it in daylight and feel it is safer to be at sea during the hours of darkness rather than entering a harbour we have never seen before. So we leave Cascais after lunch to sail through the night and arrive at Lagos next morning. The forecast is for a northerly fresh breeze and that is exactly what we get for the first eight hours. It is a wonderful sail with the wind behind us.

Mid-afternoon a solitary white adult gannet passes, leading a training school of mottled brown juveniles. It flies only inches above the water, demonstrating the finer art of dipping a wing, while its rag-tag pupils shamble behind. They aren't very good. I regret not being able to stay around to see how they manage the typical gannet dive-bombing technique, wings back as they plunge headlong onto their prey. Later we see a single youngster practicing all alone – dipping, swooping, circling – a budding Top Gun.

By nightfall the wind has become slight and we motor-sail with just one engine for the rest of the journey. Heavy rollers on the starboard quarter make us swing and toss. I do the midnight to 4am watch. It is overcast and moonless and very black with just a handful of stars behind a small tear in the heavy cloud. It is an uneventful passage but I find the darkness combined with this particular motion unnerving. I am glad when David takes over the watch and that when I get up again it will be light.

During David's watch the sea becomes slowly flatter. However, at the same time the horizon, already barely discernible in the darkness, disappears altogether as fog arrives. The combination of black night and thick, blanketing fog creates a sense of being completely cut off, for there is nothing whatever beyond your rails to give your world form and meaning, not even a light from a distant ship. And as always with fog, everything gets very wet. By the time I get up David is in his oilies, staring at the radar screen, while the cockpit drips moisture from everywhere. I make us a mug of tea each. At least with the approach of dawn it is getting lighter, and once the sun rises it begins to burn off the fog. Soon it is reduced to heavy mist until finally, as if it has become too frail to hold together any more, it falls into wispy fragments and through them we can see ahead of us the great bare brown rock face of Cape St Vincent.

Portugal is rectangular in shape and at its bottom left-hand corner is Cape St Vincent – or *Cabo de São Vicente* to address it properly – named after St Vincent of Saragossa, patron saint of Portugal. To the ancient Greeks and Romans it was a sacred promontory. It is not hard to see why. Cape Finisterre, so famous because of its gales and vicious rocky coastline, had been such an anti-climax in fine weather that David had gone below to check the GPS to convince himself that what we were passing really was Finisterre. Cape St Vincent, by contrast, towers 200 feet above you; exposed, brooding and unmistakable. As well as its height and prominence, it also takes a long time to sail round it and with nothing else to look at on this windswept corner it is in your sights for a long time.

After you've turned left at Cape St Vincent there is a feeling that you are on the last leg. You are not far from the southern coast of Spain, from where it is but a short hop to Gibraltar. And when you reach Gib you are in the Med.

Less than four miles along the coast from the Cape we are looking up at Sagres. This is where, in the 15th century, Portugal's Prince Henry the Navigator set up his famous school for navigation and began Western Europe's exploration and colonization of the rest of the world.

It begins to get hot and humid.

The last headland before turning into Lagos Harbour's entrance is Ponta de Piedade. Its stunning cliffs are made of horizontal layers in the colours of yellow ochre and sandstone. In places they have crumbled vertically into something resembling ancient Greek columns. Below them, at the base of these cliffs, are large caves. Clustered around them are open boats full of tourists under brightly coloured canopies. Their festive air is a welcome contrast to a black and turbulent night and the oppressiveness of dense fog.

On top of the headland itself there is an elegant lighthouse. As northern sailors David and I are used to lighthouses that are tall grey granite cylinders. This one is a cream-coloured Mediterranean palace with palm trees on either side. The charm of this stretch of coast is further enhanced by the fact that for some miles now the land above us has smelled of warm cinnamon.

Down on the water, meanwhile, the humid air hangs like grey gauze in the airless morning. The heat is almost tangible. And all around us small wooden fishing boats, painted in primary colours, loll motionless on a flat shiny sea.

30
Lagos

We enter Lagos Harbour at noon, pass the fishing dock and aim for the marina's reception pontoon, where a trim Portuguese girl in a beige safari suit and a shoulder bag supervises the stocky youth tying us up.

'Wow!' I say. 'There's efficient.'

When the youth has finished the girl tells David to go and register at the marina office. Once we have registered, she says, the swing bridge will be opened for us and we can go inside the marina and tie up to the berth we are allocated.

We have been warned that the Portuguese are keen on officialdom and paperwork. No other EU country seems to be interested in the movement of Europeans and European-registered boats except Portugal although so far, despite being in Portuguese waters for over a week, no-one has approached us. According to the literature, Lagos boasts a fast-track procedure. At other Portuguese marinas checking in often takes several hours.

David is gone a long time. He is hot and dishevelled when he returns. The report that follows is as he gave it.

It was a very long counter, he says, *divided off into four sections. The first was Marina Administration. A woman in her late 20s, blue and white uniform, mini-skirt, black stockings with suspenders, stilettos, rubber truncheon, torch in the eyes. She wanted our home address, date of birth (both of us), the date our passports were issued, our ship's registration papers, where we've come from, port of registry, our Small Ships Registration number, engine number and mast height.*

I hold a cold compress to his forehead and he revives a little.

It just went on and on, he mumbles. *The security code on our credit cards, pin numbers, past life experiences, the colour of our upholstery, which football team I support.*

After Marina Administration had finished with him, he and our documents had been slid along the counter to Customs – a swarthy man with a cigarette in the corner of his mouth.

Have a cigarette, Tommy. They all talk in the end, you know. Resistance is useless.

Then Immigration and finally the Maritime Police (Coast-guard).

'And the good news?' I say.

'E51 and 52,' he says. 'The whole finger, and someone will help us in.'

'Super!' I say.

The bridge across the river opens and in we go, but when we get to E51/52 it is already occupied and there are no marina attendants anywhere.

David radios the office on the VHF and tells them.

Someone says, 'Ah.' Then there is silence.

We hover for a while, then radio again and finally someone says, 'N pontoon. Someone will assist you.'

N pontoon is deserted. Not a soul. Not a single boat even, in what is obviously a new extension to the marina. So we choose a finger and tie up to it. It is 1.15pm. As no attendant has shown up we dutifully radio in our berth number. There is hesitation; we should have gone onto *M*. We gaze out across rows and rows of unoccupied finger pontoons and wait. After a long pause we finally hear, 'OK'.

David goes for a shower and to reconnoitre at 2.30pm. I stay on board with a glass of Cascais's dry white and the marina's short history of Lagos. One of the original 15th century navigators was Gil Eanes. When I look up from this booklet, the name of the contractor on the billboard of the high rise building going up just across from our stern is...Gil Eanes.

We are miles from the marina office and shower block. When David finally returns to our pontoon the card given to him by the marina will not open the security gate. He shouts for me to come and open it from the inside, but I have fallen asleep over my short history of Lagos, so he has to walk all the way back to the marina office again.

'Oh yes,' they say, 'our computer showed that it had rejected your number.'

There was one thing David *had* enjoyed about registering. On the form, the little box for the signature of the registered skipper of the vessel is headed *'El Capitano'*. David adopts this title enthusiastically, referring to it during subsequent differences of opinion and on one occasion even following it up with, 'Did I ever tell you that a ship's captain was once known as Master under God?'

'Yes,' I say, 'but it's still your turn to get dinner.'

I am as supple as a dancer now. I have no bruises any more. I shimmy and sidle past obstacles. My feet are precision instruments. I move with the movement of the boat. There is a terrible smell in the galley but I cannot track it down. It has undertones of yesterday's fish, but despite having soaped and disinfected everything in sight it is still there.

The boat is also covered in moths. They rise tremulously from our footfalls and sit in rows on the outhauls. I have visions of hauling out the sails when we are next at sea and the main and genoa floating out like lace just before they drop to pieces.

We dine on deck to the sound of Miles Davis. It is bliss. Then I finish reading the guide book. Prince Henry the Navigator (1394–1460) came to live in Lagos. It was here that he armed the caravels that began the discoveries of the 15th century and which brought gold, ivory, pepper, spices and, sadly, slaves to Europe for the first time.

As well as discovering the sea route to India, Portugal's sailors also explored Brazil, Japan and China, so that by the 16th century Portuguese was spoken in more parts of the world than any other language. During Henry's own lifetime Madeira (1419), the Azores (1427) and the Cape Verde Islands (1457) were discovered and colonized. With luck we might be sailing to all three of them.

I close the guide book and gaze out towards the west. Behind the palm trees, some little clouds which had begun as mauve are turning soft blue against a pink sky. The sun sinks behind a small brown hillock of lush green shrubs that lies between the Renault dealer and

Gil Eanes' new 4-storey building. This corner of Old Lagos is giving
way to the new. Apart from the small hillock, all that seems to be left
is the ancient little round-arched bridge between the marina and the
Pingo Doce supermarket. As dusk settles, some small feral dogs
arrive on the brown hillock opposite and bark at each other.

The water in the marina is full of tiny fish. In the darkness,
feeding on the still surface of the water, they reflect the marina's
lights and sparkle like silver. There is heat lightening behind the
small brown hill. It is still warm enough for swimsuits. Before we left
England we had put all our old records onto tapes and the rhythms
of The Temperance Seven ('formerly the Pasadena Roof Orchestra')
undulate into the soft night air.

We have all this section of the marina to ourselves for our entire
stay apart from one distant French catamaran with a hammock on
its foredeck and four small children. After dark they play tag around
a marina lamp. There is no sound from them, just their fair hair
shimmering silver, from light and excitement, like the small fish.

Next morning we make an early assault on the marina's *lavandaria*
with five bin bags full of washing. As well as clothes, bedding and
the usual kitchen and bathroom linen, some of the windows have
been leaking and we have a pile of towels that have been used for
mopping up.

On the way we encounter an abandoned supermarket trolley
and commandeer it. The *lavandaria* is unoccupied, but we have no
machine tokens. I wait with our laundry while David sets off for the
marina office to buy some. He is gone a long time.

This part of the marina is very attractive, with shops, cafés,
palm trees and benches overlooking the pontoons and boats. When
we'd arrived here first thing this morning the whole quay had been
deserted but, with the passage of time, well-pressed holiday-makers
begin emerging in readiness for leisurely boat tours to the caves.

All the decent clothing David and I possess is in the bin bags.
As I droop over my supermarket trolley in the morning heat, in
ancient T-shirt and crumpled shorts, I reflect that despite yachting's

elitist image it has taken less than six weeks to reduce me to a bag lady. All I need now is a small mongrel dog and some sympathetic soul to press a coin into my hand.

By the time David drops off the tokens, an American has filled two of the four washing machines. I load the other two and we chat. She does not share her husband's enthusiasm for sailing, so he sails their boat long distances with their sons or friends, and she flies in to join them at the places she fancies visiting. When she gets tired of life aboard she goes home.

Some time later two Scots women arrive and go into a pique because I am using three of the four washers and both the dryers, but as I try to point out, with a trolley full of laundry I'm hardly going leave machines standing empty when there is nobody else waiting. They keep drifting in and out and complaining while I wonder why they want to waste a whole day of their holiday hanging around a launderette when they can do their washing at home in a few days' time. And if they are really serious, why not wait around until a machine becomes free and put their washing in it, instead of bringing it in at irregular intervals and grumbling. I had, after all, got up at dawn for this. Things aren't helped by the fact that a standard wash takes an hour. Although besides grumbling about getting their laundry done, they also grumble about their holiday, the facilities and the available activities. As the hours pass, I wonder if grumbling is their main object in life.

In between the American completing her wash, and the Scots wandering in and grumbling, an English woman uses two of the machines. She had been a school teacher but, along with her husband, is now cruising like us. They have been doing it longer than us, however, and I find her observations interesting.

'Six months,' she says, 'seems to be the defining point. That's when it stops being an extended holiday and becomes a way of life. It's when things like a dinghy ride plus a long walk to the super-market, and the hassle of a launderette, outweigh the pleasures of life aboard.' She says there is someone she knows in that position now, in the little enclave of cruisers that has already settled in at this marina for the winter. 'She sees the people on the charter boats come in for a couple of weeks, without a care in the world, swimming all day, dancing every night, eating in restaurants and taking their laundry home. It's what attracted her to the life in the first place, but it's not like that for her anymore.'

David and I discuss the winter layover during lunch. We have been surprised to discover that so many cruisers have already stopped sailing for the year by the middle of September. But, then, we started so late that we have been at sea barely six weeks. To compensate, we want to continue sailing as long as possible and we want to spend the winter in the Med, so we will press on.

We lunch near the *lavandaria* (to be on hand to load the machines) on fried garlic sausage, garlic bread and the most delicious wedges of potato cooked in their skins with a spicy salsa and garlic dip. After that I try not to talk up close to anyone except the two Scots women. When they do finally complete their wash, they start grumbling because I'm using both driers. It is a constant problem with marina launderettes everywhere that they have half as many driers as washers and everybody gets cross. However, I say if they leave me their token I will put their wash in a drier for them when I've finished, which I do – at 4.45pm. It has taken seven hours to get our laundry done.

Back on board, I start the ironing, in the cockpit. It is a pleasant way to do a boring job like ironing, sitting in the sunshine with a glass of wine and your favourite music playing.

The dogs on the little brown hillock bark all night.

There are always items of clothing in your wardrobe which need to be washed separately, or by hand, either because they are delicate, or because the colour runs. You soon lose these along the way; about the same time that you realise that by pegging out wet clothes neatly, or folding them carefully as they emerge from the driers, you can lose the iron as well. This stage has not yet been reached at Chez *Voyager*, however, and next morning, while David shops, I wash the unreliable reds, pinks, yellows and navy blues that cannot be trusted in a machine with other items. By the time I have pegged them along our rails, however, rain looks imminent, so I complete the ironing left over from yesterday in the saloon. The iron's flex has to be attached to the barometer by a bungee to stop it wrapping itself round the table screw and sporadically snatching the iron from my hand. The sky gradually lightens so I have most of it airing out in the cockpit when the rain suddenly arrives.

Late afternoon we go for a look at the town in the rain. Its churches feature prominently in the tourist literature, especially S. Antonio with its golden altar. Unfortunately, despite being Sunday they are all closed. We splash home and cook salmon fillets julienne, baked potatoes and courgettes. We leave the hand washing out in the hope it will be dry by morning.

The dogs on the little brown hillock begin barking earlier than usual this evening.

It is Monday. We had intended to leave today but the rain is torrential. The guide book says this area has only sixteen days of rain per year. Out of three days here this is our second day of rain. We take in the hand washing, wring it out and hang it above the bath. It all has little brown peg marks on it now. We finish yesterday's Sunday paper and doze, then lunch on the most gorgeous king prawns, and a confectionary you buy by the kilo. It is heavenly, shaped like a large Swiss roll but weighing a ton. At first you think the filling is liquid apricots but decide finally it is carrot. It must be the most delicious carrot cake in the world.

The rain eases after lunch, and we go on another tour of the town. Our first stop is the post office. A sign above the counter in Portuguese and English says, 'One line only' and it moves at the speed of a glacier. We are wearing our wet weather gear for the rain but while taking root in the post office the sun comes out and the sudden humidity makes us steam. We strip off our oilies and, while David stays in the queue, I find a marble slab to sit on, with the rucksack and our outer clothing, trying to get cool.

One of life's great pleasures is to simply wander, just going where the fancy takes you. The old town is lovely, with its 16th century city walls and 17th century fort. The mosaic pavements here contain black and white medallions of swordfish and sting ray, and the jacaranda trees are in bloom with their delicate bell-shaped blue flowers. There is a two and a half mile beach with tunnels, coves and grottos along the stunning headland of yellow and red stone that we passed on our way to the harbour. The churches are still closed, except Santa Maria which is hot and packed with one of the largest congregations we have seen in many a year. Further down the same square, Liberty Square, there is a classical little building with a double arch to which we are drawn, until the guide book identifies it as the slave market (now an art gallery) built in 1441 to accommodate the first sale of Africans – but after that there is no desire to go any closer.

In Prince Henry Square there is an extraordinary statue of Dom Sebastião, who ascended the throne aged 14 in 1568. It is extraordinary for two reasons: firstly, even the local guide book says most people think it's a spaceman; and secondly, why celebrate him at all? In 1578 he armed 400 ships and set off to drive the Muslims out of Morocco. Over 7,000 men died, including most of Portugal's aristocracy and the king himself, bringing Portugal's golden age to an end. It also impoverished the country and led ultimately to its takeover by his uncle, King Philip II of Spain, and the loss of Portugal's independence for 60 years.

At a news kiosk in the square I spot the headline, 'Monica Costs Clinton Nobel Peace Prize,' on an English-language newspaper.

'Ah,' I say thoughtfully, remembering Tom's distress. 'Monica.'

The Portuguese vendor, previously invisible behind his stock, pops his head out through a curtain of magazines and says irritably, 'I don't like Monica.'

'There's a man in Cascais,' I tell him, 'who doesn't think a lot of Bill Clinton, either.'

On our return to the boat, the ever-optimistic David pegs out the hand washing. Twenty minutes later it begins raining again.

Next morning we top up our water tanks, put out and get in the hand washing (now several sizes bigger than it was, from hanging about wet for so long), shop, shower and ring the marina office to arrange our departure and also to buy diesel.

'Five minutes,' they say, and the bridge will open. We hover for ten, and get no response when we call in on the VHF. However, when the bridge does finally open there is someone on the fuel dock to tie us up, and the diesel gun doesn't spill a drop. David picks up his wallet, sighs and sets off for another interrogation during the departure formalities. *Where are we heading? Is the boat leaving with the same crew?* There is a departure form to be completed and a computerized bill. He comes running back.

'Dear God,' I say, 'what do they want now, the country of origin of our deck shoes or my bra size?'

'Our Cruising Association membership card,' he says. 'We can get a 10% discount.' This is immediately eaten up by the sales tax which no-one had mentioned wasn't included when we checked in. We get away sometime after 11 o'clock. Lunch is avocado with Cajun sauce, cheese and pizza and the last of some lovely wholemeal bread. It gets sunny and hot during the afternoon so I drape the washing around the cockpit.

At 5.20pm we become aware of a Portuguese Navy frigate on our course astern. In no time at all it is very close along our starboard side. The crew, all dressed in civvies, are lining the side deck. I smile and wave, and so do they. What happens next is the marine equivalent of having a police patrol car pull alongside going nah-nah nah-nah, and the driver's mate shouting 'Pull over!' just as the patrol car lurches in front of you and stops you dead.

First we get a *very* loud call coming out of our VHF on Channel 16 which is not surprising as the caller is only yards away. 'Portuguese Navy, Portuguese Navy calling the yacht on my port side.'

David answers, 'This is the yacht *Voyager.*'

The 277-foot long frigate (we will identify it later in a copy of *Jane's Fighting Ships* from the number painted on its side) snakes in front of us and stops, forcing David to do an emergency brake via reverse gear to avoid tailgating it. The caller asks our name again. David repeats it. And then the voice booming through the VHF tells us to remove the pink T-shirt (actually, my nightie) hanging over our starboard side. I remove everything else as well, thinking we are infringing some sort of bye-law relating to travelling at sea with your smalls flying. But it turns out that my nightdress is covering up our boat's name.

David behaves very badly. As I remove the offending item he says, 'Sorry, my wife's airing her washing.' This, as anyone who has been in a similar situation will recognize, translates as, 'Take her, not me.' It is an even greater betrayal than it first appears, because most of the colour-leaking laundry flying from the rigging is his.

It could have been worse. We had only recently remembered to return the VHF to Channel 16 from the marina's Channel 62, and would have simply ignored the frigate's call because we should not have heard it. And heaven alone knows what the protocol is for dealing with aliens who ignore a Navy frigate's challenge. As it is, David had been so startled by it that he had forgotten to turn our VHF down from high power to low – given that we are nose to tail with the frigate and not 10 miles away – and must have deafened its captain. Deafened or not, soon afterwards he is on the horizon radioing up another yacht, but we can't hear the yachtsman's reply because he has obviously remembered to turn *his* power down.

31

Lagos to Culatra

'That lighthouse ahead is at the entrance to the Faro lagoon,' says David, pointing.

'Yes,' I reply casually, as if I knew already. Actually, I've been watching it for some time trying to work out which side of its mast its genoa is flying. I may be light as a dancer on my feet now, but my visual skills have still to improve.

By 6pm gannets are falling out of the sky all over the place. 6pm must be gannet teatime here. By seven we were approaching the heads into Faro lagoon. David makes his turn with gusto and a look of extreme satisfaction, albeit prematurely. The depth gauge drops like a stone, from 42 metres to two and falling, requiring a rapid rethink and a bit of a dog-leg to get off the shoals.

'Bit choppy in the entrance,' I say, which turns out to be classic understatement.

Our destination is Culatra. It is one of the long narrow islands that lie off the coastal towns of Faro and Olhao which between them form Faro Lagoon with its 37-miles of coastline. The islands themselves are really sand dunes, with some areas barely above sea level. The lagoon's entrance is narrow, with boulders on either side. Unfortunately we have arrived at it in a wind-over-tide situation. The wind is sending a turbulent sea rushing into the entrance just as the lagoon's mid-tide is rushing out. To make matters worse, we have also arrived at twilight. The lagoon is criss-crossed by narrow channels. Much of the rest of it dries out to sand banks at low tide. We have a choice. We can go in now and navigate our way to the anchorage in the last of the light; or we can hang about among the outer shoals for a couple of hours and then go in on slack tide. The latter means we will have to try and find the unlit narrow channel to the anchorage off Culatra's village through the sand banks in the dark.

We decide to go in now.

Between the two narrow heads the outgoing tide of the lagoon meets the turbulent sea with a tumultuous roar. *Voyager* is no lightweight, but she bounces like a cork in a water chute. She lunges and surfs. When a boat surfs you have little control over it and first the great boulders of one head come rushing at us, and then the other. Just when we think it can't get any worse, the fishing fleet from Olhao begins to make its way out.

In the same way that the wind always rises when you approach a pontoon, so whenever there is a narrow and difficult bit of water to negotiate you can more or less guarantee that the entire local fishing fleet will charge out; with their local knowledge, bigger engines and dark resentments toward yachts. It doesn't matter what time of day or night it is, out comes the fishing fleet.

The effort to keep clear of the trawlers to port sends us dangerously close to the boulders on our starboard side. A natural tendency to over-steer under such circumstances sends us hurtling towards the beam of a fishing boat. We receive a wave and a friendly smile from its skipper.

I instantly forgive mine his earlier keenness to sacrifice me to the Portuguese Navy. He does well. Ultimately we surf in safely and the half dozen trawlers surge out. Looking back from the calmer water in the channel it is possible to get a better perspective. Close to the entrance's port side – the line the trawlers had taken – the water is relatively calm. So is a very narrow area close to its starboard edge. But the rest, through which we've had to come, is crashing water and when the trawlers reach the heads and turn left through it, to get out to sea, it sends them twisting and plunging too.

Throughout our struggle in this maelstrom, the local anglers on the breakwater above us have been watching impassively, casting their fishing rods or cycling away with them balanced on their shoulders and their catch dangling from the handlebars. It is pure Chekhov. Like few other playwrights, this nineteenth century Russian captured those tragi-comic moments of human existence where one character succumbs to a broken heart while another laughs on the other side of the half-open door. And as I clung to a winch and despaired of our continued existence, a passing trawler skipper gave us a cheery wave while above our heads men cast their fishing rods or cycled home to tea. But then, they have undoubtedly witnessed versions of this scenario numerous times before.

In retrospect, we should not have attempted to enter under such conditions and would not do so again. Nor would we go in at night. After David does finally get us inside the heads and into the correct channel he accidentally veers out of it briefly and our depth drops from seven metres to one in seconds. It is 8 o'clock before we anchor, and almost dark. A strong smell of unfamiliar fuels burning wafts from the village on the night air.

I wake at 2.30am. Rather than keep David awake with my fidgeting I slide out of bed and settle down in the starboard cabin. One of the nice things about having two roomy cabins is that when one of you can't sleep, or the weather is hot and humid, you can wander off across the bridge deck to another bed. With neither wind nor any discernible tide, it is so quiet the fish can be heard plinking around our hull. Through the window at my feet I can see the return of the fishing fleet that we passed on our way in. In the pitch darkness of a moonless, starless night they are visible only as a line of navigation lights, which all turn left at a red flashing buoy a considerable distance from us. Then the lights recede down the channel towards Olhao on the far side of the lagoon.

I am just beginning to doze when I hear an engine roaring. I can see nothing through the window so I open the hatch above my head, stand up on the bed and, with the upper half of my body above the hatch, stare towards the noise. It is travelling in a direct line from the lights of Olhao. Gradually I can just make out a black triangular shape hurtling towards us like an Exocet missile. A 10-foot boat might not seem much of a threat, but here some are blessed with engines far larger than our 40-foot catamaran. This makes a small boat very fast and quite lethal in a collision. Is this one being driven by a drunken fisherman, or simply an angry one returning from a really bad night on a trawler? There are no lights from the village to illuminate us and from this angle I can't see if our hurricane lamp is still alight. The impact will be colossal. And of course there will be all that spilt petrol to go up in flames when it hits us amidships. I must signal our presence. I have seconds only.

While still standing upright on the bed I manage to switch on both cabin lights. These suddenly illuminate, from below, the top half of me in white night attire. Moments later the boat zooms past, a couple of feet from our bow, and heads for the beach. With more experience I would have realised that a man who has lived his entire life on an island without electricity, and whose working life is spent on the night sea, has a night vision second to none. And that if I could see *his* unlit boat then he could undoubtedly see mine. He has simply been taking the most direct route home. For now, however, I am still very green. I do wonder, though, what the poor man made of a pale half-apparition appearing suddenly in mid-air before him in the blackness of a September night.

I am still awake at 3.30am, listening for more homecoming fishermen, when David gets up and makes us a cup of tea. At 4am a rumbling noise sends us up on deck to see if we are dragging our anchor. David stands on the chain with his bare feet to feel for any vibration, but it is just the chain straightening. Overhead low-flying charter 'planes, offering inexpensive flights at unsocial hours, head for Faro airport. I do finally go to sleep.

When I wake again, just after seven, it is light. *Voyager* has turned and instead of looking out towards Olhao, I now face Culatra and on the beach outside my window are the women of the village. As the tide recedes each day they leave their houses to collect the shellfish left behind. Some of the older ones wear skirts and are bare-legged. The younger ones wear trousers. All wear straw hats. The thing that strikes you is the quietness. They work singly and silently.

Mid-morning we go ashore. On the beach, busy little turn-stones upend pebbles with their beaks and some large, stately white birds with black wing tips turn out to be storks, the first we have ever seen outside a book. And just above the waterline is the village.

Ilha da Culatra, to give it its proper title, is an island of fishing families. Forty four of them, someone tells us later, and twenty-two family-owned bars, mostly in people's back rooms. Their neat little single-storey houses and simple church are built directly onto the sand. There are no vehicles because there are no roads, only paths through the sand, and no shops. For these the island women have to take the ferry across the lagoon to Olhao, or persuade a husband or son to take them over in his open fishing boat. One of them prepares to go across this morning. Just when you think not a single soul more could be fitted into the boat, two large dogs come running down the beach and leap in too. Their excited bodies are accommodated, their thrashing tails brought under control, and the boat lumbers away with everybody squeezed companionably but silently together.

As well as the quietness, there is a rhythm to Culatra. It comes from the women, moving slowly along the beach, bent double at the hip, harvesting what the sea has brought. It is there among the men, sieving sand where the tide scours into an inlet to the left of the houses; two men to a rectangular sieve, push-pull, push-pulling, hour after hour. It's there in the small open fishing boats lolling out on the lagoon or delivering a precarious pyramid of the island's sand to the mainland, the boat so overloaded that there's barely two inches of freeboard as it travels at a snail's pace to avoid sinking under its own wash. Once upon a time they used Portuguese water dogs here, to swim under water and drive the fish into their nets. The main concession to the late 20th century seems to be a powerful outboard engine on the back of their small traditional wooden boats.

In the small inlet, to the left of the houses, a dozen foreign yachts have been pulled higher up onto the dunes at each successive high tide until they are almost permanently aground. With the tide out, the inlet has become a large sandy area with just the occasional small pool. It is vibrant with wading birds – little egrets, curlews, sandpipers and godwits – grazing on whatever the village women have left behind.

By the time we return to the boat the morning has become heavily overcast. David sits in the dinghy cleaning unsightly black marks, caused by an old sticky fender, off *Voyager*'s port topsides. It is hot: 33 degrees Celsius. No sun. Just hot. The lagoon is dotted with small fishing boats. Sky and water are the same hazy blue-grey colour. The only way you know where the horizon lies is by the vague grey shadow of hills and buildings that is Olhao. Fish leap several feet into the air, although it is not exuberance on their part but a lack of oxygen in the over-heated water. There is not a ripple anywhere apart from the occasional fishing boat. When the shopping expedition returns from Olhao, loaded down with purchases, the small boat is so low in the water that the first couple of women to get out do so with the greatest delicacy, to avoid swamping the rest.

Meanwhile, on board, we have house guests. We brought a pair of large flying ants with us from Lagos. The two of them sat together on the windscreen all the way, hunched against the wind. They are still there. They're a lethargic species. Brush them off your clothing and they fall to the ground, land on their backs, turn over, but remain where they stand. *Standing about* seems to be as good as it gets for large flying ants; unlike Culatra's long-legged mosquitoes which are either mating energetically on the wing or biting you.

After lunch the sun comes out, the canopy goes up and so do the feet. 'Lovely,' I sigh. 'We have everything we need.' Except something for dinner this evening. The lagoon is brimming with fish, leaping high out of the water or lolling with their open mouths just above the surface. I briefly consider using a bucket to catch one but I'd still have to kill it, with its eyes rolled up at me, contemplating its own mortality. I can always open a tin of dolphin-friendly tuna.

By 3pm David is back out in the dinghy, cleaning the rest of the topsides and the back steps. I make a vegetable curry and get in the hand washing done in Lagos. It is finally dry after four days. With a lack of sleep the previous night, combined with the day's heat, I am very tired and yearn for bed. As I totter past him in my night attire David looks at his watch.

'But it's only 8 o'clock.'

'So?'

'Goodnight,' he says.

SOUTH-WEST SPAIN

⏵⏵⏵
32
Culatra to Cadiz

It is a hot, bright morning. We have breakfast out in the cockpit and a lazy day in lieu of another night passage. We weigh anchor at 4.45pm, which is the best time to ensure that we leave the lagoon on a more conducive tide than the one by which we entered. Then it is out through the sand banks, a turn to port and it's all sails up on a broad reach along the coast. And just as the River Miñho marked the place where North West Spain ended and Portugal began, so another river, the Guadiana, determines Portugal's south-eastern extremity. And once past the narrow mouth of the wide Guadiana we are back in Spanish waters and on our way to Cadiz.

There is a spectacular sunset at 7.30pm followed by a clear starry night. I cannot be sure what was in the mind of a tanker's captain, but I think one changed course for us. There seemed no other reason for his veering right and then making a sharp left turn some distance from our stern. Most kind. A second tanker does something similar an hour or two later. Not so a fisherman on David's watch. Every time David takes evasive action the man turns his trawler back into us.

By my second watch the night sea is alive with them. There are seven or eight ranged ahead of me at one point and despite our being under sail they go instantly from stationary to full speed ahead into our path. Change direction for one of them and before you can find your course again there is another one coming straight at you.

The sunrise at 7.30am is glorious. There is a line that passes through my head when the night is particularly dark, the weather worrying or the fishermen more bolshie than usual. It is, 'The sun also rises'. Hemingway used it as the title for one of his books in 1926 but like so many titles it comes originally from the Bible: Ecclesiastes 1:5. The words are a comforting reminder that no matter how dark or difficult the night, the day always comes. And when that soft blush does appear in the sky with the approach of dawn there is a sense of excitement as you wait for that first tiny piece of the sun's rim, glowing like a small gold ingot, to appear on the horizon. You watch it rise, bit by shimmering bit, first to a narrow crescent, then a semi-circle, and finally a whole blazing circle of golden light. And the instant warmth of it on your face! After a night at sea, the sun's rising is like a welcome fire suddenly lit in a cold, dark room.

By nine o'clock we are approaching Cadiz. It is most impressive to arrive here from the sea because, although attached to the mainland by a narrow isthmus, the city is effectively an island surrounded by formidable stone walls which the morning sun is currently turning to gold. The walls turn the city into a bastion and the bastion is ringed by a shimmering sea and as you get closer you can see palm trees and palatial buildings within the walls.

It was founded around 1100BC as a Phoenician trading colony and claims to be the oldest city in Western Europe, with continuous urban life for 3,000 years. Drake put it to the torch in 1587. It was described at the time as 'singeing the King of Spain's beard'. It destroyed a large quantity of stores and ships, thereby delaying the Armada by a year. The present walls, through which we now enter, were built in the 18th century.

David ties on the shore lines and hangs our fenders over *Voyager*'s sides while I steer towards the marina. It is the only one close to Cadiz and is still in the process of being completed. In fact, the facilities consist of a line of four portacabins representing the women's shower block, the men's, the office/reception and the restaurant.

The wash from passing vessels outside the marina's entrance has an awesome effect on the pontoons and on the monohulls tied to them. Even *Voyager* jiggles a bit. In the shower block I reach for the washbasin tap and a large indignant cicada rears up out of the plughole. I return to our boat and close all the insect screens.

We sleep for a couple of hours and then walk into the city along its beautiful promenade. On a plinth a large, bronze, naked maiden gazes out to sea. On a nearby bench a young man casually caresses his girlfriend's right breast. Down below the sea wall a man on the rocks casts a fishing pole 30 feet long.

Cadiz is a lovely medieval city of shady squares, narrow streets and a splendid park. We have been struck by how much space is given to parks and trees in Portuguese and Spanish cities. The trees here are glorious: palms, jacaranda, pines, oleander, feathery firs, eucalypts, magnolias, and enormous banyan trees with roots growing down from their branches into the soil to form supplementary trunks. Huge and old, beautiful and shady, they line the promenades and grace the squares. And they are cherished. Along the mosaic pavements they stand in special circles of soil edged in stone, and their roots are refreshed in the mornings by a man with a water truck. Where buildings are being demolished or extensively refurbished, the surrounding palm trees have their fronds tied up in rattan bindings, like great hairnets, their crowning glory to be let loose again only when the threat from cranes and diggers is over.

We go into one of the large and shady squares of beautiful trees for lunch. We have swordfish which is very good. As the restaurant is inexpensive, and not far from the university, it is very popular and the service so slow that we do not discover the glorious cake shop round the corner until after 3pm when it is closed. We wander streets and alleyways little changed in centuries, with their green shutters, glazed balconies, and dark, mysterious, narrow shops and bars. At night, antique wall lamps light these alleys. They are too narrow to waste space at ground level on the free-standing kind.

The park has a wide gravel avenue lined with tall, dark green topiary, and secluded paths leading down to the seafront. There is a small artificial island devoted to waterfowl, and students everywhere. The Plaza de la Flores, a small, irregular-shaped square, lives up to its name and is filled with flower-sellers. The scent from the arum lilies is heady in the heat.

We have a beer at a street café opposite the cathedral. Its walls are covered in scaffolding. It is being spruced up for the Millennium celebrations next year. Then we cross the student quarter, with its narrow houses and tiny corner shops, to get to the supermarket in search of tonight's dinner and food for the passage to Gibraltar tomorrow.

At the fruit counter, a couple press their noses and lips onto the end of *every* honeydew melon on display before choosing one, by which time I've decided I don't want one after all. And we fall foul of the do-it-yourself weighing machine. We have tied a knot in our bags. We have not realised that using the spool of sticky tape to seal them is not an option: it is wired to the scales, which will not produce a price ticket until you have sealed the bag with the tape. We buy Bonka coffee, Bimbo bread and a marbled cake called Mildred whose wrapper lists its ingredients in nine languages including Arabic. Also some fizzy white wine that will require a strong screw-driver to prize off the large metal staple holding down its cork.

We get a taxi back to the marina. It takes a circuitous route, but for a very few pesetas we get a scenic tour. Spanish taxi drivers also seem bent on providing a master class in rally driving. They push each journey to the limit and spend their lives in near-collision. Radio blaring, this one shoots forward the second our doors close and narrowly avoids flattening a small girl on a bicycle. Neither looks surprised, or even as if they've noticed particularly. One reverses slightly, one changes direction a bit. The whole journey is like that.

We are now back on Spanish time, so our clocks and watches are all correct again. I cook chicken cacciatore and spaghetti and we sit out late. A cruise ship sparkles under a full set of fairy lights, and ferries glitter back and forth across the bay. By 10.45, with *Voyager* already battened down for the night, a sudden gale blows up with thunder, lightning and torrential rain. The latter will save us spending time tomorrow washing her.

We rise late. David fills our water tanks and empties the previous night's rainwater from the dinghy. I clean the galley. The refrigerator proves the value of procrastination when the gas part begins working again. It may have been affected by condensation and dried out while being run on mains and 12-volt electricity.

When I try to take a shower up on the quay the water runs for a few seconds and then stops. I try the other showers. Then I wrap my towel around me and go round a dividing wall to the washbasins. It is the same there. Cranking a handle of what might be a stopcock above the sinks makes no difference. The door opens and exposes me and my towel to the entire commercial dock as a pleasant Spanish woman with no English enters. 'Agua?' I say, hoping that she is familiar with the system. Bless her, she tries everything. Only the lavatory cisterns produce water. I dress and stand outside the iron grille guarding the window of Reception. Two determinedly non-English-speaking Spanish men keep their heads averted in close conference at a distant desk. I go back to *Voyager* and bathe on board. The four-man crew on the yacht beside us conclude a long, jolly, boozy lunch and set out to sea.

The precursor to any sea passage is always a weather forecast. You don't leave without one. Unfortunately, we have been out of range of BBC shipping forecasts since Northern Spain. Elements at the BBC would like to abandon shipping forecasts altogether, feeling that there are so many other sources of this information that it is no longer necessary. It has, on a number of occasions, contacted the Royal Yachting Association (RYA) and other bodies suggesting the service should be dropped or drastically reduced. Fortunately, the RYA has so far prevailed in retaining the forecasts. However, the BBC has reduced their content so that the coastal forecast is now given only once a day instead of twice, and Trafalgar is included in the six-hourly shipping forecasts only once in every twenty-four hours, just after midnight. We are talking here of around twelve minutes of potentially life-saving broadcast time in every twenty four hours. Germany, by comparison, with no Mediterranean coastline, nevertheless provides forecasts for the Med. France, with only a limited Atlantic coastline, gives forecasts all the way to the Caribbean.

And it is not just leisure yachtsmen who benefit. It is a back-up to commercial vessels along with deep sea and coastal fishermen when their other systems go down – which they do. And when they do, a radio transmission at a dependable time (as well as shortening its broadcasts the BBC also keeps changing their times), albeit crackling with static and sometimes barely audible, can be the difference between life and death for someone at sea. This doesn't seem a huge amount to ask of one of history's great maritime nation's public broadcasting service.

One of the other sources of information that the BBC probably assumes is available to sailors is Navtex. All along the Portuguese coast we still had good information via Navtex but for south-west and southern Spain we do not pick up any signals at all. All maritime countries signed an agreement to put forecasts on Navtex in English 365 days a year. We will subsequently be told by other yachtsmen that Spain doesn't bother during what it considers to be the off-season and so nothing will be available until the following Spring. We don't discover this for some considerable time, however, and keep our system up and running, confident of picking up vital information eventually.

Fortunately, there is a current weather forecast on the marina office window today. It is favourable and we prepare to set off around 5.30pm. There is by now quite a strong wind blowing onto the pontoons, however, and a neighbouring monohull skipper pushing off ahead of us gets into difficulties. Colliding with the pontoon as he tries to reverse out, it takes the two-man crew plus David and a passing Finn to get the boat straight again and set it on its way.

Having seen their difficulties, we work out a strategy and the two of us get off rather well, although we have no time to gloat. It is a blind exit from the marina and we are immediately confronted by a huge container ship attached to a tug. We whiz across the tug's bows and hang around on the other side of the harbour while both vessels make their stately progress out to sea. At least the wait gives me a chance to get in the ropes and fenders in comfort, as the sea beyond the harbour turns out to be very choppy: a combination of the strong wind, last night's gale and Atlantic rollers. It is hitting our port bow and is far from comfortable. I hold us into the wind while David pulls out the mainsail and through the windscreen I recognize in the distance the yacht from the marina with the boozy crew. I also catch sight of something else.

The only way I can describe it is that it resembles a floating version of the vehicle Mel Gibson drove in the film *Mad Max and the Thunderdome* only much, much bigger. It is huge, square, and judging by the way the light reflects off its irregular corners, made of metal. While it is difficult to be sure in which direction it is actually pointing at any given moment, it always seems to be coming towards us. It dwarfs a tug attached to its far side which we glimpse only very occasionally during one of its sideways lurches. And although it is inevitably being towed by the tug, from our vantage point it looks like a close run thing as to which of them has the upper hand.

We spend so much time eyeballing this thing, trying to work out what it is, that we lose track of the boozy yacht until it gets dangerously close. Like us, they are staring at Mad Max instead of where they are going. Fortunately we miss each other, although I am somewhat confused about their intentions because the last time I'd observed them they had been nowhere near us and pointing in a different direction altogether, not sailing directly at us.

'They'll be on their way back to the marina,' says David, watching the yacht's erratic progress as we pass each other.

'You think they know something we don't?' I ask.

'Nah,' he says.

The only other vessel out here, apart from Mad Max and his tug, is another yacht. Soon this too turns and heads back towards the marina.

'Are you sure they don't know something we ought to?' I ask.

'It's Saturday,' says The Optimist reasonably. 'Like we used to go out for a sail on Saturday afternoons at Holyhead.'

Yes, and the wind always got up, and the rain came down, and drove us all back to our moorings. Only now we've got 18 hours' sailing ahead of us, not 45 minutes.

The strong wind that had made getting out of the marina such a challenge continues and we bang into it until around 7pm when we change course and it becomes a little easier. We are also able to turn off the engines and just sail. The sea state remains unnaturally turbulent for the strength of the wind and we can only attribute it to the effects of Hurricane Ivan on the other side of the Atlantic. I go below at 8.30pm. The rolling is disruptive and the squawk that always comes from the autopilot seems unusually high-pitched. It is difficult to get to sleep and I am getting a headache. I don't normally use earplugs during a passage in case of emergencies but around 9.30 I capitulate. I suppose I must have finally fallen asleep because the next thing I am aware of is both engines starting up. As they rev, rest and rev again, I rush blindly from my bunk.

'Wassamatter? Wassamatter?' I gabble as I stumble up the galley steps.

'There's a boat in front of us,' David calls from the helm.

Up in the cockpit, bleary-eyed and spectacle-less I stare past him. I am expecting a yacht. Instead my horizon is filled with the hull and blazing deck lights of a freighter.

'The bastard turned left straight across our bows,' said David. 'That's the second one tonight.'

Having travelled towards us for some distance on our port side, both vessels, several hours apart, had suddenly changed course a short distance from us and crossed our bows. This one has been the closer of the two and, had David not started the engines and taken evasive action, *Voyager* would have sailed straight into it. It hovers now, on our starboard side, as if whoever is – or should have been – on its bridge, having noticed us at the last minute, has panicked and cut his engines. As we stare at it the ship goes full-steam ahead and is away to the horizon with an awesome turn of speed. It is close to midnight and not worth going back to bed so I make us a mug of tea each and then take over the watch.

We would subsequently get into conversation with a man who said he had been Third Officer on a super-tanker. What he told us altered our whole approach to big ships. He said that most yachts didn't show up on his tanker's radar screen and its crew rarely looked out of the bridge windows. He said one night his ship nearly mowed down a large, three-masted schooner, but someone noticed a pair of crosstrees sticking up outside a window at the last minute. He also said that because of a super-tanker's weight and speed it took fourteen miles to bring it to a stop. Others since have said that it takes as much as twenty.

33
Cadiz to Gibraltar

As you change over a watch you pass on useful information. If shipping is more than a few miles away it is only a pinprick of white light, because the red and green navigation lights which tell you in which direction a vessel is travelling are not visible beyond a few miles. It is therefore helpful to be told: *that* ship is travelling north to south; *that* one is going away from us; *that* one has barely moved for hours and is probably biding time until morning; I've been watching *that* one for an hour and I still haven't worked out what it is doing, etc.

It all helps you to acclimatize quickly to the blackness, the lack of horizon and a confusing array of lights by identifying the big fast-movers, the stationary fishing trawlers, small yachts up close whose lights can be mistaken for big ships a long way off, or stars or planes, or the red lights on the tops of distant tower blocks that are a navigation warning to aircraft.

'What about that lighthouse to starboard?' I say.

'What lighthouse?'

'That one,' I say pointing.

'There is no lighthouse,' he says, not looking.

'Yes there is. It's flashing.'

'Not possible,' he says. 'There's nothing out there.'

With a noisy intake of breath I stare remorselessly at a faint flashing beacon until he is obliged to turn his head and look at it.

'Ah,' he says and goes down to look at the chart.

He returns moments later. 'That's Africa,' he says. 'Nothing to worry about.'

According to the chart, the lighthouse at Tangier can be seen 30 miles away and we are just in range. And I finally realise what it is that I have been able to smell ever since I came stumbling up from my bed. I can smell Africa; warm, woody, spicy. David sleeps in the saloon during my watch in case we get attacked by any more freighters.

Shortly after midnight, between Cadiz and Tarifa, we sail through the site of a famous sea battle. It was here, off the shoals of Cape Trafalgar, in 1805, that a British squadron of 27 ships engaged with 33 ships of the combined fleets of Spain and France in the Battle of Trafalgar. The latter lost eighteen vessels during the battle. The Royal Navy won without losing a single ship, establishing Britain as the world's pre-eminent naval power for over a century.

At one stage of my watch I am surrounded by freighters. At another, the coastline appears to be closing in, but the lights turn out to be a line of fishing boats drifting slowly towards me on the tide. One particularly active and bloody-minded Spanish trawler skipper zigg-zaggs in front of me so many times, and I change course so often to avoid him, that finally I reach a point where I say, 'Oh, sod it!' and hold my course. The result is that the trawler skipper and I are so close that I can look straight into his startled eyes but what I am really looking for are signs of whether he is trailing a net for me to run into. My irritability is not helped by the fact that I am having to wear my foul weather gear. There was a squall during David's watch and everywhere, including the helmsman's chair, is sopping wet.

We have been under sail since shortly after Cadiz, which means that the autopilot has been draining the batteries. So, instead of using the console lights, I check the instruments with a torch. The battery on the big yellow plastic one is flat, so I am using a small black rubber one which means if you put it down in the dark you can't find again. I try keeping it in my jacket pocket which unfortunately isn't big enough for it. So, having wrenched the Attack Velcro open and had it seal itself shut again four times, I have the delusion that maybe the Velcro will adhere to the matt rubber torch just enough to hold it in the pocket. But will it? Will it Hell.

'What kept dropping in the cockpit?' David grumbles when he gets up.

When you finish a watch it sometimes helps to get yourself off to sleep if you read, and after I get into bed (and one tries hard to keep one's bedding spruce) I become aware of the blackened fingers turning the pages of *Oliver Twist*. It takes more than one trip to a launderette before all traces of that wretched black rubber torch are removed from that particular bed sheet.

The Mediterranean loses more water by evaporation than it receives from the rivers emptying into it. The difference between the two is made up from a constant flow of water from the Atlantic Ocean through the Straight of Gibraltar at an average speed of two knots. With the combination of this current and a following wind it is an exhilarating sail. Our plan is to arrive at Gib after dawn. The good conditions mean we are ahead of time so when David comes up on deck to take over the watch at 3.30am we reef the genoa to slow us down.

As we approach the town of Tarifa, Channel 16 crackles out from the VHF with a Spanish voice on Tarifa Radio calling channel numbers rapidly in English. David tries all the relevant channels, but finds nothing on any of them. We sail on.

As any regular sea-goer will know, Channel 16 is used, by international agreement, as an emergency and a hailing or call-up channel. If you want to call up the coastguard, or hail another boat, you do so on Channel 16. However, as soon as you have made contact you immediately go to another channel, any one of a number of working channels, to have your conversation, thereby leaving 16 free for others to use. It is the only channel which is permanently monitored by the coastguard, and on which gale and navigation warnings are announced, along with the numbers of the working channels you can tune into to hear them.

In Britain, every mariner who is in charge of a VHF radio is required to take a course in the proper use of it and to pass a test before getting an operator's license. However, we had not been long at sea before it became apparent how much things would improve, for mariner and coastguard alike, if the people who are going to transmit information to shipping had to spend a few days and nights at sea on a small boat with standard equipment to discover for themselves the quality of a large proportion of the transmissions received aboard.

You get crackle. You get static. You get periods when all you pick up is one word in three. You get people giving information at high speed in a voice with a strong accent. You get people who mumble and young people who are clearly embarrassed because colleagues in the control room are making fun of them as they make their broadcast. There is wind, rain, sea and engine noise and atmospheric interference. The range of the average VHF radio is about 20 miles, but the nearer you are to that limit, the less audible the broadcast is. And if you happen to be on the foredeck struggling with a sail when the broadcast takes place, you are not even physically within hearing distance anyway. So for something really important, like a gale warning or a navigational hazard, a repeat announcement a short time after the original would not go amiss.

Even with the genoa reefed we are flying along and at 5am Tarifa slips quickly by. At 6 o'clock David makes the final turn towards Gibraltar and happily records in the log, 'We are in the Med!' At 6.30 he wakes me for the approach into Gibraltar Harbour.

I have been on deck only a short time when I notice that the wind is increasing rapidly, the way it does just before a squall strikes. I call a warning down to David at the chart table, assuming he will want to put another reef in the genoa.

'I think I might take it in altogether,' he says absently, 'we'll be amongst Gibraltar's shipping soon.'

'It's 20 knots,' I say, flicking my torch at the wind speed indicator again.

He remains below studying the chart.

'21 knots.'

Sometimes David can be maddeningly calm in conditions I consider stressful.

'22 knots,' I shout, starting both engines.

'All *right!*' he says, banging his head on his way out through the companionway doors. 'I said I'd take it in, didn't I!'

In the short time it takes us to haul in the genoa the wind gauge reaches 28 knots and then the squall hits us. The wind soars up to Force 8 and we pitch and toss. When running before the wind, however, it is easy to forget that the actual wind speed is greater than that shown on the wind speed indicator. To get a true reading, you have to add your boat speed. In truth, we realise belatedly, the wind behind our stern is not Force 8 but Strong Gale 9.

This is not the most auspicious moment to enter Gibraltar's waters but I begin singing *Rule Britannia* anyway. David says, 'Oh God, yes,' and pulls on the halyard to the right of the steering wheel, thereby lowering our Spanish courtesy flag. Unfortunately you can't remove a flag from this halyard from inside the cockpit. You have to climb out onto the side deck and balance there while you twiddle about with bits of fraying, knotted string. It's a man thing.

David already has one foot over onto the side deck when I say, 'One more step and I'll leave you – not that I'll have much choice anyway because I'll never be able to *find* you again in these conditions.'

A Seacat ferry, big and very fast, has recently set out from Algeciras to our left, on its way to Tangier on the other side of the Strait. We are just now crossing its wake. It adds even further to the general turbulence and David leaves the flag lying where it is, between windshield and shroud.

Our goal now is the Immigration & Customs dock and, according to the cruising guide, its entrance is identified by a red flashing light. Although it is 7.30 in the morning it is still pitch black. Driving rain is reducing visibility to almost nothing.

Suddenly an enormous hull looms up at us. We are now definitely amongst the shipping. We had seen no light to warn of its presence. After a brief panic, when we think it is coming directly at us, we decide it must be at anchor, although we are level with it before we can make out its anchor chain. The problem we have is that the anchor light on a large vessel is high up on its superstructure.

At a distance, in this murky gloom, a small white light merges into the gauzy blur of lights on the shore. In the meantime, we have been sailing blindly at its huge black hull. Another one looms up in front of us. The blackness, the driving rain, the roughness of the sea and our tiredness all become disorienting. Having negotiated our way around a second ship, we are confronted by a third. David finally spots a red light and we begin making our way towards it. Vast hulls keep looming out of the blackness, and while David steers I squint round our salty, smeary windshield, using a finger like a windscreen wiper on my spectacle lenses as I call out, 'Another immediately on your right,' or, 'One directly ahead!'

When we finally reach the red light we have been following it turns out to be on a commercial dock. But by now the sky has begun to lighten enough for us not only to make out the ships' anchor chains, but even the lines of laundry across their afterdecks. I am so pleased to finally be in the Med – although it is not the sort of conditions we were expecting – and I am particularly delighted to have arrived at Gibraltar.

We finally find the correct red light and approach the Immigration & Customs dock. It has a young Englishman in uniform standing on it with his hands in his pockets. Now, I am sure there is nothing in his manual to suggest that he might pop a bow rope round a cleat for you while you run and take care of your stern. On the other hand, nor will there be anything which says he has to start interrogating a two-man crew in a 25-knot offshore wind before their first rope goes round a cleat; not least because it puts both boat and crew at risk.

Getting a high-sided boat alongside a pontoon in a strong offshore wind is not easy. You have to stop driving the boat forward before you damage its topsides against the pontoon, but of course the minute you ease off on the acceleration the vessel begins to drift away again. Getting ashore with a rope is a matter of waiting for a bridgeable gap between boat and quay and then jumping. While David makes a sterling job of getting *Voyager* alongside I take my best chance and throw myself off the foredeck. The pontoon is slippery from so much rain and as I slither along it the wind almost blows me off the edge of it. I stagger forward and wrap the bow rope round the first cleat I come to. The boat is already being blown away from the dock and I'm desperate to get the rope tied. If David can't hold her and he has to circle, it will be doubly difficult with me on the dock and just him on board. That's supposing that the trailing bow line doesn't wrap itself around our props in the process, which in this wind would be disastrous.

'You're lucky,' says The Uniform. I assume he means my actually landing on the pontoon and not getting crushed between it and our topsides. I just wish he'd move away a bit. He follows me like there's an umbilical cord between us and gets in the way of my increasingly frantic efforts to tie up.

'Where have you come from?' he shouts over the wind.

'Cadiz.'

'Didn't you hear Tarifa Radio?'

'No.'

'Where are you going?' he wants to know.

I can't think of an answer. The Med has been our objective since leaving England and I haven't thought any further than that. He repeats his question. I straighten up trying to think of a reply for him but my mind is a blank. I look up at David at the wheel for him to answer but he is looking anxiously at our stern. In the few seconds that I have been delayed the wind has driven our stern away from the dock. In a few seconds more it will have gone too far for us to retrieve the situation. The man is close to me and blocking me off from our stern. Mortified I sidestep round him and dash for the stern line I had looped over the rail on our approach, ready for me to grab and tie up, but it is now well beyond my reach. David has to leave the controls and throw it to me. Then, while he guns the port engine to try and drive the stern back in, I haul on the rope. It is a job for a navvy rather than a middle-aged woman with a bad back and weak wrists, but desperation produces a desperate kind of strength. I gain a couple of feet, tie that off and then haul again. I am bent up double tying up the latest bit of slack as the man's shoes settle a couple of inches from the cleat.

'What flag are you flying?' he shouts at me over the wind.

My head being just above my knees, and my ears obscured by a high crackling collar, I assume I have misheard. 'Sorry?' I wheeze from the effort of hauling 11 tons against a 25-knot wind. My arms feel as if they are leaving their sockets.

'What *flag* are you *flying?*' he shouts again, only slower and louder.

I twist my neck to look upwards, at the large Red Ensign flapping furiously above our heads. It seems a strange question for an Englishman to be asking.

'British,' I reply, giving the stern rope one last pelvis-wrenching heave and tying it off around the cleat.

'Then would you please take *that* down,' he shouts.

Bewildered I straighten up and look in the direction his finger is pointing. At first I cannot work out what he is pointing at. Then I catch sight of the tiny Spanish courtesy flag cowering between the windscreen and the shroud.

Welcome to Gibraltar.

I don't think it is what I *say* that sends him scuttling off to his portacabin so much as my tone, along with a general uncertainty as to where I might shove our Spanish courtesy flag.

He turns out to be Immigration and he shares the portacabin with the Harbour Master, a Gibraltarian. Both men seem suspicious of us and unable to understand why we left Cadiz, although we explain that the 24-hour forecast for the journey was good; as indeed was the journey itself until the last hour or two. We are asked again if we heard the transmission from Tarifa and we say we were unable to hear it. They say, 'You're lucky,' again, and we don't know what they mean, but gradually this convoluted interview appears to centre on the broadcast by Tarifa Radio. They never tell us what was in it, and we don't ask. We sit quietly, waiting to know of what we are accused.

We are tired and bemused. They seem confused by us, but finally pass us onto the Customs officer in the portacabin next door whose only interest is how many cigarettes we have on board.

Once free of officialdom we tune the VHF to channel 72 and call up Marina Bay marina for directions to a berth. It is pier 4, bows-on to a concrete pier and a lazy line off the stern.

Unlike the British marina system and northern France, where you tie up to a finger pontoon, in many southern European and Mediterranean countries you tie your bow to the main pontoon by two ropes about ten feet apart to stop it swinging, and then pull up a lazy line. This is a long rope attached to the pontoon at one end and to the seabed at the other, and which you tie to your stern. In this way marinas can berth many more boats on a main pontoon, pier or quay than if they installed finger pontoons or simply let boats tie up alongside.

How it came to be called a lazy line I can't imagine, because it couldn't be more stressful. First of all, at the pontoon end, you start by pulling it up off the seabed from which it emerges encrusted with hand-lacerating barnacles, mud and untreated sewage. You then have to overhand it down the side of your boat as you walk to the stern. As the length of rope you are leaving behind you drips nasty brown stains all over your topsides and side deck, the length of rope you are pulling up in front of you is busy trying to wrap itself around your propeller. Before you tie this fetid mass to your stern cleat, however, you have to haul it in tight to keep your boat at a 90° angle to the pontoon, which takes an extraordinary amount of strength to get it tight enough to prevent a catamaran from drifting. This done, you mop up the mess, disinfect your hands, then pick up your mobile 'phone and book your husband in for a hernia repair.

A very pleasant young Englishman helps us moor, and hands me our lazy line. Tired and frustrated as we are it is a disaster-in-waiting and I allow it to get wrapped round one of our propellers. The young man is also a diver in his spare time and, for a fee of £20, when he has finished his shift he comes back to remove it. He is down for about 15 minutes and removes bits of fishing net from both propellers while he is about it.

He tells us that the border is closed again today, for the third day running; blockaded by Spanish fishermen demanding fishing rights in Gibraltar's territorial waters. People cannot get out to their jobs on the Spanish mainland, or to visit their families and it is causing endless hardship and frustration as usual.

Even when it is open, someone else says later, the Spanish border police keep cars in long lines in intolerable heat for hours on end for no reason. And no-one knows, of course, how long a closure will last. In 1969 the Spanish closed the border until 1985. The Immigration official and the courtesy flag begin to edge into perspective.

GIBRALTAR

▸▸▸

34
Marina Bay Marina

It is a super berth, opposite one of the most attractive apartment buildings I have ever seen, a row of bistros and cafés, and the kiosks for the diving school and the dolphin safaris. We have the north end of The Rock towering above us to our right, and the drama of the airport runway a few hundred yards to our left. Gibraltar has a short runway requiring a rather sharp take-off and arrival.

We have a sleep, long hot showers and a lazy meal aboard while a whisky-voiced singer entertains lunchtime patrons at the restaurant opposite. We are also more than usually grateful to have arrived safely after we realise that what we entered Gibraltar Harbour in was not a squall but the start of a gale. It continues to blow for two days, and its arrival was probably the subject of the Tarifa Radio broadcast we had been unable to hear.

The yacht on the opposite side of the pontoon from us belongs to a sailing school. During the afternoon there is a tremendous crash. We rush for'ard thinking our lazy line has given way and our bow has hit the concrete pier, only to discover that whenever one particular student wants to go ashore, instead of lowering the gangplank she simply unties it and lets it crash down onto the concrete. With the wind too high to venture out for several days, the tutor has them practicing knots, tying on fenders and studying their Competent Crew handbooks. In the few days we are there he looks increasingly strained, as if he, like his doomed gangplank, will not last out the week.

Rested and refreshed we decide the budget can afford dinner out and arrive at one of the restaurants opposite bang on for their 7.30 opening time. The seafood is delicious. There also seems to be something about relaxing after a stressful passage and, as at Tréguier, I seem to absorb my fellow diners like blotting paper. There are five people, some of them American and probably airline crew, at a nearby table; two women and three men. The youngest and prettiest of the two women is very loud and very boring, and appears to be trying for the world record for how many times she can get the word *like* into a sentence. The forty-something man opposite her begins the meal with an expression which says, 'So, she has a voice like a corncrake, but she's very attractive.' By the second course his face says, 'I'm not that desperate.' During dessert his eyes glaze over and by the time the coffee arrives he appears to have a headache.

Two enormous family groups take up half the restaurant, along with babies in bouncers, toddlers in high chairs and an elderly, sombre chap in dark glasses whom everybody entering kisses on the cheek like a Godfather. There is a highly-polished vicar with a woman in frothy lemon frills, and an aggressive-looking young woman with 'Benetton' emblazoned across her ample chest who is dining with her mom.

Today is Monday and we go into town. We drop off our films for developing, buy an English newspaper and some postcards, and collect our mail from the *poste restante* counter at the post office up Gibraltar's pedestrianised Main Street. It runs steeply up through the centre of the town and the start of it is only a short stroll from the marina. You have to cross a busy road to get there but drivers are extraordinarily attentive to crossings here, stopping the moment someone even approaches a kerb; so much so that you almost feel obliged to cross even when you hadn't intended to, rather than give offence. At the top of Main Street we browse in a book shop and buy a copy of *Jane's Fighting Ships* so that in future we shall know which vessels are accosting us at sea.

Then it is back to the boat with our mail to catch up on the news over coffee. After that we get out the bicycles and set off for Safeway's supermarket. We discover on the way that Gibraltarians don't use their indicators much. Mostly they come to a halt, smile, wave you on, and then make their turn.

Safeway's is Britain Abroad for ex-patriots. We buy our favourite Irish recipe sausages and *real* bacon, Scottish crab pâté, and organic thick cream from Somerset to have with Welsh scones and English gooseberry jam. We could have had trout from Devon as well, but decide to get something local at the fish market later.

While I put the shopping away David resumes the search for propane gas. There is no facility in Gibraltar, he is told, but there *is* a supplier in Alicante. This is becoming like the search for the Holy Grail. I tune in to Gib Radio. The presenter announces that, it being late September, Burberry and Barbour are now available in the high street and the weatherman suggests it is time to get out our winter cardies. That night, sitting out in the cockpit in T-shirts and shorts, I wonder how long it takes for your personal thermostat to adjust to Mediterranean temperatures.

I also finally see a plane take off from the runway this evening. There are very few flights each day, so despite being so close, they are a source of interest rather than an intrusion. I want to wave, but David says waving is naff. We are in bed by ten. Apart from anything else, that was my first bicycle ride in years.

The high winds continue for several days and then there is no wind at all. The mood on the sailing school yacht opposite becomes mutinous.

One day is particularly damp. 'Worse than England,' says an English neighbour of the leaden skies and deadening humidity. We write postcards in the morning, go into town to post them, collect our photographs, buy swordfish very inexpensively for dinner from the fish market, and feel grossly overcharged at the launderette. We had done six times that much at Lagos for less. 'Local Mafia,' hisses a neighbouring live-aboard, doing her washing by hand. The following day is bright, hot and sunny.

For a small place there is a lot to see on Gibraltar and it has a long history. Long before the Phoenicians, Greeks, Romans and all the rest of those early sea-borne traders and invaders found their way here it was home to Neanderthal Man. Or Gibraltar Woman, actually, for a woman's skull dating from the end of the Ice Age was found in a quarry at the foot of The Rock's steep north face in 1848. It was almost a decade later that male remains of a similar age were found in a cave in Germany's Neander Valley near Düsseldorf and gave the name Neanderthal Man to the low-browed, heavy-jawed species which walked semi-upright and pre-dated *homo sapiens*.

The Rock of Gibraltar is also one of the legendary Pillars of Hercules – the two promontories at the eastern end of the Strait of Gibraltar – the other being Jebel Musa on the African side. In ancient Greek mythology, Herakles (Hercules being the later Roman/Latin translation of his name) erected the pillars as tribute on the way to capture the oxen of the three-bodied giant Geryon, which was one of the twelve fabled Labours of Hercules.

Real-life ancient mariners had arrived here by the 8th century BC, leaving less ostentatious tributes to their gods before sailing out into the Atlantic and the unknown. In more modern times Gibraltar was successively conquered by the Moors, Spain and Great Britain. It has been British since 1704.

The Muslim invasion of Europe started in the Bay of Gibraltar, where the Visigoths sided with the Muslims by lending their ships to the Berber Chief, Tarik Ibn Zeyad, who landed by what came to be called Tarik's mountain – or Jebel Tarik (say it quickly without the final syllable) – and ended up naming The Rock as well. Its porous limestone means that there is never a shortage of water, so even when the Iberian Peninsula is arid and brown, The Rock is still green.

The famous Barbary Apes roam free on the Upper Rock Nature Reserve, and the Great Siege (1779–1783) resulted in one of the great mining feats in history. With pick and shovel, British soldiers dug 34 miles of tunnels through The Rock, from one side to the other, so that a gun could be installed to fire on besieging French and Spanish ships in the bay below.

In the winding streets at the base of the rock, the pubs of Irish Town provide hearty, inexpensive meals while old-fashioned hardware shops stock anything you want if you only look long enough. We also visit the surviving part of an early 14th century

Moorish castle on the hillside and, at the top of the town just outside the city walls, the old cemetery where British casualties from the Battle of Trafalgar are buried. It is shaded by palms and pines, divided by tidy paths and there is a great sense of peace here. Like all cemeteries, its tranquillity belies the pain of living and dying endured by those resting beneath its soil: like *Captain Thomas Norman of the Royal Marine Corps & late of His Majestys Ship MARS, who died in the Naval Hospital of this Place on the 6th Day of December 1805 in the 36th Year of his Age after having suffered several Weeks with incredible Patience & Fortitude the Effects of a severe Wound received in the great & memorable Seafight off TRAFALGAR.*

Of the three hundred and fifty men brought ashore from the battle sixty died of their wounds, some of them very young like William Forester, aged 20, who also lies in the cemetery. Although he and Captain Norman rest under individual headstones, most of those who died here lie in a mass grave while the majority of those who lost their lives were buried at sea. The Royal Navy lost 449 men that day, including its Commander in Chief, Admiral Lord Nelson, who fell in action on his flagship, Victory. Ten times that number of French and Spanish sailors died, 4,408 souls in all.

In between trips out we vacuum and iron while we have access to electricity, as we plan to leave tomorrow. We know that we need to find somewhere to spend the winter months from November to February and have a fancy for either Barcelona or a harbour near Rome that the American, Tom, in Cascais told us about. With this in mind we decide to push on as it is the beginning of October now and we still have a long way to go.

During the night some Australians, two boats down, herald their own forthcoming departure with a farewell *do*. I wake up to execrable music around 2am and a bloke yelling violently about 'Roger'. Before it becomes clear whether this is a person or the sexual act I have found my ear plugs.

We cast off from the marina around ten on a bright sunny morning, stopping off at the fuel dock before setting out into the Bay. While we wait for two Navy RIBs to take on fuel we chat to a man from another yacht. We mention our chilly reception on arrival and he explains that the authorities are very suspicious of anyone entering Gib at night or early in the morning. Considering our dawn arrival, in a gale, and showing a hated flag we are probably lucky to be leaving at all.

We motor past the dockyards towards Europa Point and are treated to our own dolphin safari. There are hundreds of dorsal fins, some of them huge, some in places dolphins don't carry them, arcing out of the water. Apart from two tankers which seem to be having a race, and the Saga Rose, in which sensible people our age go on cruises, we have the bay to ourselves. There is a great pall of yellow-brown pollution hanging over Gibraltar and the Spanish mainland.

The strong current through the Strait which had swept us into the Bay of Gibraltar five days ago flows down the centre of the Mediterranean Sea. So rather than follow the coast, we decide to take advantage of this current and by early afternoon are being borne along at 9 knots under the genoa.

It is good to be at sea again, with a bright sun, temperate sea and gentle wind. However, I note when doing the log at 2 o'clock that afternoon that the barometer has dropped 6 points since we left Gib. David begins scanning Navtex for gale warnings. Around 8pm a stunning red-gold sun drops like a stone into the sea leaving red-gold feather streaks across the sky. The wind falls to nothing around midnight, while from behind our stern a full moon bathes the boat in a light so bright you can read by it. To the south-east a shooting star hurtles across in front of the constellation Orion. The night is so clear you can easily see ships' lights 10 miles away with the naked eye.

Meanwhile, David still ponders the drop in barometric pressure and its implications for our journey.

'Perhaps I tapped it too hard,' I say.

'What?' he says.

I'd seen David tap the barometer before doing the log that morning. I'd never seen him do that before and assumed that I should have been tapping it as well. So when I'd taken over the log, I'd tapped the barometer too. It had dropped a point. I'd tapped it again, just out of interest, and it had dropped two more. Next log, I'd tapped it again.

'You're only supposed to do it once a day!' he shouts. 'In the mornings!'

Then the depth gauge produces one of its sudden drops – to just over a metre, in the middle of the Mediterranean Sea.

MEDITERRANEAN SPAIN

▶▶▶
35
Gibraltar to Almería

Our destination is Almería, at the eastern end of the Costa del Sol and at the head of a huge bay. On this stretch of coast there are very few anchorages and they are quite exposed, so we are planning to go into a marina again. David has done the last watch of the night and he is in the cockpit when I get up.

The sun is just rising as I emerge from a dim cabin with sleepy, half-closed eyes into one of those mornings that takes your breath away. The sea is flat and glossy, like floating silk. A newly risen red-gold sun has put a pink and gold sheen on it, and it undulates voluptuously, unbroken except at our wake where it curls away from our stern like cream from a whisk. The sky seems translucent. A soft pink-grey mist lies at the water's edge obliterating any sign of habitation while above it rise the soft brown contours of the Sierra Nevada Mountains, in subtle layers, bathed in sunlight. And you wonder if this is what the dawn of Creation must have been like. You go up front, still drowsy from sleep, bare feet slipping over decks wet with dew and stand on the foredeck, bathing in the unbelievable beauty of it all, wanting it to go on forever.

In less than an hour the sun has risen high and hot enough to burn away the mist and reveal an unbroken wall of high-rise concrete overhung with yellow pollution. But we are two and a half miles offshore and if you screw up your eyes a little, and pretend it is a cliff face, you can dream on a little longer.

It has been a quiet night, apart from David's brief encounter with a large stationary ship bearing a 'vessel not under command' signal – two red lights, one above the other – warning of mechanical or steering breakdown. Somebody on board had turned a spotlight on him as *Voyager* passed.

'What sort of ship was it?' I ask over breakfast.

'I dunno,' he says, 'I'd got this blinding light in my eyes.'

His own torch had gone out in the middle of his watch. We have encountered a hiccup with our rechargeable battery system. Whilst taking all day to recharge, the battery doesn't last through the night.

Some time later there is a VHF radio announcement for a weather forecast on another channel. Unfortunately I can't hear the channel number in English. In Spanish I catch only the second number – *quatro* – but by the time I have trawled through all the two-number combinations ending in *four* I have missed the broadcast. However, the weather is so calm and we are so close to our destination that, for the moment at least, a weather warning is irrelevant.

The skyline as you approach Almería from the sea is dominated by the immense Alcazaba castle, built by the Moors in the 10th century and second in size only to the Alhambra, the largest of the Muslim fortresses in Andalucía. Its fortified walls undulate over the hilltops for what seem to be miles.

The town itself was founded by the Phoenicians, an ancient race from a narrow strip of land along the eastern Mediterranean coast which is now modern Lebanon, plus parts of Syria and Israel, and which included the two biblical cities of Sidon and Tyre. They were formidable sailors, traders and settlers of the first and second millenniums BC. Their influence extended far beyond the Mediter-ranean, however, and before 600BC they had sailed to the Atlantic islands of England and Ireland, Madeira, the Canaries and the Azores and all the way round the coast of Africa. There is even some small evidence that they may have reached New England 2,000 years before Columbus made landfall in the Americas.

Almería was also a major Roman harbour after 19AD and was sacked by the Christians during the Crusades. Then ownership passed back and forth between the Spanish and the Moors until finally resting with Spain at the end of the 15th century. There is an old saying to the effect that Almería was Almería when Granada (home to the famous Alhambra) was just its farm. It currently has a population upwards of 150,000.

We arrive at 11am at a small marina, tucked behind a sea wall. We stare at a pontoon with a green awning and a courting couple on it, and what might be fuel pumps, and wonder if it could conceivably be the waiting pontoon as well. It is in a narrow inlet between the marina and an enormous wooden pier, 60-feet high, but the water itself looks very shallow. We are just thinking about nosing into it to test its depth when a marina attendant appears to our right and waves us to the short concrete dock on which he is standing. David squeezes *Voyager* in, between shoaling rocks at one end and a small cabin cruiser's beam across the other. We are the only foreign boat here.

While David goes off to the marina office and I put away our foul weather jackets, another weather forecast is announced on the VHF. The channel number I had been unable to hear out at sea turns out to have been 74 and the weather for the morrow is favourable. David returns saying that the boats here are mainly small; the area reserved for bigger boats is full; no-one speaks English and the only word he understood in Spanish was 'stay'. He has assumed that means we can stay where we are. He isn't entirely sure, however, so while he remains aboard and puts the boat to rights in case we have to move after all, I go in search of fresh bread and some torch batteries before the shops close for siesta.

When we had set out for the Continent I had expected more individual shops and markets, especially in the small coastal towns and villages we so often put into. Like England, however, most people in most places seem to shop in supermarkets. They may lack local colour, but are a boon to the linguistically-challenged. You don't get involved in queue-forming mimes while a shopkeeper tries to determine how many rashers you want, or whether you want the heads on or off. You simply pick up a pack and wander off to the checkout where a computerized till screen tells you how much money to hand over. Another advantage, when you lack road transport, is that everything is under one roof. All you have to do to find that roof is stop a fellow-pedestrian, smile, say, 'Excuse me,' in the appropriate language, add 'supermarket, please' and then *they* smile and point in the approximate direction. You pinpoint its exact location by observing the first fully-laden supermarket polybag that hoves into view and then following the line of its wash.

Between the marina and the town of Almería there is an area to cross of derelict streets, flyover supports and abandoned warehouses. It is typical of a docks area in the process of redevelopment and rebuilding is in hand. Everywhere you go, it seems, Spain is renewing herself. Once across this no-man's land you enter a new and affluent commercial centre. A woman carrying supermarket polybags cheerfully points in the direction of the building I am seeking.

Although new and bright, it is not a happy *supermercado*. There has been a gesture towards open planning and circular displays which, although attractive, leads to trolleys being pushed in curves instead of straight lines which inevitably results in collisions and bottlenecks. Also, the ticket machine at the bread counter has broken down. The queue there is enormous and edgy, and the solitary assistant looks harassed and resentful. I want something for sandwiches at sea next day, and while I'm not averse to a little crispness on the outside, I do like the inside to have a bit of *give* in it. The Spanish and Portuguese tend to favour bread with a firm texture and a very hard crust. The result is reminiscent of the half-baguettes that British Rail buffet cars used to sell as sandwiches in the early nineties, so that you turned up at business meetings with tomato stains down your blouse and mayonnaise behind one ear.

I don't join the jostling bread queue. I buy a packet of burger buns off a shelf instead. At least they flinch when you touch them and a filling stays inside so you can eat it. I am unable to find torch batteries of the right size.

In our sort of life you spend quite a bit of time looking for things. When I get back I go in search of the showers. This is a very nice marina built for local people that also provides squash and tennis courts, saunas and a gym. I find all of them while looking for the shower block as the buildings don't have any signs on them because the members already know where they are. I try Reception but both women are engaged in a long, complicated dialogue with somebody, so I go back outside. A very tall African directing car parking speaks perfect English and I enter the unmarked door to which he directs me. The large room is empty apart from a table with a model of the marina on it. I go outside again. The man is further away now but he spots me and waves me back in with a motion of the hand that says *keep going.* I continue through this empty room to another, with a woman at a counter. She directs me to the right, at the same time calling out melodiously, *'Ni-co!'* As I enter, a young man in overalls uncurls from under a washbasin, smiles and dutifully withdraws.

Like supermarkets, you develop a feel for shower blocks which range from very good to potential death traps. The worst we ever encountered had a long sloping floor of very shiny white porcelain tiles but no handholds unless you counted the loose electrical wiring to the right of the door as you stepped into semi-darkness. With the tiles wet from a previous user it was like trying to walk down a glacier on leather soles. The options were electrocution if you grabbed at the wiring for support; having your feet shoot from under you if you didn't; or hurtling painfully chest-first into the taps if you managed against all the odds to stay upright without being electrocuted. This one is currently being refurbished and will probably be very good when people like me allow Nico to finish working on it.

Although my experience is limited, every marina regardless of size seems to have three toilets and three showers; as if there is a European Union directive, or else they get them as flat packs or something. But all three of anything never work. One lavatory will not flush. One washbasin will lack a tap. One shower head will be missing. Few have adequate hooks to hang up your clothes and towel so you quickly learn to wear the absolute minimum and make a proper inspection of the facilities before committing yourself. Today, because of the renovations in progress, *two* shower heads are missing. Unfortunately the remaining one is also faulty, sending an arc of water over my head onto my towel and clothes hanging on the single hook on the back of the cubicle door. By reducing the flow to a dribble, I can retain a towel that is only moderately damp. And at least it's less water to soak my hair. In marina showers, with their high, non-adjustable shower heads, you invariably wash your hair whether you want to or not. But then the Mediterranean's hot sun and wind dries it again in minutes.

Unusually, David adjourns to our cabin after lunch. Unaccustomed heat is tiring; so are night passages with their interrupted sleep. We are also aware how very unfit we are.

At 2.30 an elderly man in a rubber dinghy tows in four Oppies. One of them has an exuberant little Angela in it. Round the edge of the high wooden pier beyond our stern I can see the castle we had observed from the sea. To the left of it is an impressive piece of civil engineering. They have erected bridges between hills, tunnelled through peaks and shored up valleys to build a road around the coast. Almería is changing. The little marina itself is where great ships would once have tied up to that high wooden pier, but either the pier was much longer then, or the harbour has silted up, for the water around it is now too shallow for anything beyond a small day boat. My eyelids begin to droop and I join David in a siesta.

We go ashore around 6pm. It is an impressive town with a lot of new building going on that gives a prosperous air to it. We stroll along a shady promenade of enormous, very old trees, and up the hill to the castle. A very bent, very old woman in black emerges from a tiny cave-dwelling in its shadow, her arthritic hand outstretched for money. Up above her an affluent young bride and groom pose for photographs under an archway using the battlements as a backdrop. In a street below her, a quartet of young, male lute players in black velvet knickerbockers, belted tunics, and sleeves slashed with red satin, wait. Their sunglasses are a modern touch; likewise the cigarettes they are smoking to pass the time until the bride and groom return from their photo session to be serenaded into the reception.

From Moorish castle, cave dweller and Renaissance musicians we meander down through old narrow streets and tiny pastel houses to a café for a beer. It is very pleasant to sit at street cafés. It's not something that happens much in northern England except during the best days of summer. It is also considerably cheaper here. Two beers accompanied by two dishes of *tapas* cost less than a single pint at home. We observe the peak-hour home-going traffic and are glad we aren't part of that any more. It is not until we are leaving our table that I read the name above the window: Café Gladys's.

I used to have an aunt called Gladys. It's not a name I've ever associated with Spain. Nor could my Aunt Gladys, nor our parents nor any of their contemporaries, have ever contemplated the life David and I are able to live now. It would have been incomprehensible to them. As with many other nations, two world wars had impoverished their generation, their parents' generation and their country.

As children during the first World War (1914–1918) many male family members had failed to return from the carnage to support them. Their working life had begun at fourteen. As adults, between 1939 and 1945, they had been conscripted into the Second World War, or into the factories that supported it, working long hours on rationed food for minimal wages out of which they paid for the hospital births of their children pending the inauguration of the National Health Service in 1948. David and I were both born during World War II.

With Britain's infrastructure in ruins, and food rationing in force until 1951, the country then struggled through a long period of post-war reconstruction and economic recovery. It is hardly surprising if food on the table, a shirt on their backs, shoes on their children's feet and aspirations to a home of their own one day were the priorities of post-war existence. Foreign holidays for the working classes had to wait until the 1970s, when improvements to the economy and cheap air fares to Europe made spending their two weeks' annual holiday abroad a possibility.

Sadly, the cycle goes on. World News, courtesy of BBC World Service and our daily contact with the wider world, catalogues – as national newspapers rarely do – the endless misery, loss and deprivation caused by one country invading another or by civil war. And you grieve in your soul for the men, women and children, not simply struggling to survive the current onslaught, but for the decades it will take them to re-establish even a minimum standard of housing, health care, education and diet. They are the reality behind the picturesque forts, crenellated battlements and fortified city walls that as tourists we all love.

There is a Saturday Night Concert in the town tonight – a woman, very loud – until 1.30am. Ear plugs are an essential part of a boat's manifest.

We had intended to leave this morning, but the latest VHF weather forecast changes our mind. The morning begins calmly enough, but by 9.30 the wind begins rising. By afternoon it has reached 40 knots, a fierce, hot wind that dries you up and leaves you torpid.

Some of the gulls are flying backwards, squawking in protest, and you wonder why they don't find shelter until the wind lessens. But then you wonder if they are actually the younger ones practicing their flying skills, because other gulls are using the ferocious wind like thermals, wings held stiffly and not fully extended, gliding sideways at high speed. Yet others conduct aerial fights in it, squabbling, being buffeted up and down by it as they turn to snap at each other, their feathers on end and in constant danger of collision with masts or one another but never quite connecting.

Unless the forecast changes drastically overnight, we might still be here tomorrow. With luck there won't be a concert again tonight, it being Sunday.

There isn't a concert and we are to remain for two days more, not one. The mornings are always deceptively mild but by noon the wind roars overhead in a sky bleached white and so bright it makes your eyes ache when you step out into the cockpit. Our mooring ropes snag against the cleats. The halyards on neighbouring boats and on the marina's flagpoles beat a deafening tattoo. The water in the shelter of the marina remains comparatively calm, but beyond the harbour wall the wind is so strong for a time that it blows the surface up into spray spirals 15 feet high. It all fades away by bedtime, leaving the boat to fall back onto the quay where the agitated water sets the fenders rasping against the concrete.

There is also a constant click-clicking around us that we cannot identify. It is loudest when you are down in the hulls. David suggests it is water lapping into a niche in the concrete pier to which our starboard hull is tied.

With sailing out of the question we explore Almería each day, glad of the shelter provided by the marina's walls to reach the town as the wind buffets and beats us, lifting us off our feet the minute we let our guard down. Yet as invariably happens, once inside the streets, parks and castle walls of any town, you would never guess that a gale is blowing just off the promenade.

I introduce David to the new supermarket. There is no queue at the bread counter today, nor fish at the fish counter either. There rarely is fish on Mondays in Spain but at present the weather is keeping the fishing boats in harbour well beyond the Sabbath. We do find what turn out to be delicious locally-made meat balls, however, to have with pasta and sauce. We also buy some eggs.

'Free range,' David says looking approvingly at the label and putting them in our wire basket.

On one jaunt we finally discover the Post Office, so reclusive it requires three separate sets of directions to find it, and stumble upon Almería's *old* supermarket. We spot torch batteries through a discount pharmacy's open doorway, go in to buy some and see wine for sale at the far end of the store. Putting a couple of bottles in our wire basket we notice a flight of stairs behind the wine racks, climb them and *bingo* – a large supermarket. It's odd how Spain hides them up flights of stairs without any apparent sign to say they are there.

Gradually the barometer grows more stable and David gets the charts out in anticipation. We are both concerned about the unsettled weather and it is another spur to hurry towards winter quarters.

36
Almería to Garrucha

We push off at 9.40 on Wednesday morning for Garrucha, 50 miles away at the start of the Costa Blanca. The boat is covered in brown dust from Almería's building site beyond our stern and the direction from which the wind has come with such ferocity during the last three days. Today's forecast is for a strong breeze from the west. The reality is light airs from the south. After days of violent wind it is now so slight that we have to motor.

It is bright sun and a rolling sea to Cabo de Gata, but once we leave this cape behind us the sea becomes calm. Just after noon, with a light breeze from the south-west, we put up the genoa. It is a warm, languid afternoon. By 5pm the wind reduces to light airs from the west and is very erratic. The genoa wafts and flaps, and we switch it from side to side several times before finally pulling it in.

We motor close to the coast until, about 15 miles from Garrucha's marina, a fisherman in a dinghy, whom I have been watching for some time, and who must have been aware of our approach for at least half an hour, suddenly roars towards us shouting and gesticulating for us to turn out to sea. He may have been laying a net between himself and a second small boat; or not, as the case may be. It is hard to tell in all that shouting. He accompanies our flight out to sea for some distance with both himself and his outboard motor in a state of mild hysteria. Then, forking an arm left when he deems it appropriate for us to turn back in, hurtles back inshore himself. All this aggravation and you still can't buy a couple of decent trout in the supermarket.

It is almost dark by the time we reach Garrucha. The marina is inside the town's small harbour. We cannot see a waiting pontoon, but fortunately a marina attendant appears and waves us alongside the fuel dock. He is a charming man who, despite no English at all, eloquently demonstrates the lowness of the concrete wharf and the need for us to lower our fenders to avoid damaging our topsides. The fuel dock has just closed so we can stay there for the night. We are grateful; it means there is no lazy line to mess about with. David goes off to pay.

A thin, embittered-looking man with a cigarette in the corner of his mouth appears. I nod a greeting but he looks through me, takes up a hose and begins spraying water over the boat across the dock from us. I go below and get the covers for our helmsman's chair and instruments before he drenches everything. On his return from the marina office David dodges the spray to plug in our electricity cable, and I have cheese omelettes, tomatoes in olive oil and basil followed by melon topped with lemon juice, brown sugar and ginger on the table by the time he has planned a course for tomorrow. We intend to make an early start.

This is an arid coastline, treeless and brown, but with groups of affluent buildings. In an English-language magazine we picked up along the way, Garrucha is described as a fishing village but it contains some very individual and impressive houses, tucked behind high walls, wrought iron gates and masses of trees. Affluence or not, Spanish pavements can be dangerous to your health. Workmen have a tendency to dig them up, or remove street furniture, leaving holes unfilled and no warning to pedestrians. Vigilance after dark is particularly important, especially here.

It is a warm night. We buy ice creams and simply wander. The streets are leafy and shadowy. There is a small market with stalls groaning with more beads and semi-precious stones than I've ever seen in my life, but no customers. The quay itself is very quiet and there seems to be no petty crime or vandalism. They even leave the linen on the tables at the open-fronted fish restaurant when they close up for the night. By 10pm we are in bed.

We are away by 5.30 into a calm sea and a dark morning with the lightest of winds. The fishing boats are still out, just beyond the sea wall. The men are working under bright deck lights that turn each boat into a splash of brilliance in the darkness. It spills over the edge of each boat, reflects off the moving water and creates a shimmering pool of light around each darkened hull.

We need the early start to get to Tomas Maestre, 70 miles away, in daylight. We have been unable to get a forecast. The only notices on the window of the little white wooden marina office are about forthcoming social events. Our Navtex is providing nothing of any use to us either. There are warnings for Croatia and France but nothing for the Costa Blanca.

The wind becomes a light north-easterly breeze and we are motoring almost into it. Half an hour later it has edged a little more to the north and we are able to put up the sails and motor-sail, close hauled on a beat. By 7am the wind speed has doubled and we can cut one engine and run the other just to keep us on course. By 9.30 it is up to 20 knots and rising. I go for a lie down on the bunk to read until David calls me to help him reef the sails. It takes me ages to get my deck shoes tied, and even then one of their wretched leather laces comes undone in the middle of reefing. I tread on it, and it snaps off. There isn't enough left to re-tie, so now the shoe won't stay on and I keep falling over.

Within half an hour the wind is gusting to near gale force and showing every sign of increasing. It is another ten hours to Tomas Maestre. We decide to make for a bolt hole instead and change course for Mazarron, an ancient centre for lead and iron-making and only three hours away. Unfortunately, this change of course brings the wind so close to *Voyager*'s nose that we can only motor. The combination of the wind's direction and strength sends large waves crashing against her bows. She rises up onto their crests and falls into their hollows. She thrashes from side to side. Waves hitting the port bow send sea spray up over the wheelhouse roof and diagonally across the cockpit to the starboard quarter. The sun catches it and makes colours out of it. We are travelling under our own personal rainbow.

At its height the wind speed reaches 34 knots – Gale Force 8 – and the rainbow spray is replaced with a rhythmic bucketful of cold seawater that hits you on the side of the head if you forget to duck at the relevant moment. It is a cold passage as well as wet, even in foul weather jackets and I'd hoped we'd seen the last of those. On deck, flying salt mingles with the brown dust of Almería. Below deck, sea water enters through a starboard vent and soaks the entire bathroom including all the towels. In the port hull the laundry bin scatters its contents, the saloon coffee table goes walkabout, several windows leak and David's favourite hat (from the Lifeboat Institution) is torn from his head and blown overboard. It is also on plunging, rolling days like this, as your foot shoots off the galley steps for the umpteenth time and every hand rail slips from your grasp, that you regret your liberal use of polish on the internal woodwork.

At 1pm, another charming man is waiting on a pier to help us berth bows on. An English couple, from somewhere down on the pontoons, also come to help hold us off which, given the strength of the wind, we appreciate very much. The attendant lines us up with the end of the concrete quay and hands us a lazy line. Unfortunately it is not in an ideal position for a catamaran and when we haul on it to hold us off the quay we are askew. Before he leaves, the attendant asks us to square ourselves up when we can as we are taking up one and a half spaces.

While David goes to pay at the office, I decide that a tin of tuna bought in Bayona would be nice for lunch. Its box is entirely in Spanish apart from a blue circle with the words 'Dolphin safe' in English, and I ponder the significance of this as I remove it. Spanish tinned tuna tends to be very oily but delicious. Unusually, this is an oval tin. The wall can opener opens only its long sides, spilling oil over the draining board and the rim of the upturned washing-up bowl. I try the manual opener but the can's edges are too distorted by now for that to work either.

Something strange and elemental can happen when you are prevented from getting food out of a tin. This is nowhere described so well as in Jerome K Jerome's 1889 classic *Three Men in a Boat* where they fancy tinned pineapple for tea but find that they have forgotten to pack a tin opener. A terrifying kind of rage descends as they attempt to get at the contents by other, increasingly violent, means and what begins in cheerful anticipation ends with the battered but still-unopened tin of pineapple being hurled into the river and the party feeling that something very close to evil has touched their lives.

Something of the kind happens with my tuna. The only way to get at it is to prize it out from under the lid with a knife, and while I narrowly avoid severing a couple of fingers on the raw edges of the tin a hyperactive fly arrives. I can't abide flies in the galley. You know they've spent the morning walking about on a garbage dump or round a lavatory bowl and now they've come to wipe their feet on your lunch. Putting down the tuna tin and the knife, and grabbing the kitchen towel, I take an irritated swipe at it. The crumbs on the breadboard – and all that pointless flour they dredge over certain types of bread – rise into the air and come down again: over the stove, the worktops, the galley floor and steps, and even part of the saloon.

Now I am angry.

I wash the tuna oil from my hands, get out the fly spray and wait. And wait. The fly soars, zooms, spirals, circles and loops-the-loop. It is the Waldo Pepper of flying circus flies, but it *will* land sooner or later and I can wait. To spray the thing wantonly in mid-air will simply spray all the food in the galley as well. Finally it lands on my bare right foot. I am delighted at its choice and spray it liberally. The fly rises from my foot and lands on the edge of the fruit bowl. Groggy but unbowed it sways there, challenging me. 'I still have the strength,' it seems to be saying, 'to traipse my disgusting little feet through your nicely-washed grapes before your fly spray finishes me.' Outraged, I bring it down with the first thing that comes to hand – the tea towel, fresh out this morning but now something else for the burgeoning laundry bin.

I resume the amputation of my fingers on the tuna tin until a very peculiar sensation in my right foot reminds me that household fly spray is a mild form of nerve gas, and rather than poison my entire system I trudge off to the heads to wash it off. When I get back, the deceased fly has been replaced by an equally hyperactive relative. The focus of its interest is the draining board, smeared as it is with aromatic tuna oil. Taking up the kitchen towel again, teeth gritted, eyes riveted on the newcomer I tense, waiting for it to land. Behind me, I hear David enter the saloon.

'Is lunch nearly ready?' he asks cheerily.

At that moment the fly lands. With a howl of rage I slam down the towel with a violence that sends the washing up bowl shooting across the sinks and into a stack of saucepans, making the whole galley rattle.

'I only asked,' he says, and wanders back outside.

The wind has dropped and, as the attendant requested, David begins to straighten *Voyager*. Naturally, when he has bits untied here, there and everywhere the wind rises suddenly so I leave the galley and go out to help. A monohull arrives and I go and briefly hold its pulpit off the quay while someone gets ashore. The two people on board are rather smug individuals. For a monohull a lazy line is much easier anyway but nevertheless they have tied up, prepared lunch and eaten it before our tuna fragments have even arrived in the cockpit. Once there, we are plagued by flies. We take our food below, and have not quite finished it before a violent bang sends us running for the foredeck. We had not been satisfied with the new setting of the lazy line and our uneasiness turns out to have been justified. It has come adrift and our starboard bow is hitting the concrete dock. Our smug neighbours come out to watch. By the time we have tied fenders over the bow, commissioned an old tyre from a pontoon to hang over the dock, retied the bow ropes and winched in the stern rope (removing a bit of cockpit gelcoat in the process) it is mid-afternoon, but we don't want to risk going into town to shop yet in case we slide forward again. So we decide to wash the boat instead.

The sun has baked the combination of salt and soil to a light brown crust all over *Voyager*. Worst of all are the windows. Indoors it resembles a nuclear winter. David gets out our hose. It doesn't fit the tap. We get out two buckets, but no water comes out of any tap anywhere on the marina. The office – which according to the hours of business listed on its door should be open – is closed. As we are reading this notice, our smug neighbours pass us on their leisurely way into town. They shrug. 'It's the off season,' they say in strongly-accented but perfect English. It is very irksome to be patronized in your own language. In the end we fill our buckets from our own water tank and soap and rinse the windows. They are still a bit smeary after we've finished, but at least light can get in and we can see out.

The shower block turns out to be rather nice, despite the huge green cicadas strolling about, and when I get back to *Voyager* a Swiss boat has arrived. The wife immediately wants to know which other languages I speak – 'French? German? Italian?' – as she finds English a bit tiring. I'm exhausted and my day is not over yet. Nor do I think my tiny repertoire of *good day, excuse me, thank you, two beers/ coffees please* and *where is the supermarket?* will make for very good conversation so I make my apologies and totter below to prepare for a trip into town. The lazy line has remained stable and if we don't go soon the supermarket will be closed for the evening. As we set off we meet the smug couple coming back. The supermarket, they say, is 1 kilometre away.

We have not gone far when the Swiss couple catches up with us and we walk into town together. They tell us they are working their way west, planning to head out of the Med and down to the Canaries, preparatory to crossing the Atlantic. They have been struggling for several weeks with bad weather and realise they have left it very late. Their experience adds to our own unease about getting to our preferred winter destination, as we are heading for where they have been trying to leave. And there are still around 250 miles to cover to reach Barcelona.

We have walked our kilometre to the supermarket when, at a fork in the road, we come upon a sign saying 'Supermercado 2' and an arrow pointing down the left fork. We mill around a bit, contemplating the meaning of the sign, having no desire for a 6 km (4 mile) walk to buy something for dinner. Our normal method, of looking out for people carrying supermarket bags, does not apply here. There are no pedestrians around, no cars even, on a street that has only building rubble on either side of it and becomes a dead-end at the harbour.

Then, as if from nowhere, an elderly, well-dressed couple appear, walking very slowly. Their clothes are dark and formal and they both wear substantial knee-length overcoats with Astrakhan collars, for this is October. The four of us are in shorts, T-shirts and a variety of hats to keep the low, late-afternoon sun out of our eyes. The gulf between our lives and theirs is very large. In a rapidly changing world, I can see us through their eyes and approach them in what I think is as non-threatening a way as possible.

Unfortunately, I forget to smile. There is hesitation in the woman's eyes. The man, older and frailer, holding tightly to her arm, looks almost afraid. 'Con permiso,' I say. She shakes her head and raises a hand to ward off my demand, whatever it is going to be. I remember to smile, and say quickly, 'Supermercado, por favor?' Her face relaxes and with rapid unintelligible words but eloquent hands she says to carry straight on and the store is on the left – but not the first left, she is most insistent, ignore the first left and take the second. I thank her and she smiles. As we walk away I hear the man beside her ask anxiously what we had wanted. 'Supermercado,' she explains soothingly. 'Ah,' he says, reassured.

First left, as she had said, is a dead-end; into apartments. Just beyond is the entrance to El Molinero. There is fresh fish – at last. I decide to be bold and by-pass all the old favourites for something quintessentially Spanish that I have seen often but never tried. I don't know what it is exactly, but feel sure it will be delicious cooked with onion, garlic, peppers and tomato in a fish stock. At the bread counter I point to a loaf that looks more pneumatic than the rest and pass over the amount on the till screen. The parcel put into my hands feels like a slab of concrete inside its tissue paper.

It does not turn out to be my most successful shopping expedition for another reason. Having got the fish home, I realise that they have scales. I sigh and take them out into the cockpit, having learned early the error of de-scaling fish in the galley. Despite my best efforts, however, the scales get everywhere. My two fish are ready for the pan as the smug couple rise from their dinner table. *We* don't eat until 9pm.

By the time the meal reaches the plates – and despite scaling them outside and cleaning up afterwards – there is a trail of fish scales through the saloon, the galley and as far as the starboard cabin. Nor are they the worst of it. I had been aware when I bought them that a third of the fish was head (with enormous mournful eyes) but what I could not have known is that most of the body was taken up with a massive skeleton. The edible bit left over has no texture and no taste, but we are even denied a good chew at it because bits of pointed bone have come loose in the cooking, any one of which could have perforated any part of our digestive tract on its way through.

As we settle into bed the night is rent by thunder, lightning and quite a lengthy hailstorm. Very noisy in a boat, hailstones. Sleep is out of the question, for a time at any rate. The hailstorm is followed by torrential rain. Having got all that over with, the night becomes blissfully quiet and we wake in the morning to a clean boat and windows that positively sparkle.

The data on Navtex today concerns an English and a French trawler sinking near Cherbourg. Unfortunately there is nothing to help a yachtsman wondering whether to leave Mazarron for Alicante. Only later do we discover that freak weather conditions are responsible for us picking up Navtex data posted by and about countries other than Spain.

While I sweep up more fish scales which have mysteriously appeared in the galley during the night, David sets off to try and find a weather forecast more recent than the five-day-old one in the marina office window. He finally gets one from the local diving club. It consists of:

'Where you heading?'

Alicante.

'Bueno!'

He decides to risk it but stay close to the coast so that we can run for cover if necessary.

While waiting for him to return I feed the young ducks swimming around us some of the bread bought in town the previous evening. Its crust is now so tough that I have difficulty breaking it into pieces for them, and I notice that instead of the usual snatch and gulp they hold each piece underwater and soak it thoroughly before attempting to swallow it.

We leave Mazarron at 10.20, taking much care over the lazy line. After half an hour the wind rises enough for us to have a sail. Twenty minutes later it drops to nothing. We take in the genoa and motor in a dead calm. A large dragonfly drifts over our stern. It is a lovely, languid, sunny, lazy day; a day for swimsuits and putting your feet up, reading and doing a crossword. It couldn't be more different from yesterday. Nevertheless, David has several bolt holes planned just in case. The first is Cartagena but the weather is so serene we sail on. The next is Cabo de Palos, but we pass that one too. It's fortunate that we don't need it, because a closer reading of the cruising guide reveals that the maximum boat length accepted there is thirty three feet, and *Voyager* is forty. As we turn this cape the wind increases enough to get the sails out again, but in less than an hour it is calm once more. With such light winds we are not going to make it to Alicante today. As we are approaching Torrevieja by early evening we decide to spend the night there.

According to the cruising guide there are two anchorages inside the harbour. The one on the right has no-one anchored in it, however, just a large commercial boat tied up to the harbour wall. If there are other yachts about and there is a large empty area some-where, it's a pretty sure bet that there is something wrong with it. There are anchored yachts to the left, however, so we drop our hook there. It is a lovely gentle evening with no flies and the big tourist town beyond the marina just a distant hum. More fish scales appear in the galley.

We are woken at 2am by the wash from a fishing boat. Sometime later we sit up and listen to a rumbling noise. We go on deck but never do work out what caused it. We also have *that noise* again. Since Almería it has manifested at every berth. They had all been concrete and I could accept the explanation of water lapping. But now we are at anchor, and the noise is still there. In fact, it is louder than ever. It is like fire crackling, or rustling polythene bags; a loud, constant clicking. We open all the cupboards and lockers to listen to the various electrics, and even stick an ear against the wall clock to see if the mechanism has suddenly grown louder. It is driving me mad. I lie in bed listening to it.

'Can you *hear* osmosis?' I ask plaintively. 'Or antifoul disintegrating?'

'Gotosleep,' he mumbles.

We lift the anchor at 10 o'clock in a calm, clear morning. We still have no forecast, but it is only 25 miles to Alicante. The wind is light and it is another bright, sunny day, another day for swimsuits, but given the erratic nature of the weather David has another bolt hole or two earmarked. Our route is taking us towards the Islas de Tabarca a small island at the western end of the bay in which Alicante is to be found. A couple of buildings are vaguely visible on the crest of the island but it looks deserted.

One might think that keeping track of one another when your living area is only forty feet by sixteen would be simple, but it isn't always. During the afternoon I leave David in the helmsman's chair, go down into the saloon, through the galley and into the starboard cabin for a book. Both of the after cabins are stuffed to overflowing with them and the one you want is usually in the second cabin you look in – or in the first one, only you didn't look properly. On the way back I hear a splash. It is only noteworthy because it is louder than normal but when I get back to the cockpit the helmsman's chair is empty.

I peer through the windscreen to see if David is on the foredeck and then down into the saloon. I rush to the stern to look for a bobbing head, and then run down into the port hull in case he's gone into the workshop. I dash back up on deck. Maybe he was lying head down into one of the foredeck lockers when I'd peered through the windscreen and I'd not been high enough to see him. I climb over the coaming and run down to the foredeck. David is nowhere to be seen. I stare out to sea again and yell his name.

Panicking now, I run back to the cockpit ready to put man-over-board drill into operation. Fortunately, because the wind had recently died, we had put away the sails and are now motoring, so all I have to do is turn *Voyager* through exactly 180 degrees to retrace the course we have taken. What horrifies me is that I should be able to see him in the water but I can't. As I scramble back into the cockpit, scraping my shin very painfully on a winch in my anxiety, there he is, just climbing back into the helmsman's chair with *A Cruising Guide to Italy* under his arm.

He takes one look at my face and says, 'What?'

'Don't ever do that again!' I roar at him.

'What?' he says. *'What?!'*

By 12.45 the buildings on the small island of Tabarca reveal themselves as a church with a walled cemetery, a tiny village, a fortress-like building and an elegant lighthouse. And two trees. When we get abreast of its north-westerly side, facing the coastline, we can see that the island is far from deserted. There are dozens of people at the water's edge which is also chock-a-block with pleasure boats and rows and rows of fishing rods silhouetted against the sky.

While we are busy noting the deceptive appearance of the island, our depth gauge drops from 39 metres to five. We had expected it to reduce sometime soon, but not that much that soon. It all had to do with the navigation buoy to our left which was guarding the shallows, and which David had insisted was a yacht, and which I'd stopped watching through the binoculars to have a look at the island instead, and we have one of those moments which are initially loud with mutual recrimination and then very quiet as we nose slowly towards deeper water again. Meanwhile, beyond our stern, a local ferry shuttles more people to the island. The next time we see Tabarca it is not a Saturday afternoon, and it looks more as it had from out at sea and much more like what it once was.

I get out some eggs for lunch. It is strange to buy eggs in a box of ten – a metric unit, instead of six – an imperial half dozen. Then I notice the picture on it.

'David,' I say, holding the box towards him. 'These eggs we bought at Almería. How did you know they were free range?'

He glances at the box, looks sheepish, and then sets off purposefully towards the cockpit as if he's suddenly remembered something urgent that needs doing there.

'It was the picture on the box, wasn't it?' I call after him. 'These chickens walking about with smiles on their beaks?' There is a clatter from the gas locker masquerading as essential maintenance. 'Ad Man's dream, you are!' I shout over the noise.

The texture of the bread is now so dense that it makes no difference whether I cut the crusts off or not. I abandon it along with the eggs and take the big fruit bowl up into the cockpit instead. Our appetite these days is for lighter food and less of it.

By 2pm the sun is so hot we have to put on protective clothing. It is hard to believe that we are well into October. The sea and sky are an extraordinarily bright blue. A plane flies low with home-going holiday-makers. David watches it. 'I bet it's raining at Manchester airport,' he says, pulling his shirt collar up to meet the brim of his panama hat and prevent the back of his neck from burning. Whenever we had arrived home from a couple of weeks somewhere warm the pilot had always announced, with a cheerfulness bordering on sadism, that it was raining at Manchester airport.

Out to sea a cargo ship's captain with a Scandinavian accent calls, 'Alicante Pilot, Alicante Pilot' amid crackle and static. No-one responds. He calls again. And again. Ultimately something incomprehensible crackles back. Communication at sea is a bit like menopause – a lot of the time it's a complete blur out there.

39
Alicante

We approach Alicante's harbour entrance neck and neck with a Spanish yacht. David says, 'Let him go first. We're in no hurry.' We have always taken the view that we are guests in other people's countries and try to act accordingly. David cuts back our engines and I wave the Spaniard through. He stares at us. Then he stops *his* engine and goes below for binoculars and returns on deck to stare at us through them. I make my gestures large: left arm extended, right arm waving him in. He puts down his binoculars and shrugs in puzzlement. Both yachts wallow. With our *entente cordiale* beginning to clutter up the harbour entrance, David decides to take the initiative and moves forward.

As we enter the harbour, a huge cargo ship leaves the commercial dock to our right and reverses out in front of us. Its skipper would undoubtedly have announced his intention to depart, but we have been too preoccupied by our *pas-de-deux* with the Spanish yacht to notice. Then the cargo ship begins its ponderous 90° turn to point its bow towards the harbour mouth and the open sea – and straight at *us*. A small power boat emerges from behind its stern and roars down its starboard side. This is also the only route we can take to avoid the cargo ship, so we have no option but to head in the direction of the small power boat. Then a large power boat roars out behind the small one, followed by a jet ski. They all hurtle down our port side. For no reason other than that its owner wants to have a look at *Voyager*, the large power boat then crosses our stern, roars down our starboard side, across our bows and back up our port side again, effectively circling us at high speed. The wash is incredible and sends us plunging. I am on the foredeck, ready to spy out the marina's waiting pontoon. Clinging to the rails in a desperate attempt to stay upright, I look back at David to see why he isn't steering into the wash. But he isn't at the helm. With our boat's name being called repeatedly on the VHF as we enter a foreign port, and given our proximity to a large commercial ship in the process of manoeuvring, he had felt obliged to go below and answer it. It is the Spanish yachtsman asking what we wanted.

'I was inviting you to go first,' says David.

'Oh!' says the Spaniard.

There is a pause and then the line goes dead.

At the fuel-cum-waiting dock a young man with a friendly face and neatly dressed in navy blue gets ready to catch my bow rope. But at that moment – in accordance with the laws of sailing which require the wind to rise dramatically whenever you approach or leave a pontoon – the slight breeze by which we had entered rises to an onshore wind of 16 knots and my rope hits him in the face. He accepts my profuse apologies with a touching courtesy.

A couple of holidaymakers in dark glasses and bile-green T-shirts are on the dock when we arrive. They both stare fixedly at us for the whole half hour that it takes to tie up, refuel and be allocated a berth. It is eerie and I wonder if this is what it must be like to be famous. Two Spaniards in uniform, with guns in their holsters also come and look at us then go away again. Meanwhile, in a corner, I spot that magic word *Lavandaria*. Washing machines!

We are allocated a finger pontoon down the far end of the marina and the wind does its best to drive us onto it in the most awkward way possible. In the circumstances, however, we berth almost gracefully. I am particularly glad when I spot the smug couple from Mazarron a few boats down, watching us like hawks. Even if we had fouled it up, though, I feel we could still have claimed the moral high ground. Because, unlike them, we hadn't slipped out of Mazarron without paying the mooring fee. Inevitably, we have no sooner finished tying up than the wind drops away to nothing.

The marina's office is closed until 5pm. Since we can't register until then, our next job is a trip into town to find an ATM. It refuses to yield up any money but we are approached by a very polite young couple with excellent English who say they are having difficulties changing money and want to do a deal with us for our English currency. It is siesta, the streets are empty but for us. We anticipate either being robbed when our wallet comes out to oblige them, or becoming involved in something illegal like currency dealing or money laundering that will involve a long stretch in a Spanish prison. So we make our excuses and leg it to another ATM which obliges with some cash. Everywhere is closed except the restaurants, of which there are many.

Before we left England David bought a couple of short-sleeved rugby shirts in a sale. One of them is in Australia's green and gold and sports the national rugby team's kangaroo motif on its breast pocket. I hate it because it bleeds copious amounts of yellow dye everywhere the moment it comes into contact with water, and in consequence has to be washed separately from everything else. It had, indeed, been among those hand-washed items drying in the cockpit the day I fell foul of the Portuguese Navy. David finds it very comfortable and has put it on for the trip into town. It is pure coincidence that Australia's rugby team has very recently beaten England's.

Sitting in one of the restaurants fronting the marina are four stiff-necked, middle-aged, choleric English types – two in blazers and grey flannels, two in frocks. Observing David approach in his green and gold rugby shirt one of them mouths 'Bloody Australians!' to the other three. All four glare at us, the speaker's grim memsahib the hardest of all. David gives them a huge grin as we pass their table. 'G'day Poms!' he says in his best Rolf Harris. 'Good game, eh?'

At 5pm, equipped with funds, we arrive in the marina's reception area – all marble floors and leather settees – to register. On a wall near the vast reception desk there is a huge and haunting painting of three women – old, middle-aged and young – and a boy, staring out of the picture. They form the base of a triangle. At its apex is a man, his head cut off by the top edge of the canvas. On its right, the wharf they are huddled on is slipping inexorably into the sea, under misty bowsprits and a grey, threatening sky. Trying to guess its meanings fills up the time for me while David fills in a form.

Mast height?

Why, is there a bridge?

How many engines? How much horsepower?

Why do they want to know?

Engine number?

'*I* don't know!' says David.

'Invent one,' hisses the Englishman beside him, also filling in a form. 'Nobody ever knows their engine number.'

It is £5.50 for the night with water and electricity included. We are provided with a disc to get into the showers and a fitting to enable us to connect our water hose to the tap on the pontoon. We have little fresh food left and it is too late to bother with shopping. With so many restaurants within walking distance, we decide to go into town and treat ourselves to dinner out.

I set off for a shower. We are about as far away from the main facilities as you can get, but happily there is a small building housing two showers at the end of our pontoon. Its door refuses to open no matter what I do with the disc. This requires another long walk round this large marina to get a replacement disc from Reception. It is no longer any surprise to me that cruisers are rarely overweight.

Finally within reach of a shower, I am just taking off my shoes at a leisurely pace when two middle-aged women enter: one short, dark and plump, and one tall, grey and thin. Wearing dressing gowns and slippers, they come through the door talking non-stop. I shove my shoes under the bench and dart past them into one of the two shower cubicles. In marinas there are so few facilities between so many people that you soon become light on your feet. And from form-filling to second disc it has taken an hour and a half for me to get to this stage.

The two women talk and talk; not loudly but with extraordinary consistency. I wonder briefly if perhaps they are sharing the other shower, as their voices remain at such a constant level. Were one outside the shower and the other inside, surely the timbre would change as they talked over the noise of the water. Not that I pay too much attention as the water cascading over me is cold and most of my attention is given to getting out from under it as fast as possible. I dry myself and dress and when I get out they are still where I'd left them, in their dressing gowns, barely drawing breath. 'Cold,' I shiver. 'Frio?' says the plump dark one, and shivers too. And they both leave. Still talking. I see them again next day, pushing an empty pontoon cart between them, still talking.

As it is nice to honour one's host country by eating its national dishes we choose Spanish that evening. We should have stuck with the starter. It was generous in its proportions and very tasty: cheeses, salamis and small fresh fish. The wine was also good. I have never been over-fond of rice dishes but assume that paella prepared by Spaniards in Spain will be the best of all possible worlds. It is dreadful. A large pork bone, some bits of chicken, two cockles (one still firmly closed) and a huge plateful of odd-tasting, yellow rice. We leave it and move down the street to an ice-cream parlour for a gigantic sundae to take the taste away. It is very good.

A disco somewhere beyond the quay continues until 6.30am. Fortunately it is far enough away to be just a hum, along with the traffic and the local dogs; unlike the noise in our hulls, which is louder than ever. We have rats behind the linings. There can be no other explanation.

We spend Sunday morning exploring the town. It is only a short walk through the marina, past the *al fresco* restaurants, and you are on a busy road. Cross that and you are on a wide promenade lined with cafés under big, beautiful trees. There is an orchestra playing on the bandstand and little wooden chairs have been put out to enable music-lovers to linger in comfort.

We wander through small leafy squares and narrow streets. We find a bread shop open, and learn that everything will be closed on Monday for Constitution Weekend. We stop at a church dedicated to Saint Sylvestre, with a dark blue tile cupola and bell tower. There are healthy-looking, twenty-something beggars at the door. A service has just finished and the well-dressed, mostly middle-aged-to-elderly congregation is filing out. Their exit is impeded by the young beggars, hands extended, in the narrow doorway. There is tension in the air, as the Christian concept of alms for the deserving poor collides head on with the cynicism of professional begging. Supplication meets resistance and falls back momentarily, only to push forward again more aggressively. As the ebb and flow of conflict spreads out into the narrow street, we take the opportunity to slip behind it and go inside. The church is dark, old and worn. It is also still very crowded. There is obviously a strong religious community here. We gaze at Saint Sylvestre's skull in its glass case; and at a statue of Saint Rita and wonder how she met her martyrdom, not having heard of her before.

The route back to the boat takes us past Alicante's ruined castle which towers above the town and the marina. The promontory on which it stands is very high and very steep but has an elevator from the street which takes you to the top for only a few pesetas.

There is another English catamaran opposite ours, with people on board, so we go over to say 'Hello.' Jim and Betty are from Kent and staying for the winter. They are very hospitable, dispensing much useful information along with the drinks. They are amazed to discover how cheap our rate is. 'Grab it,' they say. Theirs is two categories higher. We begin to think we should. A cheap winter in an excellent marina so close to such a nice town is not to be lightly ignored.

Later the same afternoon a Spanish/Dutch couple from Valencia tie up alongside. Their English is excellent, and learning we are new to the area they lend us a book of aerial photography of the coast which is extremely useful for assessing anchorages.

We decide on another evening meal out, but this time choose Italian. It is dreadful. The 'seafood pizza on a bed of mozzarella cheese' promised in the menu turns out to be four very small prawns on a bed of very greasy Cheddar, like cheese on toast only tougher. In a lot of places you can eat cheaply *and* well. This bit of seafront, this week, isn't one of them.

I am sorting washing on Monday morning, ready for an early dash for the *lavandaria* when a Swedish couple with a son and daughter arrive. We help them tie up and introduce ourselves, then I head for the *lavandaria* and David for the office to pay for two more nights and get the winter rate confirmed.

Early or not, I have missed the washing machines. Both of them are in use. Pointing to the one on the right, Laura from Suffolk says, 'That one's nearly finished.' And with a nod to the left adds, 'My last load's in that one.' As she speaks, the machine on the right goes into its spin.

'Great!' I say, eyeing the long line of bags on the table beside her which is obviously her completed wash. 'I was afraid this was going to take hours.'

David enters looking crestfallen. A different woman is on duty today and says that the weekend receptionist made a mistake. We are category 7 not 2. We can have the first night at the original rate of £5.50 as we have already paid for that, but … David had talked her down to category 6, which is £15.50 per night, and although we would get 15% off for paying 3 months in advance, water and electricity would also have to be paid for. As compensation she has given him a laundry token worth 600 pesetas, around 25 pence. I suggest he go and tell Jim and Betty what our true rate is in case they are tempted to go and argue the toss in Reception and end up getting their own rate increased as well.

Laura empties the contents of the machine on the right into the dryer but, as I reach for one of my bags, the laundry door bursts open and a small, dark-haired dynamo in her late thirties enters and starts throwing the contents the bag she is carrying into the machine. I begin to protest. She sweeps a magisterial hand towards the long line of bags on the table beside Laura while at the same time explaining that here your bags are your place in the queue, and her place is next. To reinforce the point she picks up the box of washing powder from beside the line of bags, measures some into the machine, drops in a token to set it going and sweeps out again.

I look again at the long line of bags on the table beside Laura. 'I thought they were yours,' I say. She shakes her head.

'They're Annie's,' she says, adding, 'She's from Humberside. I only had two loads.' She points to the left-hand machine again. 'This will be finished in a minute.' I wonder if Annie has some sort of radar relating to washing machines and will sweep in again when that one is emptied, too.

In the meantime I return to the subject of winter berthing charges increasing almost threefold and say that, although we know a winter layover is inevitable, having begun cruising so late in the year we are not really ready to settle down yet. She asks if we have considered The Balearics. She says she and her husband lived there for some years and sailed throughout the winters, albeit beginning later and finishing earlier as the weather got colder. She suggests that David and I talk to her husband after lunch.

The left-hand washing machine completes its cycle and as Laura empties it I scan the horizon through the window for the approach of the small, dark-haired dynamo from England's North East. The minute Laura straightens up from the machine's drum I cram my first load in with rather indecent haste. As she leaves she says she will tell her husband to expect us after lunch. Before I leave myself I make a note of the time the cycle takes so that I can get back before it finishes and establish my claim. Before leaving I carefully line up my bags. If this is the system then as far as the left-hand machine is concerned any queue forms behind *me*.

I get my second load in unmolested but, when I return to put in a third, Annie from Humberside is rattling machine doors. Her washing machine and the solitary drier have both finished their cycles but their doors will not open. She goes off to find an attendant and returns with a man in overalls who ferrets about in a fuse box. Unfortunately, instead of releasing the doors, both machines restart their cycles. He shrugs and leaves. Annie watches her clothing embark on its second cycle with resignation. 'I don't know what size it'll be when I get it back,' she says.

David has lunch ready by the time I get back to the boat. While I eat, with one eye on the clock, I tell him what Laura has said about The Balearics. Then I hoof it back to the launderette to get my latest load out of the machine and put in another; assuming, of course, that Annie's problems haven't spread. When I get there she has just fetched the attendant to her machine again. While I empty and refill mine she is disposed to talk.

There comes a time for many cruisers when a lot of things go wrong in a short space of time and it can mean the beginning of the end of cruising for them. She and her husband have recently had their boat broken into and virtually everything of value stolen. They still have a flat back home they cannot sell because, as in our own locality, the property market has died. And the income they had been depending on to support their venture has just taken a sudden and dramatic dive. As if that weren't enough, coming through the Strait of Gibraltar their boat had been caught in a drift net.

'It was awful,' she says. 'It was a Saturday night and the fishermen were all drunk. They surrounded us and fired flares over us. They were still burning when they landed on our deck. It went on for hours. I was terrified.'

The drier stops again and she goes off to fetch the attendant once more. I abandon any hope of using the drier short of spending the night here and take my laundry back to peg around the boat rails.

We have a cup of tea with Laura and her husband, then I leave David to learn about locations and anchorages while I retrieve my last load of washing. Annie is now operating the fuse box herself every few minutes to get the drier to finish its current load. She looks balefully at the renegade washing machine. It has 50 minutes on the meter.

'Every time I re-set the fuse for the dryer,' she says, 'it starts the washing machine's cycle again.'

Another cruiser arrives, weighed down with bags, and fixes a predatory eye on my machine. Mentally I multiply the number of bags of washing Annie still has waiting to be done by the cycle times of the washer (55 minutes) and the drier (45 minutes) and then double it to allow for two cycles per machine per bag. 'You planning to spend the winter in here?' I ask her.

'At least it'll be warm,' she says.

I bag my own washing and stop off at Laura's boat. Her husband has been very helpful and has given David lots of ideas for winter cruising. Back on our own boat I festoon the remaining empty rails while David digs out what little information we have on board about The Balearics. We are beginning to like the idea of going there.

Such is the warmth of a Mediterranean evening in mid-October that by the time we have dined our laundry is dry.

Tuesday morning we have a mammoth shop-up at the big two-storey market building. Typically it is up a steep hill and miles from the marina. It has no name on it, just 1921 in big numbers on the front. It is packed with stalls, big and vibrant and bulging with produce, everything you could imagine. Swordfish steaks are ridiculously cheap and you buy bay leaves on the branch. There are different types of spinach, four kinds of melons, great pyramids of locally grown tomatoes and fresh dates straight off the palm tree and still on the stem. The dates are just as you see them growing on the trees along the town's streets, like big, plump, buff-coloured acorns, not yet dark and wrinkled and packed into long narrow boxes with white doily edges and little plastic twigs down the middle like we get at home at Christmas. By the time we have added wine and mineral water from a shop around the corner we return to the marina like pack mules.

After allowing time for our thoughts to settle we have begun to think seriously about The Balearics. We want more information and ask around for a bookshop which might sell books in English. We are told that El Corte Inglés, Alicante's premier department store, sells books and will probably have cruising guides in English. After a considerable hike to get there we find nothing in English nor any charts or guides in any language, but I spot a very nice swim suit and

David finds a hat to replace the Lifeboat Institution one that went overboard.

Back at the marina we stop off for a chat with the Swedish couple next door. Their children are chalk and cheese. The little girl, around eight years old, prefers to spend her time reading below. Their son, about ten, is out in their dinghy, in his element creating a wash, outboard engine buzzing like an angry gnat, shouting excitedly to his father and filling the air with acrid blue petrol fumes.

On board *Voyager* we have a crew meeting and decide to abandon plans to winter at either Barcelona or Rome. Rome, we have decided, is just too far away. Barcelona's harbour, our neighbour Jim tells us, is very dirty and causes your hulls and propellers to foul up at an alarming rate; although we are later told by somebody else that the city's social and cultural life makes up a hundred-fold for anything the bacteria in its water can do to your anti-fouling. For us, however, the desire is to go on sailing as long as possible and the best place to do this through the winter months seems to be The Balearic Islands.

With the public holiday over, there has arrived that long-sought-after event: the refilling of our two gas tanks. Despite being in daily use for cooking, water heating and refrigeration since Tréguier, over two months ago, the current one is still going. But we cannot expect it to last much longer and having failed to get refills in Coruña, Bayona and Gibraltar we really have to succeed now. Jim is not encouraging, however. The local taxis won't carry gas tanks, he says. *He* hired a car, but with a minimum three-day hire it made the gas quite pricey. We decide to try anyway and ask the marina's receptionist if she will telephone the local taxi service and ask if one of their drivers would be prepared to carry gas tanks. The taxi service asks what time we would like the cab. We put our flaking, 13kg tanks in bin liners to protect the taxi driver's boot.

It is quite a long way out of town, these places usually are, but at least we get to see a little of the countryside around Alicante. The driver delivers us to the gates, and we carry the tanks in. Two men accept them, and then the entire workforce goes off for a tea break. The taxi driver very kindly volunteers to wait, indicating that we might have trouble getting another cab way out here to take us back. The men ultimately return, fill the tanks, send us off to pay and the taxi driver loads them into his boot. When we get back to the marina, and before we are even out of his cab, he has them out of the boot, and into a cart ready for us to wheel them down the pontoon to our boat. We think this is splendid service, and tip him accordingly.

As we heave our two tanks aboard, the Swedish couple's son buzzes about in their dinghy making an even bigger wash than usual. It looks suspiciously like an attempt to drown his sister who, against her better judgment, has allowed herself to be persuaded into joining him. She sits pale and stiff, clinging on with white knuckles, determined not to be hurled overboard as he throws the tiller violently from side to side. The family leaves late afternoon.

Meanwhile we make our preparations to move on as well. The weather is so wonderful it is difficult to believe that winter is actually approaching but, even had we been ready to settle, £15.50 a day plus electricity and water would have made for an expensive winter. We top up our water tanks and tidy the boat. David then goes to recover our deposit on the disc for the showers and the pontoon water connector and returns shaking his head. He has picked up a copy of the marina's price list. For our size boat it quotes £5.50 a day for winter rates including electricity and water. We say farewell to the people who have been so helpful to us and cast off. Fortunately the marina provides a weather forecast, as today's Navtex warnings are for the Adriatic.

40
Alicante to Calpe

Our destination is Calpe, 34 miles along the coast, chosen as a convenient jumping off point for The Balearics. There is a light wind, a choppy sea and bright sunshine. At around three o'clock we are sailing parallel with the coast and about three miles off when, after miles and miles of a hazy green and brown shoreline, a strange white patch appears in the distance as if all colour has been bleached from the land. As we get closer, and with the help of binoculars, it looks like several miles of huge broken teeth. Sometimes at sea your brain simply cannot make sense of what your eyes have in front of them and you say, 'What am I looking at?' and sometimes neither of you has a clue and you just have to wait until you get closer. David is at the chart table, however.

'What *is* that?' I call to him.

'Benidorm,' he calls back.

I fiddle with the focus on the binoculars, screw up my eyes and realise that what I am looking at are multi-storey hotels and apartment blocks.

There was an episode of Star Trek, in the seventies from memory, in which the Star Ship Enterprise visits a planet so over-whelmed by its own population that when the ship's crew looks out through its portholes all they see is an endless slow-moving mass of people wedged shoulder-to-shoulder. I find myself wondering what would happen if all the guests at Benidorm decided to leave their rooms and go out onto the beach at the same time. Would there be room for them all to stand on it, even shoulder-to-shoulder? In the 1960s Benidorm was still a village and the beach was where the men carried their boats after a day's fishing. Tourism makes a lot of changes.

The marina at Calpe is monumentally crowded and rather confusing. We just keep plodding slowly into it and after a while up pops the

Swede from Alicante, just his head and shoulders, waving to us, his boat invisible behind a mass of others.

'Seen the waiting pontoon?' I shout.

He points to another huddle of masts and somewhere in the middle of them we find a pontoon with a notice on it saying 'Visitors Pontoon' and what looks to be an imperative to 'Await Attention!' in Spanish. I am just tying up when a long-haired malcontent arrives waving his arms saying we can't stay. I am unsure whether he means at the waiting pontoon or in the marina generally. I just say *one night please* and after mouthing off for a while he points vaguely in one direction and disappears in another. I untie us, climb back on board and we set off in the direction he has indicated.

We finally find him standing on the quay. Then begins an undignified performance.

'Bows on?' I signal to the malcontent. 'Or side on?'

Side on, his irritated arm signals inform me, and he is standing resolutely where a marina attendant would stand if we were going to tie up sideways on to a quay. I ask again, to be sure that is what he wants. He screws up his mouth and shoots his arms to his feet in a way that now says, *Bows on!* I tell David and he abandons a rather nice approach in a very restricted space, reverses and re-aligns himself to tie up bows on.

No! the man signals manically, *side on!* I throw the rope and let him get on with it. Only he doesn't. He merely catches it, drops it onto the quay and walks off. Because of the angle we have ended up at, plus an offshore wind, it becomes rather difficult. We are just hauling her in as best we can when I look up from the bow to see a pulpit and anchor nosing under our ensign and about to hit our cockpit combing. A 40-ft mono, without power, is being pushed by a small boat whose driver is looking in the opposite direction to the one he is travelling in and whose owner stands over the pulpit with that annoying look of people with large overhanging pulpits that says, 'I'd like to do something, but as you can see I can't reach your boat to fend off, and from experience your boat will be the one to get damaged so I'm OK.'

With David yelling at me to tie on the bow rope I drop it instead, scramble on board and grab the importunate pulpit. I can't push it backwards because the small boat is driving it forward with more force than I possess so I shove it sideways and the rest of the boat follows down our starboard side without damaging anything. David says the pulpit wouldn't have been a problem if I hadn't abandoned the bow rope and allowed *Voyager* to get blown away from the quay and, still struggling to tie up *Voyager* in a rising offshore wind, we have a brief but unseemly row on the quay. The woman running the office comes out to watch. I don't like Calpe.

David goes to the office to pay. Its door and windows are all tightly closed and it is like a sauna inside. The German yachtsman in front of him has forgotten his reading glasses, so filling in the form takes a long time, and then the man's credit card won't work. By the time he returns, having been charged £14 for the night with no power or water, David isn't keen on Calpe either.

Meanwhile the Swedish kid is out in his dinghy producing a wash and filling the air with petrol fumes. At least being tied up side-on to the quay we've no lazy line to bother about, and we couldn't be more sheltered, tucked in under the huge rocky outcrop called Peñón de Ifach which forms the tip of the headland, and is shaped like a miniature Gibraltar. In fact, Calpe is the name the Greeks gave to Gibraltar.

After dinner we have a wander round the marina and an ice cream on a stick before bed. The showers are nice, although the door to the block – which is only yards from a public road – doesn't close let alone lock, making the security key redundant. The shower cubicle doors are of the Wild West saloon type and, given the unlockable entrance, leave one feeling somewhat vulnerable.

The seagulls here are given to huge belly laughs. But apart from that it is a quiet night until the fishing fleet begins unloading its catch at 4.30am, just before a party of carousing Germans returns from the bar. Still wide awake long after they have settled into their bunks, and with the noise in our hull destroying any chance of going back to sleep, I reach for a free sailing newspaper we've picked up somewhere, to take my mind off night thoughts about rats.

There is an article in it about a single sailor who, driven almost to the point of madness by rodent activity in his boat, dismantles over a period of days everything that can be dismantled to locate and dispose of the infestation. On finding that the scuffling and scratching is still there, and now close to certifiable, he is found by a fellow-sailor one evening with an inspection lamp and an electric saw, about to carve through those areas of a boat's timbers which should never be breached while a vessel is still in the water. After listening to his ravings for a while, the Good Samaritan prizes the electric saw from the man's fevered hands and leads him and his inspection lamp up from the devastated bowels of his boat and out onto the pontoon. Once there, he aims the beam of the inspection lamp just below the boat's water line – at the fish energetically nibbling at the marine growth on the bottom of the demented man's hull.

I take our big yellow torch outside and shine it down into the dark water. The shoal of grey mullet enjoying an early breakfast off our own hull barely gives me a glance.

Next morning the marina's touch-screen computerized info system fails to respond to David's touch, but after waiting through a series of videos he does finally get a weather forecast. Then with great panache he reverses out of the berth that caused us so much strife to get into last night, which is usually the way when there is nobody messing you about. We have main and genoa out plus both engines to enable us to reach our destination in daylight. It is a roly poly sea again like yesterday.

THE BALEARIC ISLANDS

▸▸▸

41

Calpe to Ibiza

The towering Sierra Nevada Mountains that dominate southern Spain – along with several lesser mountain ranges – do not end at the coast but continue out into the Mediterranean Sea where their exposed peaks form what are today called by English-speakers The Balearic Islands. In the official Catalan they are called *Illes Balears*; in Spanish *Islas Baleares*. The Romans gave this group of islands the name *Insulae Baleares*, possibly derived from the Phoenician term for islanders resisting attack with stones and slingshots. There are four main islands. In descending order of size they are Mallorca, Menorca, Ibiza and Formentera. We are currently heading for Ibiza.

Around 11am David and a small container ship en route for Alicante make way for each other, after which its skipper calls David on the VHF for a chat and signs off by wishing us a safe journey. Lunch is soft white bread and gazpacho soup.

At 4pm a tiny green finch lands on the main outhaul. Even powerful seabirds sometimes become tired when battling overlong against strong winds or adverse weather. This is a very small bird which should really be in a tree somewhere sheltered. Even so, it exhibits the same instinct for survival and sea-savvy as any seabird ten times its size. When exhausted at sea, birds seek out the nearest vessel and then perch on it until they feel strong enough to fly again.

The tiny green finch takes a walk under our doghouse roof but disturbed by our presence it flies down the length of the cockpit to the dinghy, as far away from us as it can get. It perches on one of the davits for a minute or two, but with 17 knots of wind buffeting its soft green feathers and all but dragging its tiny, needle-thin feet from the shiny stainless-steel, it quickly returns to the shelter of the doghouse and perches inches from us on the top edge of one of the open companionway doors. Aware of our little guest's dilemma we sit quietly, so as not to cause it undue stress. When it has had the rest it needs it swoops off astern. The island of Ibiza has become visible, looking like a large jagged tooth.

At 6pm, within range of Ibiza, the GPS quits. We have begun to wonder if it suffers from stage fright. Just when you need it to perform it goes all bashful.

When planning our time of arrival we had failed to allow for the fact that we are travelling east and that the sun sinks earlier. We arrive in Sant Antoni's harbour at 7.15 in a stunning sunset. By the time we have anchored it is dark. It is a joy to anchor again, to have a cold bottle of wine open and dinner started within minutes of arriving; instead of putting out fenders and ropes, tying up to a waiting pontoon, waiting to be allocated a berth, untying again and moving to the berth, tying up again, re-adjusting all the fenders and putting on springs, then a long trudge to a hot office to fill in forms and pay. To simply drop the anchor is bliss. And of course it is free.

A little way down the beach from us is the hotel where we stayed on a holiday here nearly twenty years ago. We may have changed but the hotel doesn't seem to have. It still has the little straw umbrellas over the tiny tables you put your drinks on, and the beach huts near the outside shower where you can change after your swim in the sea.

The sea tonight is like a millpond. There is a fair on the quay, but very little sound, and two very tall, illuminated, inverted Vs which we assume must be municipal sculpture or something. They turn out to be supports for what seems at this distance to be a communal bungee. After dinner we see the first cage full of holiday-makers hurtle up and down between them, flying way above the pinnacles of the two Vs. It looks horrendous. There is a long delay between launches. David reckons this is while they hose out the cage. I don't want to contemplate this so soon after eating. There do seem to be more people watching than participating, however, which must be counter-productive as far as the operators are concerned because quite soon nobody gets into the cage at all.

It is a very quiet, still night. The fishermen, the ferry boats and Sant Antoni's infamous revellers are a long way away.

It is a cold, damp morning. The rope on one of the davits slips as we are lowering the dinghy. I sprint down the back steps and support the outboard before it can go under water. I find my responses much improved of late. I also squabble less with ropes and knots. We sort out the dinghy and motor into the marina. The chandler here carries exactly the sort of cruising guide we want for The Balearics, in English, and also provides directions to the supermarket.

The streets are deserted apart from one young man who looks as if he was one of last night's revellers and should not yet be abroad. He is pale, with drooping eyelids and the kind of cough that a long night of heavy smoking and drinking produces. He totters from his doorway into a car and drives away.

We turn too soon for the supermarket and end up in something that is half bar and half small corner shop. The barman has that wistful, other-worldly look of someone who has been up all night and whose thoughts are longingly directed towards his bed. His half-dozen customers, at separate tables and each drooping over a glass, look like characters from Eugene O'Neill's play, The Iceman Cometh, who spend all their days in a bar room because they cannot face life in the outside world.

These young men sit silently, gazing into their drinks and we wonder if the products on the shelves are really there for them – orange juice, milk, breakfast cereals and snacks – so that they have no need to leave until the clubs open for business again. Erupting among them like this seems a little like intruding on private grief and we leave quietly without buying anything.

We find the real supermarket eventually and while David heads for the shelves to do the bulk of the shopping I join the queue at the meat counter. I am second in line, and only want some breast of chicken for a pasta dish, but the man in front has a brochure of the week's specials in one hand, and an elderly woman's elbow in the other. He is filling his mom's freezer for her.

The butcher is slicing half a sheep into wafer-thin chops, cutlets and roasts while the customer talks to him. Unfortunately, every time an answer is required of him, the butcher stops cutting, turns around, makes his leisurely reply and then returns to his chopping block. After he's wrapped the lamb cuts into little parcels, tied them with tape, till-rolled and poly-bagged them, he starts on the pork specials. When these have all been neatly wrapped, he lays waste to the trays of chicken.

When my turn comes the only piece of chicken left is a large leg with a long if scrupulously clean yellow foot on it. I am weary and my back aches. I have been standing too long. I fear that if I ask for breast meat the butcher will disappear through the two large stainless steel doors of his freezer and return a short lifetime later carrying great bins of meat and begin totally restocking his massive counter before he gets around to serving me. It has happened before. So I point to the solitary leg. He weighs it, then holding it aloft with one hand asks with a cutting motion of the other if I want the foot removed. I shake my head. I just want it gift-wrapped and handed over so that I can go. I leave the parcel with David at the till and totter out to sit on a wall in the sunshine until he emerges with it, along with bread and milk, wine and fat red grapes, fresh fish and picture postcards.

We weigh anchor at noon. The day is hot and sunny. There is little wind and what there is blows straight on the nose, so we motor. With no other boats around and not another soul in sight it is also a day for abandoning clothes. We put up the awning and our feet. It is bliss. The coastline here is sheer and the water deep so you can sail very close to the cliffs. The rock formations are fascinating, the pine forests are a lush green and it is all very beautiful. We have a lovely, leisurely, scenic trip in utter solitude, for it is estimated that Ibiza's half a million annual visitors are largely concentrated in half a square mile, mostly around the Sant Antoni night club district. The rest of the island is largely deserted, with lots of empty bays to swim and laze in.

Mid-afternoon we anchor in one of them, Clot d'es Llamp, a small bay on the north-east coast. The water is so clear that you can see the sandy waves on the bottom six metres down. Like much of Ibiza, this little bay has a fascinating geology. You find yourself just gazing at the cliff face, following with your eyes the great curves and sweeps of different colours and textures, and trying to imagine the tumultuous primeval eruptions that created them.

Another nice thing about being at anchor is that, except when opposed by a stronger current, an anchored boat will always point into the wind, however slight. *Voyager*'s opening bow windows take full advantage of this. We open them now, and her other ten hatches, and a cooling breeze circulates through the boat and out into the cockpit, dissipating the afternoon heat. The sea is lapping on the rocks. Everything is switched off, including us. It is time for a glass of something cool and refreshing.

The sun disappears behind the cliffs by five o'clock creating a delightful early evening, shady but warm. We listen to World Service news while dinner cooks: Chile's General Pinochet has been arrested in London; there are 250mph winds in India and a typhoon is heading for Japan.

To our left there is a most un-fort-like little fort overlooking the sea, with big windows and impossible to defend. David reckons its garrison must have spent a lot of time practicing surrender drill – *Our flag* down, *two three – wait for it, wait for it – white flag* up, *two, three.* The water remains aquamarine until dark. It is a fantastically starry night. Orion is positively glowing in the northern sky, very close and very bright.

Later, as we resume gazing up at it through the hatch above our bunk, and drowsiness begins to overtake us, David wonders if the tiny green finch we had on board earlier in the day made it safely back to land. I listen to the furtive buzzing near my right ear and wonder how it is that mosquitoes know so precisely the very moment you are about to fall asleep.

42

Ibiza to Mallorca

When we leave the anchorage at 7.30 next morning there is still a tiny sliver of bright moon. The water is so clear that even in the dawn light you can see the anchor rising from the seabed. There is a particularly beautiful sunrise at 8.15. It is not just the return of the sun that is so captivating but the way everything around you changes from a chilly grey-blue with a hard edge to warmth, colour and soft contours. The sea takes on a pink sheen this morning and two dolphins come to bask in our bow wave. We go up front to keep them company. We invariably will, on all our journeys, except in bad weather or on solitary night watches. It seems discourteous not to.

At 1.30 pm there is a cry of 'All ships, all ships' from the VHF. We sit through the Spanish broadcast but the only words we recognize are 'Menorca' and 'ocho' – eight – presumably a warning for Menorca to expect winds up to Gale Force 8. But we are not going to windy Menorca, we are heading for Mallorca, the largest of the Balearic Islands. As well as discovering the beauties of the island, we have also arranged with David's brother Tony to have our mail arrive there at the same time we do.

Mallorca has been inhabited for at least 6,000 years, the earliest traces having been found in a cave near Sóller. Around 1200BC the Talayot, or tower culture, flourished. Then came the Phoenicians, Carthaginians and Greeks. The Romans arrived in the 2nd century BC and stayed until 5AD when Rome itself was overrun.

The Romans called Mallorca 'Major' and Menorca 'Minor', hence the names Majorca and Minorca familiar to many visitors. The Vandals and the Corsairs ravaged Mallorca after the Romans left, but prosperity returned in the 10th century with the arrival of the Moors. The combined armies of Catalonia and Aragon drove the Moors out in 1229 and destroyed the Muslim capital of Palma.

The thirteenth to fifteenth centuries were Mallorca's golden age and many buildings from this period, including the cathedral begun in 1230 on the site of a former mosque, survive. By the 15th century Palma had become an important trading post between Spain and Africa but as the 'new world' opened up so the island gradually declined into a backwater and succumbed to pirates.

Arriving at most places by sea is pleasurable because the harbour is often the oldest and most interesting part of a coastal town or city. Settlements tended to originate at the water's edge and then spread inland later, the sea providing food, trade and transport long before agriculture and land routes had had a chance to develop. Approaching Palma, from the huge *Bahia* or Bay of Palma, is particularly impressive with its castle up on a wooded hill, the vast Gothic cathedral towering above the old town and the remains of medieval walls.

The late afternoon is still warm and sunny as we mill around a bit, hunting the waiting dock of the Réal Club Náutico marina. We need fuel as well as a place to stay for the night. Finally we spot the fuel dock, and beyond it, invisible until you actually reach it, a sign saying 'Visitors Quay'. A yachtsman tells us the fuel dock is closed until nine tomorrow morning and that there are no berths available. He suggests we raft up to somebody. A marina attendant in a yellow T-shirt arrives by bicycle and says we can stay on the fuel dock until it opens at 9am. David goes off to the office with his wallet. The woman inside says, 'Full up!' We can't stay.

In any country, on land or water, in hotels, offices, shops or marinas, you are fairly safe in assuming that discourtesy, unhelpfulness and arrogance by staff will increase in proportion to the affluence of the clientele. In this marina the clientele is best described as *rich*. It is also predominantly absent; most luxury boats being occupied for only a few days a year.

David and another yachtsman persuade the receptionist to reconsider and she demands our ship's papers. David has forgotten to take them with him, and he makes the long trek to *Voyager* and back to the office again.

We are allowed to remain for the night but there will be no time to look around tomorrow morning as hoped, so we postpone our evening meal and head for Palma's old town instead. It is *gorgeous*. Sometimes a couple of hours in a place can be as enjoyable as several days when you get a series of beautiful mental snapshots to take away with you. On this occasion they are of lovely old buildings, secret cobbled courtyards, and some stunning restaurants with cavernous interiors and great church-like doors that suggest that they were once wineries; a green pool with black swans; beautiful trees and elegant boulevards. There is a Sunday evening service in the enormous cathedral, a busy little square in front of it and a maze of alleyways behind it. This old town, behind the cathedral, contains the few remaining streets and buildings from the Muslim period. We also work out the fastest route to the main post office, and note its opening time tomorrow (8.30am), so that David will be able to collect our mail before we have to leave.

I cook a supper of monkfish in a tomato and basil sauce with large sweet prawns added for the last few minutes, baked potatoes and broccoli. We dine under the stars and admire the floodlit castle on the hill to our left; and the floodlit cathedral to our right; a panorama of the harbour and the town, the town quay and three cruise ships with all their lights on. It is a warm still night, dry and bright and very lovely.

Unfortunately, at 4.30am Palma's fishing fleet goes out at speed, a dozen large boats, one after the other in a line - *wap, wap, wap, wap* – directly opposite our berth. Their wash is *extraordinary*. I fear our mooring lines will snap. We have only just stopped bouncing off the dock when another four rush out. When their wash finally subsides I make us a cup of tea. At 7.45 I set off for the showers. They are closed for cleaning. So, for £14 we have had no water, no electricity, no showers and broken sleep. David returns from Palma with our mail, fresh bread, tonight's dinner and a day-old English Sunday newspaper.

Meantime, the pump operator has opened his kiosk and I am taking on fuel. Water, he says when David picks up the hose, also has to be paid for. 'We've paid,' I say, waving our berthing receipt at him. I've read the back of it – *including agua* it says.

'That's *theirs*,' he says. 'This is *mine*.'

I feel we've had little enough for our money here – not even basic courtesy – so David and I drag the boat back from the fuel dock to where we can reach the marina's hose. We are accosted by a marina attendant, a different one from the previous evening.

'Already paid,' I say, waving our receipt. He inspects it and then checks every detail on it with the office via a hand-held VHF. 'OK,' he says, and then we must go.

The weather forecast at the marina is two days old. Navtex is giving forecasts for Toulouse, Biscay and the Adriatic. So, again resorting to local knowledge with a vested interest, on his way back from the post office David had enquired at a local yacht charter office. The man there had said confidently, 'Not much wind, thunderstorm possible, but if it's not here by 10am we won't get one.'

It is well after ten by the time we have filled up our fuel and water tanks and washed the dirt from the fuel dock off our decks. There has been a brief rumble of thunder in the distance and a cloud has passed over us delivering a spatter of rain drops but now the sun is shining again. The barometer has fallen only 3mb since our arrival the previous afternoon in a light breeze from the south-east. There is no wind at all now. Given these factors we feel safe to set off for Porto Colom. A number of other boats set out at around the same time, one of them a ketch flying a Spanish ensign.

43
Mallorca: Palma to Porto San Petro

About an hour out of Palma we are romping along on a broad reach under full genoa and main in a strong easterly wind gusting up to 22 knots when the VHF crackles 'Securité, Securité, all ships, all ships ...' but when we retune to channel One Zero as advised there is nothing there. The barometer shows no change, and we are not concerned since whenever we have listened to these local warnings they have always been about windy Menorca.

By 1 o'clock the wind is in the mid-20s and rising, so we reef the genoa. Several monohulls around us are still blithely un-reefed, although heeling madly. The radio crackles another 'All ships, all ships ...' We turn to Zero Three for Palma Radio as instructed – nothing. We alter course past Cabo Blanco, which brings the wind to less than 45° off the nose so we take down the sails and motor. The Spanish ketch behind us, still under sail due to a slightly wider course than ours, gradually overtakes us but remains in sight. The other yachts fall behind us and gradually disappear from view.

The radio crackles with another 'All ships, all ships ...' We turn to One Three as instructed but there is only silence on Channel 13. The barometer is reassuringly steady, having dropped only 1mb since we set out. However, with a following sea on our starboard quarter, and the wind almost on the nose, it is not a comfortable passage. I raise a speculative eyebrow at David. 'Nothing doing here,' he says, so I go below and stretch out on our bunk with the Sunday newspaper he brought back from Palma this morning.

In time I become aware of distant thunder and that it is getting choppier. But an eleven ton cruising catamaran doesn't roll much normally, so when the view through the window at my feet begins to lurch from leaden sky to deep troughs of equally leaden sea I stagger above to see what is going on. David is standing in the doorway, blocking my view.

'Everything OK?' I ask clinging on to the companionway doors for support. Pencil-thin lightening is zigzagging into the sea around us.

'Yes,' says David, in a small, strained voice that is struggling to sound normal.

A couple of miles off our stern, and visible over his right shoulder, is a waterspout. It is a mortifying sight; a smooth, black column spiralling up from the sea and joined at the top to a black storm cloud. Grey spray rises from its base up a quarter of its length. The spray is jagged from the violence of the energy propelling it upward. It is one of those things you never wanted to see. You only find brief references to them in books, usually followed by a comment about yachts having been lost in them. What is most worrying is that it is getting larger and this could be because it is getting closer to us.

It's the sort of thing you keep looking over your shoulder at and wondering what avoiding action you can take. But when something appears to be travelling at you against the prevailing wind, and is huge and powerful, what can you hope to do?

After about ten minutes it splits into two unequal columns and the thinner of the two collapses like a fountain suddenly switched off. Shortly afterwards the larger column, also losing its energy, buckles and falls into the sea.

Relief is short-lived. Around 15 minutes later another water spout appears in roughly the same place behind us. The wind has risen to 35 knots and the sea is now tumultuous. Our progress slows as we rise on each crest and crash into each trough.

On our port side there is a long, dense, grey cloud, stretching as far down the coastline as the eye can see. From its depths it spews rain from some parts of itself and lightning from others. It is very low, scraping across the top of the cliffs, and travelling with the wind; that is, in the opposite direction to which we, and the waterspout, are moving. It is eerie and elemental and we can only stand and watch in awe. It is one of the images that comes to mind now whenever people in television studios talk about 'controlling nature'. This cloud is darkening by the minute, as its convulsive, seething ferocity prepares to unleash itself. We are just grateful that it is moving down the side of us and not into us. With that directly on our bows and the water spout behind our stern we should soon be reduced to very small flotsam. As the monumental cloud grows ever darker, David says sympathetically, 'Looks like Palma is in for a real humdinger.'

Immediately above *us*, however, the sun has broken through and when we look behind us the waterspout has disappeared. The barometer is still steady, and the sky ahead of us appears to be getting lighter. Admittedly the cloud to our left is now deepest black and has obliterated the coastline, but it is three miles off and travelling away from us. We seem to have passed south of the threatened storm and be leaving it behind us.

At around 2.30, however, the wind backs suddenly through 130 degrees so that instead of being just off our bows it is now directly behind our stern. It also brings with it the cloud that has been hanging over the land. Like some monstrous, computer-generated demon making a U-turn to pursue some small item of prey, it is now following us. Gradually it begins to overtake us. As it gets closer, the rain contained inside it spatters us. It quickly becomes torrential and, with the force of the wind behind it, horizontal. An open wheel-house can provide no cover from it and it beats remorselessly at our backs. With 39 knots showing on the wind speed indicator, we leave the steering to the autopilot and retreat to the saloon to keep watch from there.

The wind increases. Above its howl there comes a rattling sound which takes a moment to identify; the rain has turned to hail and is pinging off *Voyager* like grapeshot. Visibility drops to a few yards. If anything is ahead of us, we have little chance of avoiding it. We turn on the radar and can make out the coast on the screen, so we know we are maintaining our course. Unfortunately, it is not identifying the location of other vessels and thus the possibility of a collision. The problem with radar is that it produces echoes from heavy rain, hail and a troubled sea which then appear on the screen as a mass of dots. It is, therefore, impossible to tell if one of those dots is a boat, and we know there is at least one out there: the Spanish ketch. The sea is heaving now, churned up by the violent change in the wind. After being pushed by strong winds from the north-west all morning, the water is now being driven back on itself by a gale from the south-east. The wind rises to a roar. The hail stones hammer against the companionway doors.

David is checking our course on the GPS so, when its screen shows a sudden change in our direction, he is immediately aware that the autopilot has given up the unequal struggle to hold a course in a quartering sea and we have taken a 45° turn to starboard. He rushes outside to steer manually but the autopilot regains control as he reaches the helm and he stumbles back inside almost immediately.

'I think I've an idea now,' he says, rubbing his face, 'what it feels like to be stoned to death.'

In the few moments that the doors have been open for him to go out to the helm, and then to return inside again, the saloon has resembled one of those glass paper weights you shake to make 'snow' fall softly on the scene inside. Only this is hard and painful as hail-stones the size and texture of marbles shoot horizontally into the saloon and ricochet off the bow windows. While David keeps watch again I scoop them up from the chart table and upholstery and throw them down into the galley sinks before they can melt and soak everything. With this one exception, our autopilot has functioned in all conditions, but we have sailed with friends in monohulls whose autopilots could not withstand heavy waves on either quarter. We wonder about the helmsman on the Spanish ketch, standing exposed at his wheel.

The hail becomes so heavy that it flattens the sea, and with a gale-force wind behind us we begin to pick up speed. Staring out through the bow windows it is like being transported into the unknown inside a small, dark, grey cocoon. Even the vague outline of land has vanished from the radar screen.

David checks our course on the GPS again and plots it on the chart. We are being pushed slightly off course but fortunately out to sea and not towards land. As a land creature there is a tendency in dangerous weather to feel you would be safer closer to land, but on a boat you are safer well out to sea: away from hazards such as shallow water, rocks and reefs, and especially other boats. When he has reassured himself that we are not being driven ashore David stands by the companionway doors with his back against the bulkhead. From here he can keep a look out on either side of us, watch the GPS and radar screen, and also make a fast exit to the wheel if necessary.

Confronted with something you can't control, there is comfort in focusing on something you can. A crash of thunder overhead stirs in me a memory about the safety features David had valued when we had chosen our boat.

'Don't we have a big steel A-frame supporting the mast behind that bulkhead you're leaning on?' I ask.

'Yes,' he says, lightning forking past the window beside his left shoulder.

'And don't lightning strikes usually hit the mast and travel down?'

'Yes,' he says.

'Well, do you think you ought to be leaning there, then?'

He takes a step forward and leans against the side of the chart table instead. I go back to staring out through the bow windows and watch the anchor gloomily. I had tied it onto the port bow roller after our last anchorage. It is now lolling over the side of the roller and my knot appears to be slowly unravelling. All we need now is an anchor crashing about the foredeck. I am also worried about what is behind us; whether the waterspout has re-formed again and is about to overwhelm us, carried along by this horrendous wind. How much worse, I wonder, is this going to get?

The hail gives way to rain. Without the hail's calming effect, the sea rises again. We resume our violent, hobby-horse motion, rising up onto the wave crests and plunging down into the troughs, while the spray from breaking waves washes over the deckhouse roof. The constant slam of our hull against the sea makes my back and head ache. Holding on with both hands, I flex my knees to reduce the impact on my spine of each succeeding crash and stare out at the few grey yards of foaming sea that is all that's visible in front of me. The wind is ripping the white crests from the wave peaks and running them in long thin streaks of white foam ahead of us down the dark grey sea. I have only ever seen this kind of sea once before, in a photograph in *Reed's Nautical Companion* illustrating a Force 9 Gale driven by wind speeds up to 47 knots.

I turn and look at David. He is calm, watchful, ready to act. I dread panicking; letting us both down. 'Dear God,' I say silently, 'forgive my sins and if I'm going to die please let me do it with a little grace.'

The wind increases. The white crests become longer and deeper and indistinguishable in the gloom from yacht hulls crossing our bows. But each time one seems to have solid form and I go to shout 'Vessel ahead!' it rolls over and disintegrates, and another forms somewhere else. I try to remember what the next photograph in *Reed's* looked like, the one illustrating Storm Force 10. I can't, but it doesn't matter. I feel sure now that we shall not come out of this alive, but at least I am calm. I recall reading once the different sounds the wind makes at different speeds. The one that has always stuck in my mind was Force 12, the hurricane. It was said to scream like a single note on a crazed church organ.

Then, as suddenly as before, the wind veers, almost back to its original position. The rain eases. Light and visibility begin to improve a little. Through the bow windows I see two yachts. They look ghostly among the foaming grey water in the strange grey light, but their white hulls are discernibly solid. The one on our port side is on a course which must have recently taken it across our bows. The other is close in front of us, to starboard, and has obviously also just crossed our bows. We have probably missed one another by only minutes. As visibility continues to improve we can see that the Spanish ketch has maintained its course and is off to starboard.

Moments later David is able to make out the lighthouse at Pointa Salinas. Safety harness clanking, he grasps the handle of the companionway doors but they don't move. We put our shoulders to them and force our way out. There's a mound of hailstones wedged behind the doors and the cockpit is slippery with them, like trying to walk on ball bearings.

It is still raining and despite the change of wind direction, or because of it, the sea has lost none of its turbulence. Meanwhile, on our port side, shimmering against the coastline is the biggest, lowest, brightest rainbow I have ever seen. Far from hovering in some indeterminate, distant place like rainbows usually do, this one is between us and the land, not above the cliffs but in front of them. Only a short while ago I had contemplated death in that eerie, violent greyness and unaccustomed as I am to prayer it had been a genuine one. Now a long-dormant memory comes to mind and I realise with surprise that it's an Old Testament one, of the rainbow as God's sign to mankind, after The Flood had subsided, that His act of destruction was at an end and would not be repeated.

Sight of Point Salinas lighthouse means it is time to alter course and while David makes the necessary change to the autopilot I observe the dinghy. The violence of our passage has loosened it on the davits, so that it lurches back and forth with every movement of *Voyager*. It is not helped by the fact that it is also much heavier than usual, being half full of hailstones. I can envisage us losing it.

'I'll see to it,' says David, watching me watching it.

'Oh no you won't!' I say. 'Either I go or nobody does.' I know which side my survival's buttered. If I go over the stern there's a good chance he'll get me back on board. If he goes, we are probably both done for. I join my safety line to his and with him reeling me out I slither to the stern and tighten the davit handles. The dinghy weighs a ton and is still askew when I stagger back into the cockpit, but there's no longer any threat of our losing it.

The wind is gusting 38 knots and our new course brings it directly onto the nose. As we hit each fresh wave pattern *Voyager* judders, slows to 2 knots, then slowly gathers speed again just in time to hit the next big wave. As a result we are averaging only 3 knots. To continue to Colom at this speed will mean entering an unknown anchorage in rough weather in the dark instead of the mild sunlit afternoon we had been anticipating when we left Palma. It also means another three hours of very uncomfortable sailing.

David consults the cruising guide and settles on Porto San Petro – St Peter's Harbour. It is an hour closer, so we will arrive in the last of the light. We hug the land to take advantage of the slightly calmer water there and arrive just before 6pm. Several boats are anchored already. Faces stare out from them in that impassive way yachtsmen have when they have been safe and dry for some time, or have sat out the storm altogether, and a boat arrives carrying weary people in sopping oilies.

Our anchor bites first time and in half an hour we sit down to that old stand-by, cheese omelettes, with fresh Palma bread and a bottle of dry white wine. I had planned a larger meal for this evening but we have no appetite for one. We have come through the worst experience of our brief sailing career and are exhausted.

Over coffee we browse through our new Balearics cruising guide. It mentions, in passing, that 'in Spring and Autumn water-spouts may be encountered'. It is silent on the subject of hail driven by Force 9 winds. We expect widespread damage from its intensity. In the event, the damage is restricted to the cockpit: the glass on the log is cracked, the top of the shore power socket has been sheared off, and our flexible solar panel is badly pock-marked. We have heard the Mediterranean described as sailing for non-sailors. This must have been one of its off-days.

44
Mallorca: Porto San Petro

Porto San Petro is a glorious bay, and next morning it is bathed in sunshine. The village is at the far end of it and there are tiny, tidy boat houses fronting part of it. The local fishing fleet seems to consist of an elderly man in a faded blue shirt and a straw hat.

We set about drying out our boat, carting out half a dozen wet towels from the bow windows and opening up every hatch and window to let in the sun and warm breezes. The other yachts in the anchorage leave during the morning and we move to the most sheltered spot, although we needn't have bothered because the weather has become so mild. At noon we take the dinghy into the harbour. We tie it up between a small wooden fishing dinghy and a glass-bottomed tourist boat and go for coffee just above the ramp. Halfway through our coffee we leap from our chairs when a second glass-bottomed tourist boat arrives and heads straight at our dinghy. They are very good-natured about it, and hover patiently while we extract it.

In the tiny 'supermarket' the proprietor is deeply suspicious of us. It is undoubtedly the backpack and the fact that we have split up, with David at one end of the L-shaped little corner shop trying to determine which white wine is *secco* and how much it costs, as there are hardly any price tickets; and me up the other end head first into the huge chest freezer among the calamari and shellfish. She keeps running between the two of us looking anxious. In the end, as a gesture of goodwill, we lean our backpack against the side of her counter and she relaxes. Then *we* get anxious about our valuables inside it every time another customer comes in and stands over it. We enquire about a post office, but the nearest one is five miles away.

Despite being the only boat in the anchorage, when a German yacht arrives for lunch it settles only a couple of yards from us.

'Why so close?' I mumble at David.

'*I* don't know, Sandra,' he mumbles back. 'Maybe they put their beach towel on this bit of seabed before we got here.'

There are four people aboard. As soon as they are anchored they turn on a radio, talk very loudly over the top of it, and take off all their clothes. One of them, the largest, keeps leaping into the water, clambering out, and leaping overboard again.

'Call me a prude, if you like,' I grumble, 'but I can't help thinking that most people look better with their middle regions veiled from public view.' I've always felt that this applied especially to the overweight, the sporty and those well past the first flush of youth. The person currently throwing herself repeatedly off the stern of the neighbouring boat falls into all three categories.

'You're right,' says David. 'You are a prude.' But I notice that he keeps his eyes averted from the over-abundance of airborne flesh alongside him.

The yacht leaves after lunch and we have the bay to ourselves. It is a luminous afternoon. We rig the dinghy and take it for a sail. We drift in and out of the coves, feet dangling over the sides, with just enough wind to carry us along. It seems strange to be floating around this tranquil bay in bright sunshine and light airs after the nightmarish journey of yesterday. A few hours at sea can be a long time.

45

Mallorca: Porto San Petro to Porto Colom

Next day we set off for our original destination, Porto Colom, five miles away. The cruising guide describes it as the best natural harbour and anchorage in Mallorca, its dogleg entrance effectively turning it into a sheltered lake. It has wooded hills all around it and the small town of Porto Colom at its western edge. We are anchored just off its town quay and plan to remain here a little while as we have some jobs to do.

The area of Porto Colom's waterfront closest to us has a general store, three cafés, two banks and a traditional meat shop and deli which sells lovely cheeses and delicious homemade cannelloni and sausages. The sausages are chewy and so full of lean meat that they leave no fat behind in the pan.

Further down the quay there is a terrace of small identical houses with wooden doors and window shutters painted dark green. One morning, hard up against the door of one of them is a van delivering a large quantity of parcels. The quay itself is spread with fishing net; miles and miles of it, in all shades of blue. It is a blue sort of morning, with the fishermen working on the nets wearing navy blue, the bright blue Campsa fuel kiosk and the blue sea and sky. I'm in blue, too: light blue shirt and dark blue sailing trousers. In fact, if I stood against the horizon I'd probably disappear. A little further on, at the small marina, we find an up-to-date weather forecast. Force 6 today, possible 8 later.

On the way back to the boat we stop and read a very small notice on the terraced house door that had had the van backed up to it earlier. The notice says: *11.40am–12.10pm Mon–Fri*. We have found the Post Office.

Back on board, David tackles the leaking vent which let rain and seawater into the bathroom during the recent storm. We also have replacement kits we bought out with us from England for the four main hatches, so that they will stay open by themselves like they used to and we won't have to prop them open with sticks any more.

However, after considerable difficulty, with bits of metal and rubber that don't fit where they are supposed to, and having to catch them in mid-air before they disappear overboard as they ping off again, we discover we've been sold the wrong kits.

Leaving David to put the old bits back on the hatches again until we can get the proper parts, I write a birthday card and a couple of cheques ready for posting. I also finish a long letter on the computer to David's brother Tony and his wife Pam. Affronted by the postcard David had sent them from Lisbon ('This is Sintra. We haven't been here. Hope you're both OK. We are.') I thought they might like a résumé of what we have been doing, as they are providing us with backup. While trying to print this letter off, however, the generator packs up, so that's another job added to the list.

Tired of maintenance at last, we take the dinghy on a jaunt to the southwest corner of the bay. The water gets shallower and shallower until it is barely a foot deep and the colour and clarity of green glass. We tie the dinghy to a tiny jetty at the end of a row of little white boat houses like the ones at Porto San Pedro, and walk up a small beach scattered with pine needles and wild flowers. Beyond the pine trees a road winds up a hill. At the newsagents half way up it, an English newspaper headline says: *Government U-turn*; another says: *Palace Crisis*. Nothing new, then, since we last bought a paper about a month ago so there seems little point in troubling ourselves with another one just yet. Distance lends perspective and while the detail may change the substance seems to remain the same. At the top of the hill we discover an SYP supermarket.

Known to British expatriates as Save Your Pesetas, SYP actually stands for *Servicio y Precio* – service and price. And you really can't fault the prices or the quality either. With regard to service, however, this depends on your criteria. In particular, *speed* does not appear to form part of the Spanish concept of service, while wrapping up fresh food nicely does. Unfortunately, for anyone with hopes of a life beyond a supermarket's meat and cheese counters, this can be a source of some frustration.

In Spain the butcher cuts your meat, weighs it, puts it on a slab, turns to a large roll of high quality paper behind him and tears off a strip. This paper has an attractive pattern on one side and is grease-proof on the other. The meat is put on the greaseproof side (in some establishments it is even put on a separate piece of thin greaseproof paper first) and the two long edges are rolled into a pleat. The short ends are then folded back to make a neat parcel. This is then put into a transparent polythene bag, along with the price ticket from the weighing machine, and the bag is tied up. It is all beautifully done, but not with any sense of urgency. The same process is then gone through at the cheese and the cooked meat counters.

At the checkout, the cashier unties the bag, takes out the ticket, reads it, rings it up, tears it, puts it back inside the bag and re-ties it. Meanwhile the queue lengthens. This is not helped by the fact that most Spanish checkouts have rollers which do not roll, and means that the cashiers have to drag every item over them to the till. Today's cashier saves a little time by not untying and retying the bags but slashing them with a long purple fingernail so that on the way home the mushrooms spill out and the chicken breasts mingle with the swordfish steaks. We have the swordfish for lunch, cooked in garlic, olives, parsley, lemon juice and with a few smoked mussels. It is delicious.

In the afternoon I get out the computer again. Its opening sequence says that the clocks in England have gone back an hour, although in mainland Europe they won't change for another week. I look up at the big brass clock on *Voyager*'s bulkhead. It says 5pm. In England, when the clocks go back for the winter, it is already dark by 5pm and, being late October, it tends to be cold, grey and damp as well. Across the way, between *Voyager* and the boatyard ramp, there is a lot of shouting. A small ketch has anchored there and two very overweight men and a plump youth are swimming off its stern in the warm sunshine.

An hour later, as I am preparing dinner, there are male voices talking, very close to my ear. I look up. The ketch is now on the other side of us and slowly passing my galley window. The two older men are sitting in the cockpit chatting animatedly; the lad is fishing from a large dinghy tied to its stern. Next time I look up, the boat is well past us and heading slowly for a French sloop. The two big men still talk; the lad still trails his line in the water. I am filled with admiration for yachtsmen who can be so laid back about dragging their anchor.

The next time I look up the ketch is drifting slowly but remorselessly towards the bay's exit and the open sea and I wonder why they don't do something. They are saved the trouble by the arrival of a tall, thin man in a dinghy. He stands at the tiller of his outboard engine but because he is too tall to reach the tiller from a fully-upright position he has to bend one knee. This gives him that forward-leaning pose most usually seen in statues representing heroic workers in soviet collectives. He tows the ketch back to a mooring buoy not far from us.

The older man briefly stands to watch and I see him properly for the first time – not very tall, but so wide that he is almost a sphere. He looks like a sumo wrestler. At first I fear he is naked, then realise he is wearing a pale pink tracksuit. Their ketch is no more than 30 foot long and its old-fashioned design means there is not much room aboard. It certainly explains why the lad spends so much of the day in the dinghy. I wonder how all three of them get inside to sleep.

After his fleeting interest in the mooring of his boat, the man in the pink tracksuit reseats himself and resumes his conversation with the younger man. The lad remains in the dinghy, fishing. When they reach the mooring the younger man goes to the bow and waves a boat hook ineffectually at the pick-up buoy, but misses. The tall, thin man in the dinghy picks the buoy up, hands it to him and watches him hook its rope over a cleat. Then he resumes his former heroic angle at the tiller and phutts away. The two men on the ketch talk late into the night.

In the small hours the wind gets up and there is heavy rain. The promised Gale Force 8 has arrived. David moves to the saloon sofa with a book to maintain a watch. Left below in our bunk, and freed from any concerns about dragging as David will fetch me if I'm needed, I still can't sleep. Apart from the gale, there is something loose in the rigging on the ketch and, tossed by the wind, it rattles and clatters against the main mast. Even after putting in earplugs to cut out the sound, my body still feels the toss and tug of the water against our boat. It is said that people flock to light comedy when under threat of war or economic depression, and only relish the dark and dismal when times are good. I only know that when the night is stormy, and a snatching anchor chain sets the nerves on edge, it is not a psychological thriller I reach for but *The Wind in the Willows*.

Next day, calm weather returns. David works on the generator and fixes the davits so that we can raise and lower the dinghy more easily. He also puts a shackle on our new spare anchor, with its shiny white rope, ready for us to use as a stern anchor at Porto Cristo's town quay, our next port of call. I begin sorting through three packs of photographs.

We put our photographs in albums; otherwise they end up as dozens of unidentified packs in a locker. Putting them in an album means we sort out the best ones or, even if they are a bit fuzzy, those that recall people and places we most want to remember. The rest we throw away, which saves valuable locker space from being filled with snaps we shall never want to look at again. We've found that the maximum number of packs it is prudent to accumulate before sorting for the album is three, somewhere between 70 and 100 prints. Any more than this and we get so confused about where the pictures are from that we put off sorting them. Then the pile gets so big that it becomes too onerous to even make a start. Even with only three packs it usually takes both of us to identify where all the pictures were taken.

Determined to maintain at least a semblance of personal respectability, despite our new relaxed lifestyle, I also give us both a haircut. They are our first since leaving England two and a half months ago. We had begun to look a trifle ... wild.

On one of the afternoons I begin to adapt my letter to Tony and Pam into a newsletter for other relatives and friends. It is David's idea and a good one. The trouble with postcards and letters is that after a while you can't remember what you've sent to whom and become either repetitive or neglectful. A newsletter will also relieve David of any guilt about writing letters home without any effort on his part as we both know who will be producing it. I don't mind, however, and I won't be short of material.

Since starting out I've kept a journal because I couldn't help myself. I found our experiences so new and captivating that the urge to write them down was irresistible. In addition, I knew that the many places we were visiting, often for a very short time, would quickly blur into a very few; which would be a pity because each was unique. And I knew that all the things that are happening to us would soon become a jumble, and could envisage a future time in which we would be unable to agree about what happened where and when and how and to which one of us, because memory is so fallible. And I feared that, with advancing age, memory might fail us altogether and I wanted to capture for that future time these challenging, life-enhancing, frightening, funny, maddening, magical, sun-filled days of unexpected liberty.

Liberty had not been part of the equation when planning improvements to our health and quality of life. We had not considered that for most of us living on an increasingly over-populated planet it is the sea, not Space – except for a tiny minority – that is the *final frontier.* And that for the present at least the great oceans of the world are still an unpredictable, ungovernable environment that is largely unrestricted, un-nationalized, unmonitored, untaxed, unprotected by social legislation, unrepresented by quangos, impervious to 24-hour news media, untrammelled by lawyers and emotional trauma counsellors or health and safety directives and not remotely politically correct.

We need a name for our newsletter and finally settle on Claytons' Progress. I ask David what he feels he is progressing towards.

'Unresponsibility,' he says.

I misinterpret this and he says no, not *irr*esponsibility, just not being responsible. Although David rarely brought his work home, or complained about anything or anybody, I can imagine that a staff of 350 and a long list of customers with pressing deadlines for more than a decade is at least one area of responsibility he has not been sorry to shed. The rhythm of our life is dictated nowadays by the weather and the hours of daylight, waking with the sun and heading towards bed not long after it gets dark. Its pace is mostly 5 knots, so that when we do eventually get behind the wheel of a car again we will hurtle along at 20mph, mortified by the manic speed around us. Unable to get the generator working we have to abandon any printing for the time being and lower the dinghy for a jaunt instead.

At the north end of the bay there is a fishing village called La Colonia. Every inch of its quay is filled with small, traditional wooden fishing boats as if, instead of the family car, every household has a family boat. All are painted white except for the wood-stained and varnished tops of their high prows, and in lieu of license plates each has its registration number on its bow. They are all immaculate and identical. To the right of them is the now familiar row of small, low, white boathouses. The village itself is captivating; a place of sleepy dogs, steep narrow streets, and a big, old stone church – lit up at night and one of our transit points – with a shady, dusty square across the narrow street from it.

We time our return to coincide with the thirty-minute opening of the post office. Its inside is as unlike a post office as its green-shuttered outside. A well-built, jolly man in navy blue sits at an old wooden desk strewn with rubber stamps, ink pads and mail. He takes our envelopes, keys the price of the stamps into his pocket calculator, shows the total to us with a smile and then drops our money into a small tin cash box. The walls of the small room are lined with shelves. Over these, and the floor, parcels tumble in cheerful profusion. There is a Christmassy smell of a recently-smoked cigar. This is the Santa's grotto of post offices and unlike any other Spanish post office we will ever encounter.

Back on board *Voyager*, the two heavyweight men on the ketch opposite talk non-stop. Their conversation seems to be focused on whatever it is that's dangling by a wire from their main mast and which is out-chattering even them. During the afternoon they send the lad up the mast. During his long sojourn up there with a pair of pliers, he is harangued by the younger of the two men with endless instructions as to how the job should be done. Then he is stopped from working altogether while the man takes photographs of him from the bow and the stern. Because of the direction of the wind, however, all this is only a vague hum.

At around 5pm a rusting old coastal cargo boat, registered in Amsterdam, moves out of its berth on the end of the town quay. Its bridge is painted blue and has the words *Ship of Fools* written across it and there is a dead tree festooned with pale blue fishing floats on its foredeck. It lurches towards the bay's entrance, lurches back, forwards again, and then anchors just where everybody enters or leaves the bay and is about as inconvenient as it could get.

I wake around 4am, disturbed by shouting, and go up on deck into a soft, still night. Apart from drunken revelry, which this isn't, the sound of people shouting in the early hours usually means a marine emergency of some kind. When I get outside, however, it becomes clear that there is a humdinger of a row taking place on a boat that arrived yesterday: wooden, pretty, but of a type with no standing headroom inside. I think being unable to stand upright must cause a lot of stress when the first novelty of cruising has worn off. There is a long wail of weeping, strangely unconvincing, like a child's when it can't get its own way. Then a woman's voice emerges, accusing. Then a man's voice, louder and clearer, utters a trio of unflattering expletives.

Lights come on in the house on the shore behind them, and on a nearby motor yacht. The woman's accusations, only partly heard, appear bizarre; not unlike the exercises in my ancient teach-yourself Spanish book. One such runs along the lines of, 'You have a towel! If you have a towel, why can't I have a towel? And if you go, you will drown.' Part of me feels guilty about being there, listening; another part wants to shout, 'Speak up a bit! You're not making any sense!' For after all, it's their fault that I've left my bed at four o'clock in an otherwise tranquil morning. There is obviously a lot more shouting to come before they are done, so I search out my ear plugs before getting back into bed.

It is probably not the content of the present argument that is the problem, whatever that might be, so much as the tensions of living in a limited space with a limited income; when a boat that began as a dream of freedom becomes a form of imprisonment. And there's not a lot of privacy on the water in which to work things out, either. Beyond them, at the bay's entrance, the black and white striped lighthouse blinks with such a frail light that a hamster on a treadmill could produce it.

Next day we dinghy down to the small marina for a weather forecast and then up to the little stone jetty with the translucent green water and tiny boathouses. We cross the small beach with the pines and wild flowers and climb the hill to the supermarket. There is a bit of a wait at the meat counter – behind a man with one of those shallow, circular wicker baskets of the type restaurateurs seem to favour – while each cut of meat is individually parcelled up and bagged. It is an extraordinarily well-stocked counter, and with its selection of dressed game birds and rabbits it reminds me of the old high street shops of my childhood, before everything came in polystyrene trays and plastic film.

We leave Porto Colom at noon with the wind on the port quarter and the genoa up. We have no log – probably weed around its paddle wheel – and the autopilot is not working. We arrive at Porto Cristo at lunch time and aim for the town quay for a variety of reasons. Most importantly, we're not sure that *Voyager* will fit between the marina's finger pontoons. The public quay is also closer to the town, and a night's stay there is a quarter of the cost of the marina.

It says in the cruising guide that stern anchors are required at the quay. So while still out in the bay, along with fenders and ropes, David has hauled our new Danforth anchor with its pristine white rope out of the forward locker and set it up ready for me to drop off our stern while he aims our bows at the quay.

When we reach the public quay, however, we find it now has lazy lines, making our stern anchor unnecessary. Unfortunately, and unbeknown to us, the boat on our starboard side has pulled up the wrong lazy line and it is lying across the space we are trying to enter. Out of sight below the water, and not where you would expect it to be, this lazy line gets caught around one of our rudders, bringing us to a halt short of the quay. The man who comes to help us I assume to be from the harbour master's office, but he turns out to be a visiting English yachtsman, and very patient. It all provides endless entertainment for the people lunching outside the restaurant on the quay.

Before David can finally tie on the lazy line a woman in a blue uniform arrives at our bow. They always arrive while your hands are brown and stinking from a fetid lazy line and you're sweating buckets from wrestling with mooring ropes in the hottest part of the day.

'Money?' I rub my fingers together. 'Si' she says smiling.

'Five minutes?' I signal hopefully.

She looks at her watch and shrugs amiably. 'Five minutes, ten. Within an hour.' She hands me a form to complete. I leave nasty brown finger marks on it. She ambles away.

Her office is on the quay to our right, just below the restaurant. It is a white-washed, flaking room in an old single-storey building with green shutters and a big atmospheric black-and-white photograph on its back wall showing what the area where *Voyager* is currently berthed looked like before development. It is similar to other pictures we have seen of fishing villages from around the 1880s. She observes our interest. Large numbers are always difficult to understand in a foreign language so she automatically writes down for us the year the photograph was taken – 1990. A lot has changed in eight years in Porto Cristo. She then provides us with a map of the town from her fax machine and directions to the post office, supermarket and laundry. As well as all the usual stuff, we still have the pile of towels used to mop up seawater from the leaking windows and vent during the recent storm. Although we had dried them out the following day, we have since had no opportunity to wash the salt out of them. Neither San Petro nor Porto Colom had a launderette and we did not have enough fresh water on board to do them by hand.

It is a lovely berth. Our cockpit faces the headland with its palm trees and four stunning arcaded houses. Our bow faces the quay and the restaurant. To its right is the old whitewashed stucco and green-shuttered office of the Harbour Master. To its left is a truly disreputable toilet that constitutes the quay's ablutions facility, with a door that someone appears to have put their foot through; then trees and a small rose garden. Despite its being the end of October, the dark red roses fill the warm air with their perfume and the trees are filled with songbirds. Beyond the rose garden the buses gather and their drivers shout the odds to confused tourists studying timetables.

We are surrounded by boats. Both sides of this long narrow harbour are jam-packed with them and most of them are German. Some are of the older, traditional type which I find rather beautiful, but for some unaccountable reason *Voyager*'s unusual lines are the central attraction of the quay. An endless procession of people stop to discuss her, stare at her, and pose for photographs in front of her.

You have to choose your time to go ashore for fear of ruining some-one's holiday snaps by suddenly popping up in the middle of them.

It is a still, balmy day and utter bliss. After a bath and a late lunch we wander into town. There are a lot of tourist shops and in among them is a small shoe shop. My trainers have a hole in them and I am wearing my hated deck shoes. On board, over time, I have learned to avoid catching unwary toes under cleats or on the pointed corner of a low-lying window frame. This has allowed me to spend most of my time aboard barefoot and only resort to footwear when going ashore. Accordingly my deck shoes have never got any more comfortable and, even on so short a trip as this one, they are currently killing me. On a wire rack in the shoe shop's doorway I spot just what I need. I go inside and point to the blue denim loafers. They are the kind the elderly fishermen out on the quay are wearing.

'Senor's' explains the elderly lady assistant and tries to draw me over to a rack of women's shoes.

I ignore her invitation, sit down, remove my deck shoes and present my wide, irregular feet for her inspection.

'Ah!' says the elderly lady and shouts the shoe's name and my size to the even more elderly man in a small back room. He emerges and tries to give them to David and is puzzled when *I* reach for them.

'Senor's,' he says politely.

I offer my feet for his inspection.

'Ah,' he says. He hands the shoes to me and returns to his stockroom.

Wide, seamless and comfy, I tour the town in them. They will last for years.

The town's laundry says 48 hours on its window but because today is Thursday we can't have it back until Monday and we want to leave before then. So we take our bedding and towels home again.

At Porto Cristo's town quay you buy electricity and water by the day. So we pay for a day's water, fill our two water tanks and do our laundry. David treads the larger items in the bath while I do the smaller ones in the galley. We festoon the boat as discreetly as possible but it reduces *Voyager*'s potential as a photographic backdrop considerably. Then we refill our water tanks.

We dine in the cockpit by candlelight, on chicken breasts marinated in honey and lemon juice and cooked in garlic and olive oil, served with baked potatoes, carrots and small French beans. There is an abundance of fruit in the shops at present, too, so the fruit bowls are brimming with juicy nectarines, pears, melon and grapes the size of damsons.

The dog-leg entrance to the harbour makes it very sheltered. It is also very beautiful with a heavily-wooded hillside curving round to the left of us. The trees on the waterline are lit from below at night and look like a grotto. To the right of us, behind the marina's pontoons, is the affluent, colonnaded building of the Club Nautico with a restaurant on top and lots of palm trees, also magically lit at night.

It is all utter bliss – until bedtime, after which a German man with a booming voice on a boat in the marina directly opposite, talks non-stop into the early hours.

Mallorca: Porto Cristo

First thing next morning we get a 'phone call from our estate agent in England. We have received an offer on our house. It is considerably less than the current asking price, which has already been reduced twice, so we make a very reasonable counter offer. The response comes in the time it takes the agent to redial our mobile 'phone: *this is a cash offer; we want to be in before Christmas* (seven weeks away); *take it or leave it, no negotiation.*

We remember this man and woman coming to look at the house some months ago. They are both divorced with two children apiece and setting up home together. At the time, however, they both had a house to sell. Face to face he was also more civil. Presumably financial leverage has imbued him with a sense of power for the agent tells us that the man has now sold his own house and that contracts have been exchanged on his partner's. He is particularly insistent that the family move in before Christmas.

It is the only offer we have so far received. A number of people have been interested, but all have yet to receive offers on their own houses. The market locally is dead. We could wait for a better offer, probably next spring or summer, but in the meantime we will continue paying all the costs of the house: insurance, council tax, general maintenance and heating throughout a long, cold northern English winter. A cash offer, with no complicated chain to drag the process on indefinitely, and the speed of the desired completion finally tips the scales. The whole thing will be done and dusted in less than seven weeks and we shall be back in Mediterranean warmth for Christmas. We decide to accept the offer and suggest a very reasonable price for carpets but as we set off to find Porto Cristo's supermarket I am decidedly irritable.

It is a long walk from the quay and I find the upper town depressing. The streets are narrow but without the usual Spanish small town charm – or pavements, so you're constantly at risk from traffic or from people stepping out of shops or houses. After a long walk uphill the supermarket's fresh produce turns out to be old and unappetizing. All we buy is a famous brand of frozen lasagne for the evening and two enormous, over-ripe bright-orange Sharon fruit.

It is a very hot day. Too hot. But it isn't just the heat that is oppressing me. I want to sell the house as much as David does, but as my tiredness increases, so does my irritation. I know that refusing this offer would be what my father called *cutting off my nose to spite my face*, but I feel an irrational desire to tell the agent to leave our house on the market and the purchaser to take a hike. David says if I want to, I should do it, which makes me even madder and we have the inevitable argument. We eat the lasagne, which is awful, in silence and retire to separate beds hot and exhausted at 8.30. Two boats' away a German man with a very loud voice talks all night over a recording of Beethoven's Ninth Symphony. The wind gets up and there is a bumpy sea, so all in all it is a disturbed night.

We rise late next morning and discover *Voyager* askew. Our lazy line has come adrift. And I am still grumpy. The trouble with intuition is that you can never be sure until later if intuition is actually what it is, or whether it is something quite different: such as resentment, feeling that you are being stampeded into something, taken advantage of, or just plain irritability. Whatever the reason, I have a bad feeling about our purchaser but unfortunately he is all there is. However, having accepted the offer our next task is to find somewhere secure for *Voyager* for a few weeks while we clear the house and complete the paperwork. David consults the Cruising Association's Mediterranean Lay-up Notes and settles on Mahon, the capital of Menorca.

A guillemot hovers by our port hull, then dives under it and emerges with its breakfast wriggling in its beak. Out in the town a fishy treat awaits us, too. An anonymous metal shutter, lowered yesterday, is raised today revealing a pristine wet fish shop. There is no need to make the long hike to the supermarket. I buy fresh cod and prawns to take with us, and salmon for dinner tonight.

I have never before been to a place so completely dominated by a foreign nationality. This is doubtless how other nations feel about going to parts of Tuscany or Provence and finding that nearly everybody there is English. Porto Cristo's harbour and lower town, meanwhile, is full of Germans. This wouldn't matter if they didn't keep you awake all night, or insist on walking three-abreast along narrow streets and expecting you to leap into the traffic to get out of their way. Even the Spanish woman in the baker's greets me in German. I fear I am a little short with her.

Nevertheless, we relish her soft-centered, crusty bread with hard Spanish cheeses and salad for lunch, followed by the Sharon fruit that we bought from the over-ripe supermarket yesterday. They have split since being washed and we scoop the flesh from their skins with a spoon. It's like apricot jam, sweet but not sickly and utterly delicious. We will buy them again, in other places at other times, but they never taste as good as these.

It is another very hot day. David does not seem to feel the heat like I do and after lunch is happily working at the bench in the workshop. I feel exhausted. He needs some screws to finish what he is doing and is about to set off into town to find some. Just the *thought* of being out in the white-hot glare of mid-afternoon makes me wilt.

'Just sit in the shade and have a rest,' he says. 'Put your feet up. We're retired now. You don't *have* to do anything.' I sink back onto the cockpit cushions. No sooner has he gone, however, than the gang-plank begins to graunch and groan with every rise and fall of the boat. I get up and go to the bow. Oddly it isn't the plank scraping on the dock, as I'd expected, but the rope around the cleat on our bow. It is soon so loud that I begin grinding my teeth and the customers at the restaurant opposite all have pained expressions. I try retying the rope but that makes no difference. Then I tie on a second rope, to spread the pressure on the cleat. That stops it until I get back to my seat, when the noise immediately starts again. I go back and tie more rope around the original one, to inhibit the friction.

A middle-aged woman with a large fishing rod appears and points to our stern. She tries hard to engage me in an arrangement, but finally resigns herself to my failure to understand what she wants and goes away. I know very well what she wants – to fish off our stern. Every Spaniard is an angler, and every angler will do anything to get an extra forty feet out over the water. Had I relented, in half an hour the stern would have been full of them. What with anglers at the back, and a perpetual photo shoot at the front, I'd get more peace on the centre strip of a motorway.

There is a telephone call from the estate agent. The purchaser has halved our moderate valuation of the carpets. Take it or leave it. Letters are being exchanged. The rope begins graunching again. Desperate, I try a damp floor cloth between the rope and the cleat. As I form it into a garrotte I think about our purchaser's neck. The estate agent had also said England is experiencing severe gales and flooding. It will at least be a relief to sell the house before the winter really sets in. I suppose.

There is no reduction in the noise from the rope. I am becoming demented. The restaurant opposite has emptied. Its proprietor leans expressively on his door frame, arms folded, watching me and sucking his teeth. I have a brainwave. Haul up the gangplank; relieve the pressure on the rope completely! Why has it taken me so long to think of this? I have just sat back down thankfully in the shade when I hear David calling my name. He cannot get on board until I lower the plank for him. I get up and go to the bow again. 'Did you manage to get a bit of a rest?' he says.

At sundown there are hundreds of garden birds in the trees on the quay and the smell of roses is headier than ever after the heat of the day. I've just put salmon julienne on the cockpit table when a boat bearing six young Germans motors past. Finding no space available further up the quay, they reverse and begin to squeeze in between us and another German boat. This leaves only three inches between their gunwales and ours. We move fenders to accommodate them, give them one of our lazy lines – we are currently using two to try and keep *Voyager* straight – go and scrub our hands and return to our dinner. People invariably arrive just as you sit down to a meal.

We have a home-recorded video for our evening's entertainment. We didn't choose it specifically. Our movie collection still
resides in large plastic storage boxes at the back of the big saloon
locker, which was where David stowed them when he loaded the
boat at Emsworth ready for our departure at around the time he did
in his back. The boxes are unmovable, so you just reach in at arm's
length and rootle around until your fingers prize out something you
haven't watched lately. Like most of our home recordings it has a
short on it, usually a half-hour comedy programme, to fill up the
spare tape left by the film. This one has on it a half-hour episode of
Dad's Army, the popular TV series poking gentle fun at British character traits via the members of a Home Guard platoon on the south
coast of England during World War II. With our six new German
neighbours sitting on their deck only inches away, however, we both
leap for the volume button as its signature tune – Flanagan and
Allen's *Who do you think you are kidding, Mr Hitler?* – booms out. So
much for not mentioning the war. Fortunately our neighbours have
gone out for the evening by the time the main feature, the classic
film, *Cabaret* set in 1930s Berlin, gets underway, so they miss the
Horst Wessel song.

'I bet they'll return at 2am and sit on deck talking for the rest
of the night,' I grumble as we prepare for sleep. Whatever time they
do return, we do not hear them.

Mallorca: Porto Cristo to Ratjada

We leave Porto Cristo after lunch. Despite the wind rising momentarily, just as David reverses, we make a tolerable exit. Better than our arrival, anyway. We motor the thirteen-and-a-half miles to Ratjada and arrive around 3.15 in the afternooon. The wind is mostly 5 knots until shortly before our arrival, when it rises briefly to sixteen. We tie up port-side on to the visitors' quay facing out to sea. The barometric pressure has dropped seven points since this morning and, because the stretch of water between Mallorca and Menorca is known for its high winds, we *must* get a forecast before we set out tomorrow.

A lone Frenchman, with a beard and ponytail, arrives in a small sloop and circles. The wind rises again, just as he approaches, and blows him off the quay.

'You help me?' he calls, pointing to a spot behind our stern. 'I come in here'. We run to grab the light little sloop's rails before its topsides can collide with the concrete as he drives it hard at the dock to compensate for the wind. It is difficult for single-handed sailors sometimes, and this one is nervy and fretful. We hold onto his boat until he has enough ropes tied to be secure and then leave him to himself. He ties and reties his shore lines and springs a number of times but still does not seem entirely happy with them.

While I set-to in the galley a couple of jet skiers emerge from the marina and roar up and down alongside us. Then they spin in tight circles and perform a few aerobatics. Their wash sends *Voyager* and the little French sloop crashing against the quay, the twenty-foot-high jets of seawater shooting up from behind their seats splatters in through our open hatches and their exhausts fill the air with evil fumes. As I grip the edges of the sink to keep my balance, I can see through the galley window that they look extremely pleased with themselves, gazing about to see if anybody aboard the two moored yachts is admiring them. Jet skiers would be despised less if they sought somewhere more challenging than a visitors' dock and its captive audience to go through their paces. When they've finished their display, they throttle back and make a decorous return into the marina at the speed of rowing boats. Yet surprisingly, when other water users shout obscenities at them, jet skiers always look surprised and hurt.

With the jet skiers' wash still receding I observe a kindred spirit through my galley window. A cormorant on the ramp opposite has spread its wings to dry its flight feathers and stands there in a state of tranquillity until one of a pair of nearby seagulls takes an unprovoked lunge at it. With a look of almost human resignation, the cormorant leaves the ramp and flaps off to settle onto an adjacent rock jutting just above the water. The rock is only just big enough for one pair of webbed feet to balance on it and, offering its laundry up to the breeze again, the cormorant glares resentfully at the gulls.

We have an early dinner of succulent thick cod and large tender prawns with fresh crusty bread, tomato in olive oil and basil and a green salad, followed by an apple Danish bought this morning at Porto Cristo's bakery. On our way out of the harbour for a walk around the town we stop to look in at the marina's window but the forecast there is two days old. As it is now Saturday evening there is little chance of there being an up-to-date one tomorrow morning.

Ratjada turns out to be quite a large town. In a small square a scene for a movie is being filmed by a German film crew which somebody says is starring TV actors. The director, in a little motorized cart, looks grey-faced and anguished, while the boom operator leaning over the set looks as if he suffers with back problems. When they get to a wrap, the Director says, 'Thank you' in English.

Back on board I smoke a cigarette on deck before bed, and observe the French boat at our stern. With every movement from passing vessels it ducks and dives, leaps, plunges and chafes at its ropes. Rather like its anxious owner. And I wonder if yachtsmen become like their boats, as dog owners are said to resemble their pets. If so, David and I are likely to end up broad in the beam and bandy-legged.

49
Mallorca to Menorca

It is 8 o'clock on the morning of November 1. All Saints Day. Spanish clocks went back overnight. David sets off into Ratjada in search of an English Sunday newspaper and a weather forecast. He returns empty-handed. The news stands are closed and neither the marina nor the yacht club has a current weather forecast on display. David makes another sortie at nine.

While he is gone a young officer of the Guardia Civil appears on the end of the quay. I go and ask him if he has a forecast for the day. He is very pleasant and does his best to help. 'Probably like yesterday,' he says. David returns from the town with a newspaper this time, but still no forecast. On his way past the French boat, however, he finds its skipper hunched over his SSB radio listening to the French forecast. He is having great difficulty hearing it but finally straightens up with a triumphant, 'West 3–4!' It is currently Variable 1 and the only hazard of the day turns out to be the fishing buoys off Ratjada's harbour mouth. An upturned wooden crate with a twig stuck in it may be a cheap option for local fishermen, but it is almost impossible to see with the glare of a low, bright sun behind it.

Once clear of the crates, and of Mallorca, David sets a course for the south-east tip of Menorca and turns on the autopilot. The Windy Isle attracts only light and variable winds all day and we have a sunny motor there with the current behind us. As we approach the island our autopilot stops working, which is at least a change from the GPS packing up.

Menorca is the second-largest of the Balearic Islands and the most easterly. A mere 26 miles by eleven, its strategic position in the western Mediterranean means it has been coveted as a naval base by maritime nations since the Phoenicians. By mid-afternoon we have entered the long, narrow, beautiful bay which leads up to its capital,

Mahon. Between 1708 and 1802 the island changed hands six times and each time the prize was the port of Mahon.

As you sail up to it you can see why: deep water for a fleet of warships, surrounded by hills offering protection from bad weather and an easily defended entrance. For us it is a voyage through part of British naval history since many of the fortifications lining the north shore date from Britain's occupation in the 18th century.

Near the far end of the bay is Isla Pinta, an island joined to the north shore by an isthmus and the most prominent part of the naval base. It is a complete surprise. The words *naval base* conjure up barracks and an industrial environment: cranes, workshops and fuel dumps. The last thing you expect is long, low white-walled buildings with terracotta roofs set in immaculate lawns with a white stone balustrade around the water's edge. More like a Governor's residence really.

Just before you reach the naval base you come to the first of two floating 'islands', in reality large square wooden pontoons attached to the seabed to which around 20 boats can tie up using lazy lines. One is completely full while the other has only a single yacht tied up to it. A young French Rastafarian emerges from this boat and comes over to help us tie up, for which we are very grateful. He has colonized one end of the pontoon with diving gear and other equipment which, when he goes ashore shortly afterwards in his dinghy, he leaves in the care of a very large German Shepherd. We are getting low on water but do not attempt to attach our hose to the water tap as it is alongside the dog's bowl. We decide to wait until the young man comes back.

At sunset, from somewhere unseen on the naval base, The Last Post echoes softly into a feathery red-gold sky. The afterglow of the sun's dying rays warms and deepens all the colours of the waterfront. The pretty white houses scattered along the lush green hillside, and their white steps meandering down to the water's edge, all turn a soft pink.

50
Menorca: Mahon

Monday dawns fine and bright. After breakfast the French Rasta begins preparing his boat in readiness to leave by filling a large number of water containers. He has no English and I have little French but we manage. He is off to Gibraltar. I was very grateful for his assistance in coping with the lazy line yesterday so although he seems very self-sufficient, as solo sailors usually are, I risk asking if he needs any help.

'Meteorlogica?' he asks, without much hope of one. We actually have a forecast for today, off Monaco Radio. I tell him Easterly 4 to 5, which pleases him. It should do. Had he been contemplating the opposite direction, towards Corsica, he could have expected Force 9 or 10.

The French boat is soon replaced by an English one. The couple aboard have been here before and warn us that the lazy lines on this pontoon are unreliable, which explains why the other pontoon is so popular. They lift what they judge to be a sound one and we help them tie up. I am delighted to find someone even worse with mooring ropes than me. She says her husband is planning to write a book called *Single-Handed Sailing with Your Wife*. Despite their best efforts in selecting a lazy line, in no time their boat is at a crooked angle to the pontoon. Then our port bow starts bumping against it, too.

We adjust our own lazy line and with their offer to protect *Voyager* from mangling her bows in our absence, we set off in the dinghy for a look around the bay. As well as providing a secure environment to leave our boat, Mahon looks like a very pleasant place to come back to for our coveted warm dry Christmas. I have already begun working out how to cook a traditional Christmas dinner with all the trimmings in an oven a quarter the size of the one at home. All we need now is a safe berth.

Our first stop is the other floating island. In terms of security it is ideal, since as well as being offshore it has all these other yachtsmen dug in for the winter. And their pontoon has reliable lazy lines. However, it is full to capacity and no-one is planning to leave. They have obviously established a community here if the camaraderie and the small Scandinavian paddling pool in the middle is anything to go by.

From there we go to have a look at the marina down the far end of the bay, but it is virtually empty and there is no security. The moorings on the town quay are exposed too. In both places anyone so disposed could simply step onto your boat and there is no-one to notice. Then, on a walk down the quay we see a T-shaped pontoon behind a locked gate. A notice on the gate gives the address of an office further along the street where its manager, an Englishman called Joss, offers us winter rates we cannot refuse. He and his family have been resident in Mahon for some time and have recently bought a house here.

Joss is a man of infinite patience, good humour and useful information. He apologizes for the fact that, because of necessary repairs to a damaged stretch of pontoon, we shall have to go on the inside of the T and it will be a tight fit. It is. And naturally, by the time we get *Voyager* over there, the wind is gusting 15 knots. It is also a long jump down from the bows onto the pontoon, where I tie up and fend off while David takes care of the lazy line but, since there is no-one around to see, we manage rather well. There are a handful of other boats but none is occupied. We are to have this little stretch of Paradise all to ourselves.

Our companionway doors and cockpit open onto a terrace of five three-storey houses – two white, three cream and pale apricot – with terracotta roofs, green shutters and white chimney pots. They are domestic above, with casement windows opening onto small balconies, and garages or businesses below. One is a restaurant, with a dark timber interior and blue and white check table linen. Another sells locally-caught shellfish, including large lobsters. Behind them is a high, sheer cliff with a palatial white building and palm trees on the top.

Outside the houses the leaves on the sycamore trees lining the pavement are turning yellow. A few brown ones lie crackling in the street. A narrow two-lane road runs between the houses and the water. A low wall prevents its traffic from encroaching on the waterfront and at the same time creates a protected, narrow promenade. Directly opposite us, on the other side of the water, are the long low white buildings and manicured lawns of the naval base. To the left of them are three long docks for warships, although the only resident is a 225ft Patrol Boat. We can identify it precisely thanks to that copy of *Jane's Fighting Ships* we bought in Gibraltar.

Once we are settled we walk down the quay to the office, pay two months' mooring fees, and tap Joss for local information. Our two priorities are a launderette and a travel agent who speaks English. The *lavanderia* up in the town is closed for the winter, and the one that is part of the public shower block down on the town quay, just below our berth, is closed for renovations. We get directions to the English-speaking travel agent, however, but as we are leaving a worried-looking staff member rushes in shouting, 'Utopia's missing! Utopia's missing!'

'Oh dear,' says David, 'I rather thought we'd just found it.' It turns out someone has moved a very expensive power yacht of that name further down the quay but forgotten to tell anyone.

From Joss's office we turn left up a steep wooded hill to the town, above the white chimney pots of the terraced houses on the quay behind our boat. We tell the travel agent we expect to be off in two or three weeks' time, and ask how much notice is needed to get a flight. 'Just don't leave it too close to Christmas,' she says.

We make only a brief acquaintance with the town today. When you are going to spend a while in a place you can afford to take your time getting to know it. As with a person, it is best done slowly. Even on our first day, however, I'm afraid we fall in love with Mahon, with its whitewashed houses, terracotta roofs, palm trees and narrow, cobbled streets. A big horse feed store and saddler's seems incongruous where streets are either pedestrianised or grid-locked by cars, while a tribute to trust and honesty is the king's ransom of artists' materials left on another shop's doorstep. The people are very courteous and everywhere is very clean.

We wander into the large porch of a church in a row of buildings and discover it is a monastery, with a small grille in the far wall and a bell to summon a brother. We have no desire to intrude so we tiptoe out again. Outside, at pavement level, there is an open service hatch. I bend down and peer in. There are rusting metal implements hanging on the wall.

'Good lord!' I whisper, 'I thought hair shirts were as far as it went these days.'

There is a shout and a loud bang within, and I back quickly out. Two steps further on we discover the cellar is not part of the monastery but underneath the police station. We walk swiftly on. Looking out vaguely for food shops, we follow a number of people into a building we take to be a market, but once inside find it is the Department of Social Security.

At sunset, and back on board *Voyager*, The Last Post echoes across the water again. Although now that we can see directly into the naval base it is apparent that the seaman lowering the Spanish flag does so to the accompaniment not of a lone trumpeter, as we had assumed, but a scratchy recording coming from one of the buildings.

We decide to celebrate finding such an ideal berth with dinner at a restaurant along the quay and order a bottle of wine to go with it from the affable waiter.

'House white?'

Yes, please.

'Mineral water?'

Yes.

'Still?'

Yes. Get a lot of English in here do you?

'Yes.'

Mahon gave the world mayonnaise. Originally called *Mahonesa*, it is based on the local aioli sauce. While the actual circumstances of its creation are disputed, it probably dates from a brief period of French occupation in the mid 18th century. The restaurant serves a local variety, with crusty bread, as a starter. It is an enjoyable meal with friendly service, and inexpensive.

Back on board we sit out in the cockpit in the warm evening and look at the stars and the terraced houses on the quay, with their windows lit and fleeting glimpses of the lives lived within. It takes such small things sometimes to make life very pleasant and here even the street lights are designed to throw their light over the road where it is needed, instead of blazing upwards and blotting out the stars.

51

Winter Sun

A new day and another sunny one. A few yards up the quay from our berth there is a small square. From there a flight of wide, white stone steps takes you up to the town. It is lined with feathery pines and palm trees and its borders are still bright with summer flowers even though it is now November. As you stand at the top, to let the muscle spasms in your legs and the rasping in your lungs subside, you can enjoy an unimpeded view of the harbour. It is only the *second* time you climb these steps that you think to count them – there are 153 – and realise with relief that you are actually fitter than you thought.

At the top of this flight of steps is a steep, narrow, irregular-shaped village square. At its far end is a Carmalite church: huge, square, built of stone and locked. Beside it is a flight of steps up to another square stone building, unmarked but not unlike a town hall. Its entrance is busy with people going in and out. Remembering yesterday's blunder into the Department of Social Security we enter with caution.

It turns out to be the cloisters of the church next door, complete with stone columns and classical capitals. An escutcheon on one of the columns dates it from the 1770s. It is a beautiful building in the process of being renovated as a very up-market market hall. There are stalls along one side, for fruit, vegetables and flowers, and one corner is ablaze with great maroon chrysanthemums, white daisies and pots of green herbs. While a friendly woman serves us fruit and vegetables, she explains how many English words – along with those of every other occupier of this island over the centuries – combine with Catalan and Spanish to form the island's unique Menorquin language. Opposite her stall are small, specialist shops: one for red meat, one for poultry and another for cheese. I indicate a large slice from a huge, delicious-looking cheese. Fortunately the man says tentatively, 'Butter?' before he starts cutting and then guides me to something that really is cheese.

A few doors down from the market is a bread shop: not a baker's, more an odd jumble of a shop selling bits of grocery, soft drinks and mineral water. But behind the counter in wooden racks is kept the day's delivery of bread, *soft* bread, and on the right-hand side of the counter, in a glass case, the most heavenly crème caramels, the first we have encountered since Tréguier. Across the square is an old-fashioned bottle shop with modestly-priced wines and a cheerful, elderly lady behind the counter.

At the bottom of the square is the fish market which, from outside its high green gates, looks more like a luxury villa than a fish market. It is single-storey cream stucco with a terracotta roof, and built around an open courtyard where the fish is delivered each morning and the empty trays washed ready for return in the afternoon. The long low rooms around the courtyard contain the stalls where the local women sell the fish their men have caught. On the wall behind many of them hangs a painting of the family boat. The fish is very fresh and very reasonably priced. These are the kind of shops I had envisaged when we first set sail.

We amble away from the old square laden with fish, fruit, vegetables, cheese, fresh bread, wine and a couple of orgasmic crème caramel pastries. Mindful of the climb needed to get back up here if we have forgotten anything, David pauses at the top of the long flight of steps. Raising the shopping bags he is carrying he asks, 'Do we have everything we need?'

I look from the bags of fresh, delicious food up into his tanned, relaxed face which only recently had looked so tired and unwell, and then out over the breathtaking beauty of Mahon Harbour sparkling in the Mediterranean morning sunshine. Yes,' I say, 'we have everything we need.'

We have also achieved our two major objectives in setting out: a warm, dry climate and an improvement in our health. The latter has been achieved partly thanks to the former, but an active outdoor lifestyle has worked wonders as well.

David has lost weight now that he no longer sits at a desk or in a car all day, or snacks on chocolate bars to keep alert during the 40,000 miles he used to drive every year. The reduction of allergens in his life – especially traffic fumes, dust and pollen – has had a dramatic effect on his respiratory system to the point where not only have the chronic sneezing and congestion disappeared, but so has the sleep apnoea. He is also fitter and stronger.

As for me, I've had chronic back and joint pain with periodic bouts of fatigue since childhood. There have been a variety of conflicting diagnoses over the years but none of them treatable without side-effects arguably worse than the condition itself and no guarantee of improvement. I had learned to live with it.

Living with it had become harder, however, around the time of that cold, damp winter evening five years ago, sitting before the fire – David wheezing and me aching – when he had first suggested a fundamental change to our lifestyle. The pain had become much worse and the fatigue more or less constant. It had a lot to do with my age, an increasingly damp climate and a stressful, sedentary job. On the other hand, I had not been convinced that the dramatic change being proposed would provide any improvement, and part of my initial reluctance to living on a boat had been how I would cope physically. Now, thanks to the regular exercise required by a life afloat – combined with a better climate – I have more energy and am fitter, stronger and more comfortable than I have been in years.

There have been changes in other areas of our lives too, like the challenge of acquiring new skills and increased confidence in our capacities. For instance, while learning everything he could about the handling and safety of a yacht, David knew that seasoned sailors would feel that he did not have the experience necessary for what we were setting out to do. Then, on our very first passage, to Alderney in the Channel Islands, he had made a mistake with the tide tables. Ever since, he now admits, he has constantly checked and rechecked all data for fear of making another. But his diligence has paid off and in the past four months we have navigated our way through some of Europe's most difficult and dangerous coasts (the Channel Islands and Brittany), anchored comfortably and safely in gale force conditions (the Spanish *rías*) and endured storm-force conditions with a potentially-lethal waterspout (Mallorca). We have also survived man-made hazards, including commercial ships with no lookouts suddenly changing course and the occasional attack fisherman.

Our odyssey began with the surprisingly similar thoughts of two dissimilar people, an English Anglican bishop and an American explorer. The former asked, 'How much is enough?' The latter said, 'I live more simply now and am happier'.

But what *is* happiness? And can you be *well*, in the fullest sense of the word, if you are not happy? If I have learned anything at all by this stage in life, it is that happiness comes from within not without. There is no direct connection between happiness and, say, giving up everything to become a beachcomber any more than there is in devoting your life to relentless acquisition. Happiness seems to result from the way in which the things that you do each day, and with whom, make you feel.

In the western world, where we are spoilt for choice and have the trappings of celebrity and wealth constantly in our faces, it is easy to pursue goals which do not ultimately bring happiness. What helps us to be happy is to understand who we are, what we *really* want that is within our reach, and then working to achieve it.

Many of the things that appear glamorous, in reality are not. Cruising is not glamorous, although from the outside it may look as if it is. For example, your living quarters are small, your wardrobe negligible, there is little money for restaurants, most entertainments are home-made, and anybody who has read this far can be in no doubt about the effort needed to fill the fridge or do the laundry.

But we like our new life and our new home, and not simply because it is warmer and less stressful than the old one, or that we feel fitter and healthier. We have been overwhelmed by the sheer beauty of the world and the extraordinary courtesy and kindness of the people we have met. And next year, if we feel ready, we shall think about crossing the Atlantic.

Glossary for Non-Sailors

Antifouling – paint put on the hull below the water line to stop marine growth and shellfish becoming attached and reducing the speed of the boat.

Autopilot – device to hold the boat on a set course automatically.

Beat – when sailing with the wind coming from in front of you rather than from behind or to the side.

Bluewater cruising – long distance ocean cruising.

Boom – a movable beam which holds the bottom of the main sail and allows it to be set in various positions to catch the wind.

Broad reach – when the wind is directly on the side, or beam, of the boat.

Coaming – raised edge on deck to prevent water entering the cockpit.

Courtesy flag – acknowledges that you are in someone else's country and recognise its jurisdiction.

Davits – two small hoists to lift and hold a dinghy, usually at a boat's stern.

Dead reckoning – the process of plotting a course or position from a known point using charts and tide tables.

Ebb – the tide is going out.

Flood – the tide is coming in.

Gelcoat – the hard shiny outer layer covering the fibreglass from which our boat is built.

Genoa – the large sail in front of our mast.

GPS – global positioning system which tells you where you are.

Hard – abbreviation for hard standing, when a boat is lifted out of the water to allow work to be done on its hull.

Heads – specifically the marine toilet, but also refers to the room it resides in, including our bathroom.

Heeling – when the force of the wind on its sails inclines a boat from the vertical.

Knot – a unit of speed used by ships and aircraft, equal to one nautical mile per hour. One nautical mile equals roughly 1.15 land miles.

Lines – ropes. See also Mooring lines and Shore lines.

Log – a speedometer; also a written record which in our case includes weather, location, direction, etc.

Luff – edge of the sail closest to the mast.

Main sail – the large sail behind the mast.

Mooring lines – ropes used to tie a boat to the shore.

Neap tide – occurring soon after the moon's 1st and 3rd quarters when high-water is at its lowest. (See also Springs or spring tide)

Navtex – receiver for international weather forecasts in English, either on a screen or as a print out.

Osmosis – when the outer protective skin (gelcoat) on a fibreglass hull becomes porous and allows water to attack the inner fibreglass core.

Outhaul – rope used to haul out a sail.

Port – left-hand side of vessel looking forward.

Raft up – when mooring space is limited, one boat will tie up to a pontoon or quay and a second boat will tie up alongside the first one.

Red ensign – the official flag for British Merchant Navy ships and British leisure boats which is a red ground with the Union Flag in the top left-hand corner.

RIB – stands for rigid inflatable boat; a high-speed rubber dinghy with a rigid, glass fibre bottom.

Royal Yachting Association (RYA) – the national governing body for water sports in the UK, founded 1875.

Sheets – ropes used to control a sail.

Shore lines – even when boats are rafted up (moored side by side) good practice requires the outer boats to take lines ashore to prevent the combined weight of all the boats from being borne by the inner boat's mooring lines.

Shrouds – multi-strand, stainless-steel wires which hold the mast in place.

Spring – while a mooring line ties a boat to a pontoon fore and aft, a spring is added diagonally to prevent the boat from surging back and forth.

Springs or spring tide – the highest tide, occurring on days shortly after new and full moon.

Starboard – right-hand side of vessel looking forward.

Stay sail – small sail between the genoa and the mast.

Squall – sudden increase in wind-speed, often accompanied by brief but heavy precipitation.

Wind over tide – when wind and tide travel in opposite directions, thereby producing a turbulent sea.

Winch – used to put tension on sails.

Windlass – used to raise the anchor.